THE CALIFORNIA COOK

Also by Diane Rossen Worthington

The Taste of Summer
The Cuisine of California

THE
CALIFORNIA
COOK

CASUALLY ELEGANT RECIPES
WITH EXHILARATING TASTE

Diane Rossen Worthington

Wine Notes by Anthony Dias Blue

BANTAM BOOKS
NEW YORK TORONTO LONDON SYDNEY AUCKLAND

THE CALIFORNIA COOK
A Bantam Book/June 1994

Library of Congress Cataloging-in-Publication Data

Worthington, Diane Rossen.
The California cook : casually elegant recipes with exhilarating
taste / Diane Rossen Worthington.
p.   cm.
Includes index.
ISBN 0-553-09179-4
1. Cookery, American—California style.   I. Title.
TX715.2.C34W67   1994
641.59794—dc20   93-40445
                                                              CIP

Published simultaneously in the United States and Canada

Bantam Books are published by Bantam Books, a division of Bantam
Doubleday Dell Publishing Group, Inc. Its trademark, consisting of the
words "Bantam Books" and the portrayal of a rooster, is Registered in
U.S. Patent and Trademark Office and in other countries. Marca
Registrada. Bantam Books, 1540 Broadway, New York, New York 10036.

PRINTED IN THE UNITED STATES OF AMERICA

FFG   0 9 8 7 6 5 4 3 2 1

For My Daughter, Laura,
With All My Love

CONTENTS

ACKNOWLEDGMENTS

ix

INTRODUCTION

xi

A NOTE ON WINES

xv

Appetizers and First Courses

1

Soups

39

Salads

73

Pasta, Pizza, Polenta, Risotto, and Eggs

115

Seafood

159

Poultry

193

Meat

227

Side Dishes

269

Breads
309

Desserts
343

Basics
391

Menus
427

INDEX
431

ACKNOWLEDGMENTS

There are always those people behind the scenes that help the author and the book reach its goals. Many thanks to:

- Don Cutler, my agent, for his thoughtful insights
- Fran McCullough, my editor, who always had another way to look at a problem and solve it
- Chris Benton, for her precise copyediting and incredible patience
- Nydia Olivares, for her tireless assistance and helpful suggestions
- Brigit L. Binns, for her accomplished recipe testing and researching skills
- Denise Smith, for her loyal friendship and generous recipe testing
- Anthony Dias Blue, for his exceptional knowledge on pairing California food with California wine
- Kathy Blue, for her insightful suggestions and critical palate
- Susan Silverberg, for teaching me to trust the process
- Dee Worthington, for her skillful editing
- Ginger Worthington Paca, for always being there
- Denny Luria, for being the best friend that anyone could ever ask for
- My colleagues Laurie Burrows Grad, Janice Wald Henderson, Ellen Brown, Jan Weimer, and Ciji Ware for their gracious assistance
- The Huntington Library for the generous use of the rare library's Helen Evans Brown Collection
- To all the California chefs and cooks who continue to inspire me daily
- My brothers Richard and Bob, my sister Marcine and my parents Ruth and Allan Rossen, for being great tasters
- And finally my husband, Michael, and daughter, Laura, for all their love and support

INTRODUCTION

YOU DON'T HAVE to live in California to be a California cook—what you do need is a California spirit. That means having a sense of adventure about food, an appreciation of the freshest seasonal ingredients and a desire to reinterpret familiar dishes with unexpected twists.

Simple, lively and bright tastes are the heart of California cooking—and it's all put together with casual elegance. It can be enjoyed anywhere, as long as you have access to fresh produce and enjoy bold flavors.

In this book, it means serving gravlax "Asian-style" with a ginger-mustard sauce, firing up lettuce and vegetables on the grill and tossing them with sweet smoky shrimp, and roasting sea bass with a blend of Mexican salsa and Dijon mustard.

As a "native" California cook, I have been fascinated with flavor ever since I can remember. Even in grade school I wanted parsley on my deviled eggs or a dash of curry in my Campbell's tomato soup. I was probably the only teenager in Los Angeles who kept a volume of Escoffier on my nightstand and would read myself to sleep with thoughts of Rôti de Bouef and its variations. Clearly, I was captivated with the magic of cooking.

Years later, I pursued this love of food at the Cordon Bleu in London and later in Paris. I would walk through the open air market and fill my basket with fresh produce, cheeses and breads to prepare exquisitely simple meals. I learned firsthand the exhilarating impact fresh farmer's market–quality ingredients can have on cooking.

I had that same sense of excitement when I returned to Los Angeles in the early 1970s and found a new cuisine emerging. California cuisine was a movement toward freshness, simplicity, and originality defined by the use of the freshest local produce, herbs, fish, and dairy products. Grilling, marinades, and California wines were key elements in this evolving style, which originated in the restaurant kitchens of Chez Panisse and Zuni Cafe in San Francisco and Spago and the West Beach Cafe in Los Angeles. Chefs were experimenting with fusing influences from different cuisines, and each of the leading restaurants could be identified with a particular influence—Mediterranean, Mexican, Japanese, Italian. The common bond of these new California chefs' food was their insistence on the freshest ingredients.

When I was writing *The Cuisine of California* in 1982, I had to rely on chef friends and produce managers to provide me with ingredients like radicchio, arugula, shiitake mushrooms—specialty ingredients I was sure would soon become available in all supermarkets.

Ten years later, as I walk through the supermarket aisles I see chanterelle mushrooms, orange and yellow sweet peppers, purple potatoes, ancho chiles, fresh herbs year-round, sun-dried persimmons, and fresh goat cheese. California's culinary landscape has most certainly changed, and the rest of the country is catching up fast.

While the immense variety of fresh ingredients is the cornerstone of contemporary California cooking, there are other factors. One of them is simplicity and it comes from several sources. Kitchen technology has produced the hand blender and food processor, which have made food preparation much less labor-intensive and cooking far more enjoyable. The hand blender is a particular favorite of mine as I'm now able to create beautifully textured soups right in the pot.

Another simplifying change since publication of *The Cuisine of California* has been my growing fascination with high-heat oven roasting. This technique gives chicken and vegetable dishes more flavor, crispness and caramelization than roasting at a medium temperature. It's also a lighter alternative to sautéing. I even make my stocks this way, using only one pan, with great results.

Barbecuing, marinating, and the use of vinaigrettes and salsas remain signatures of modern California cooking. Salsas in particular have become an indispensable taste enhancer. They provide an enormous amount of flavor and an appealing texture. It's amazing how so few calories can heighten the flavor of simple grilled dishes. Who would have thought this California Rancho tradition first introduced in the early 1800s would be reinterpreted with combinations like oranges, grapefruit, scallions, chiles, and mint?

California cooks have always benefited from eclectic ethnic influences. In the late 1700s, the Spanish missionary fathers established themselves from San Diego to Sonoma and brought with them corn tortillas, chiles, beans, dried fruits, and chocolate from Mexico. Their grape seeds and olive pits flourished in the famed California soil, producing the region's first wines and olive oil.

California Rancho kitchens taught us to cook with olive oil instead of lard, to grill meats over wood coals and to complement those smoky meats with zesty salsas. During the Gold Rush and with the arrival of Chinese immigrants, California cooks were first introduced to such contemporary ingredients as fresh ginger, soy sauce, dried mushrooms, sourdough, and peanut oil. We Californians have a great appreciation for our diverse heritage that is reflected in these recipes.

Like everyone else, California cooks have a range of cooking moods. Sometimes we want a fresh, quick last-minute dish while on other occasions we're delighted to spend an entire afternoon playing in the kitchen. Consider the West Coast Dungeness crab cakes surrounded by pink grapefruit sections and drizzled with a grapefruit sauce. While crab cakes are more involved than simple orange-mustard grilled chicken, the joy of preparation and the taste experience are well worth the extra time.

When shortcuts work, I use them. Ready-made wonton skins make fast, delicate, and delicious pasta for butternut squash ravioli without having to fuss with dough. For make-ahead entertaining there's an easy baked vegetable rigatoni with tomatoes and smoky provolone cheese or a lasagna with roasted vegetables. I serve these casually elegant dishes during the holidays because they have complex layerings of flavor, and they're very easy to prepare.

California cooking has a sense of sparkle and freshness not bound by tradition. A leg of lamb emerges "California-Indonesian" when marinated with a grainy French mustard and exotic star anise. A grilled scallop brochette is delicious with a lemon butter sauce, but instead it's topped with a toasted almond caper relish. These are ideas that have originated in restaurant kitchens, adapted here for the home cook.

While there are no specific rules in planning a menu, I consider balance of flavor, richness, color and repetition of ingredients. Menus in this Pacific rim state tend to be cross-cultural and might include a southwestern-style first course soup (Black Bean Soup with Lime Cream) followed by an Asian-style main course (Grilled Swordfish on a Bed of Pasta with Asian Salsa) ending with an Italian influenced dessert (Orange Almond Olive Oil Cake).

Contemporary California cooking has a logical and healthful base. For example, in reinterpreting the warm spinach salad, I thought about the traditional version with crumbled eggs and a bacon dressing. Then I remembered my countless hours on the treadmill. While retaining the crunchy bacon, I eliminated the bacon grease, added a light olive oil dressing and for color added tomatoes along with egg quarters. The result is a more healthful, satisfying twist on a classic salad, logical and simple.

Perhaps the easiest recipe in this book is grilled lamb chops with a cranberry-rosemary marinade, another simple but logical idea. In my research, I discovered that the California Rancho cooks marinated lamb with pomegranate juice. They must have chosen this juice for its availability and its pungency to compensate for the gaminess of their lamb. Today lamb is much milder so I substituted a lighter version of the pomegranate taste and came up with the cranberry juice–rosemary marinade.

Healthful food that maintains the basic integrity of a dish is very important to me. I don't substitute tofu for red meat, but I do reduce indulgent levels of cream, butter, and other fats, especially when the result remains incredibly satisfying. Spicy marinades, herb coatings and simple reductions help create lighter but brightly flavored foods. Fresh herb combinations are terrific flavor enhancers and provide excellent substitutes for salt.

But when you want something really indulgent for a special occasion, those recipes are here too—Chocolate Truffle Brownies can make your reputation as a cook. I am a working mother with more than a full-time schedule and family responsibilities, so I want the food I prepare to be all things simultaneously—quick to prepare, fresh, and exciting. If there's a faster way to prepare a delicious broccoli soup using a hand blender rather than a food mill, I'll take advantage of the latest technology. If I need fresh tomato salsa and don't have time to prepare it, I'll trust a quality supermarket version. And if I can substitute low-fat yogurt successfully for sour cream or crème fraîche I do.

The California Cook is a convergence of all these ideas, to accommodate busy lifestyles and our increasing sophistication and cultural diversity. The result is a cooking style that produces food that's tantalizing but also familiar to the palate. I hope you will find the techniques, tips, and advance preparation notes that are a part of each recipe valuable, and I sincerely hope these foods bring you much pleasure.

—Diane Rossen Worthington

A NOTE ON WINES

THE WINES SELECTED for a meal should flow from one to the next. It is just as important for the second wine to relate to the first as it is for the first to relate to the dish with which it's served. Just like the meal itself, the wines should offer a beginning, a middle, and an end.

Appetizers would be very easy to match with wine if they weren't followed by a main dish. If they were on their own, you'd simply select a wine to balance the flavors of the dish and leave it at that. But when the appetizer is part of a full meal—which it is by definition—other important considerations are involved in choosing the first wine.

The accepted way to provide a deftly orchestrated range of wines is to move from light to heavy, from white to red, from dry to sweet. Thus an appetizer that calls for a spicy red may have to be matched with a less assertive white to preserve the sequence of the meal.

—Anthony Dias Blue

THE CALIFORNIA COOK

APPETIZERS AND FIRST COURSES

PEAR, PISTACHIO, AND CHICKEN LIVER MOUSSE 3

SMOKED SALMON AND CAVIAR TORTA 5

SMOKED FISH MOUSSE 7

ASIAN GRAVLAX WITH GINGER-MUSTARD SAUCE 8

GINGER-MUSTARD SAUCE 9

SHRIMP SALSA 11

ASSORTED GRILLED VEGETABLES 13

ROASTED PEPPERS WITH MINT VINAIGRETTE AND GOAT CHEESE
CROUTONS 15

CHILLED ARTICHOKE HALVES WITH RED PEPPER AÏOLI 17

GREEN OLIVE TAPENADE 19

SUN-DRIED TOMATO TAPENADE 21

GREEN PEA GUACAMOLE 22

ASIAN GUACAMOLE 24

GOAT CHEESE WITH RUSTIC SALSA 25

BAKED BRIE WITH SUN-DRIED TOMATO PESTO 27

GRIDDLED QUESADILLAS WITH CARAMELIZED ONIONS,
CHICKEN, AND JACK CHEESE 29

CALIFORNIA CAPONATA 31

RICOTTA CORN CAKES WITH SMOKY SALSA TOPPING 33

TUNA TARTARE 35

PEAR, PISTACHIO, AND CHICKEN LIVER MOUSSE

SERVES 8 TO 12

CALIFORNIANS LOVE FRUIT in just about everything, including pâté. In this fluffy mousselike pâté, juicy Bosc pears and softened black currants add an intriguing essence, while pistachios bring a buttery flavor and crisp texture to the mild chicken liver base. Look for a domestic pear brandy. It's less expensive and will still provide the right flavor. Serve this mousse with mild crackers or sliced French bread.

For a large party, double the recipe and pour the mousse into an 8- or 9-inch springform pan. As a more elaborate alternative to the simple pistachio and parsley garnish, decorate the top with cherry tomato quarters arranged as flower petals, a chive stem, and an outer border of dill. When ready to serve, unmold the mousse and cover the sides with finely chopped parsley. This mousse makes a wonderful gift for the holidays.

RECOMMENDED WINE: My first instinct here would be to suggest a late harvest wine to balance the sweetness of the fruit and the richness of the chicken liver. Keeping in mind the next course, however, it may be better to opt for a crisp, off-dry (1 to 2 percent residual sugar) Riesling or Gewürztraminer.

2	tablespoons dried black currants
1/4	cup pear brandy
3	tablespoons unsalted butter
2	tablespoons olive oil
1	medium onion, finely chopped
1	medium Bosc pear, peeled, cored, and finely chopped
2	garlic cloves, minced
1	teaspoon salt
1/4	teaspoon dried thyme leaves

1/8 teaspoon ground allspice
1/8 teaspoon white pepper
1   pound cream cheese, softened and cut into 2-inch pieces
1   pound chicken livers
2   tablespoons coarsely chopped unsalted pistachios

GARNISH
shelled unsalted pistachios
parsley sprig

1. Soften the currants by pouring the pear brandy over them and letting them steep for at least 4 hours and up to 24 hours.

2. In a large skillet over medium heat, melt 2 tablespoons of the butter and 1 tablespoon of the oil. Add the onion and sauté for 3 to 5 minutes or until softened. Add the pear and continue cooking until softened. Add the garlic and cook for another minute.

3. Transfer the mixture to a food processor fitted with the metal blade and puree. Add the salt, thyme, allspice, white pepper, and cream cheese and process until pureed.

4. Heat the remaining tablespoon of oil and butter in the same skillet and sauté the chicken livers over medium-high heat until the chicken livers are cooked through and just slightly pink (about 5 to 7 minutes). Strain the pear brandy from the currants (reserving the currants) and add the brandy to the skillet. Ignite the brandy with a long match, averting your head and making sure any overhead fan is off.

5. When the flame has gone out, add the liver mixture to the onion-pear mixture in the food processor and continue to process for about 30 seconds or until the mousse is smooth. Add the softened currants and the pistachios and process until just combined, making sure the currants and pistachios retain their texture. Taste for seasoning.

6. Pour into a 4-cup crock or mold and decorate with the whole pistachios and a sprig of parsley. Chill for at least 4 hours before serving.

ADVANCE PREPARATION: Can be prepared up to 3 days ahead, covered well, and refrigerated.

SMOKED SALMON AND CAVIAR TORTA

SERVES 6 TO 8

THIS IS PARTICULARLY festive for a cocktail party or as an appetizer at a more formal dinner party. Layers of crunchy cucumber and velvety smoked salmon star here. Combining ricotta cheese with the cream cheese base lightens the mixture.

Sparkling beads of colorful red and yellow American "caviars" make a dazzling design on the top of the torta. Purists insist that only the processed roe of the sturgeon can be called caviar, but you can find jars of various other processed fish eggs labeled caviar in most specialty stores. Here salmon and whitefish caviar are used.

Ask for the less expensive lox or smoked salmon end pieces since you will be chopping them anyway. Accompany with simple crackers or toast so that the full flavor of the torta is highlighted. Follow this with Rack of Lamb with Mint Crust (page 244) and Confetti Rice Pilaf (page 305).

RECOMMENDED WINE: A crisp, dry sparkling wine does well here. The shimmering bubbles underscore the festive quality of the torta. A fresh Sauvignon Blanc will also do the trick with the smokiness of the wine complimenting the smokiness of the salmon.

1/2 pound ricotta cheese
1/2 pound cream cheese
1   tablespoon finely chopped fresh dill
1   tablespoon finely chopped fresh chives
1   tablespoon fresh lemon juice
1/4 teaspoon salt
     pinch of white pepper
1/2 cup peeled, seeded, and diced cucumber
7   ounces smoked salmon, finely chopped

GARNISH
2   ounces salmon caviar
2   ounces golden whitefish caviar
    fresh dill sprigs

1. Oil a 3-1/2- by 6- by 2-1/2-inch loaf pan. Place plastic wrap inside so that it is tucked into all the corners, leaving enough to cover the top after you've made the torta.

2. Process the ricotta, cream cheese, dill, chives, lemon juice, salt, and pepper in a food processor fitted with the metal blade until completely blended and softened. With a rubber spatula, spread one third of the softened cheese mixture on the bottom of the pan. Make sure the layer is even.

3. Carefully spoon one half of the chopped cucumber on top of the cheese mixture, patting it in an even layer. Top with one half of the chopped salmon, patting it in an even layer.

4. With the rubber spatula, spread another third of the cheese on top. Again, make sure it's an even layer. Repeat with the remaining cucumber and salmon. Spread the remaining cheese mixture on top, making sure the salmon and cucumber do not show through. Cover the torta completely with the plastic wrap and refrigerate for at least 4 hours or until well set. (If you have any cheese mixture left, refrigerate it and spread it on toast or French bread.)

5. To unmold, fold back the top layer of plastic wrap, lift the whole torta from the pan, and invert it on a rectangular platter. Remove the plastic wrap and garnish the top with alternating stripes of golden whitefish and salmon caviar. Garnish the sides with dill sprigs. Serve with slices of freshly toasted French bread or a simple cracker.

ADVANCE PREPARATION: Can be prepared up to 1 day ahead through step 5 and refrigerated.

SMOKED FISH MOUSSE

MAKES 1 CUP TO SERVE 4 TO 6

THIS QUICK APPETIZER always wins raves from my guests. Ask to taste the smoked fish before buying it to make sure it's evenly balanced, not too oily and not too smoky. Add the lemon juice sparingly since it tends to bring out the saltiness of smoked fish. Remember to make this ahead, even a few days, so that the flavors can blend and the saltiness mellow.

RECOMMENDED WINE: Try a crisp and slightly smoky Sauvignon Blanc (Fumé Blanc), which offers nice balance to this smoky mousse.

1	**small shallot**
1/2	**pound lean smoked trout, whitefish, or bluefish, all bones removed**
3	**tablespoons mayonnaise**
2	**tablespoons cream cheese**
1 to 2	**tablespoons fresh lemon juice to taste**
	pinch of white pepper
	pinch of cayenne pepper
1	**tablespoon finely chopped parsley**

GARNISH
parsley sprigs

1. With the motor running, mince the shallot in a food processor fitted with the metal blade. Combine all remaining ingredients and process until pureed. Taste for seasoning. If the mousse tastes overly salty, don't worry; it will balance out as it sits. Spoon into a 1-1/2-cup crock and serve with a simple cracker or lightly toasted, thinly sliced egg bread. Garnish with parsley sprigs.

ADVANCE PREPARATION: Can be prepared up to 3 days ahead, covered well, and refrigerated.

ASIAN GRAVLAX WITH GINGER-MUSTARD SAUCE

SERVES 8 TO 12

GRAVLAX—CURED FRESH salmon—is traditionally marinated with dill. This California variation uses the stronger, more aromatic cilantro along with fresh ginger and spicy Sichuan peppercorns. Sometimes called *anise pepper* or *Chinese pepper*, Sichuan peppercorns can be found in Chinese markets. If they aren't available, use white peppercorns.

The fish is actually cooked, or cured, by the marinade, but the curing takes time, so begin four days before you plan to serve. Serve the gravlax with sliced sourdough or French bread. Follow with Braised Stuffed Shoulder of Veal (page 260) and Roasted Winter Vegetables (page 274).

RECOMMENDED WINE: A crisp and lively Sauvignon Blanc is ideal with the gravlax.

2 to 2-1/2 pounds fresh salmon fillet (1 large piece)

3	tablespoons sugar
2	tablespoons kosher or coarse salt
2	teaspoons Sichuan peppercorns or white peppercorns
1	teaspoon coriander seed
1	tablespoon finely chopped fresh ginger
4	large bunches of fresh cilantro

GARNISH
lemon wedges
cilantro leaves
Ginger-Mustard Sauce (recipe follows)
thinly sliced French bread

1. Lay the salmon on a sheet of wax paper. Combine the sugar, salt, peppercorns, coriander seed, and ginger in a small bowl. Rub the salmon with half the mixture. Turn the salmon and rub with the remaining mixture. Press down firmly on the salmon to make sure the seasonings coat the fish evenly.

2. Arrange 2 bunches of cilantro on the bottom of a large, shallow nonaluminum pan. Place the salmon on top. Then arrange the remaining 2 bunches of cilantro over the salmon to resemble a sandwich.

3. Cover well with foil or plastic wrap; place a weight on top—a heavy pot lid, brick, or large can—and refrigerate. Turn the salmon twice a day for 4 days. Make sure the cilantro and peppercorn paste is evenly distributed.

4. To serve, remove all the cilantro and the peppercorn paste. Lightly pat the salmon dry with paper towels, making sure all the salt and sugar is removed. Slice very thinly on the bias and serve with the garnishes.

Ginger-Mustard Sauce

MAKES 1 CUP

THIS SWEET MUSTARD herb sauce has a texture similar to mayonnaise. It's great with poached salmon or gravlax.

1/4 cup Dijon or grainy mustard
3   tablespoons dark brown sugar
2   tablespoons cider vinegar
1   teaspoon dry mustard
1/3 cup vegetable oil
1   tablespoon finely chopped fresh ginger
2   tablespoons finely chopped cilantro
1   tablespoon finely chopped parsley

1. In a food processor fitted with the metal blade or a blender, mix the mustard, brown sugar, vinegar, and dry mustard and process for a few seconds. While the machine is running, add the oil in a steady stream until the sauce is thick and smooth. Blend in the ginger, cilantro, and parsley and process for a minute.

2. Pour the sauce into a small bowl. Chill for 2 to 3 hours or until ready to use.

ADVANCE PREPARATION: Can be prepared up to several weeks ahead and refrigerated.

SHRIMP SALSA

MAKES 6 CUPS

THIS VARIATION ON one of my favorite recipes, Guacamole Salsa from my last book, *The Taste of Summer*, blends sweet cooked shrimp with crunchy, colorful vegetables. The spices here are Mexican, but you can use fresh basil or dill instead of the cilantro. Warm crisp tortilla chips (page 324) are my first choice for dipping. For a lighter appetizer, try Belgian endive leaves, celery ribs, or even jícama sticks.

RECOMMENDED WINE: A slightly off-dry Gewürztraminer would be a spicy complement to this spicy appetizer. The salsa also works well with a wood-aged Sauvignon Blanc.

2   large tomatoes (about 1 pound), peeled, seeded, and diced
1/2 medium red bell pepper, diced (about 1/2 cup)
1/2 medium yellow bell pepper, diced (about 1/2 cup)
1   cup peeled and diced jícama
1/2 European cucumber, diced
1/2 cup corn kernels, preferably white (about 1 medium ear)
2   tablespoons finely chopped cilantro
2   tablespoons finely chopped parsley
1   jalapeño chile, seeded and finely chopped*
2   tablespoons fresh lime juice
1   teaspoon salt
1/4 teaspoon black pepper
1   ripe medium avocado, peeled and cut into 1/2-inch pieces
1/2 pound cooked and peeled medium shrimp, diced

GARNISH
cilantro leaves

---

* When you're working with chiles, always wear rubber gloves. Wash the cutting surface and knife immediately.

1. Combine all the ingredients except the avocado and shrimp in a medium mixing bowl. Refrigerate for at least 1 hour.

2. Spoon into a serving bowl. Right before serving, add the avocado and shrimp and taste for seasoning. Garnish with cilantro leaves and serve with the chips or crudités as described.

ADVANCE PREPARATION: Can be prepared up to 6 hours ahead through step 1 and refrigerated.

ASSORTED GRILLED VEGETABLES

SERVES 6

PICTURE A LARGE platter of colorful vegetables, each with its own grill marks, decoratively arranged. Pretty barbecued vegetables are one of the signature clean flavors of California cooking. This is an elegant beginning to lunch or dinner as well as an excellent side dish.

Don't restrict yourself to these choices. Whatever is fresh and at its best is appropriate for the grill and your table. Roma tomatoes, asparagus, Belgian or California endive, and small rounds of corn are other good choices.

A drizzle of olive oil, a squirt of lemon juice, and a sprinkling of fresh herbs heighten the pure flavors of grilled vegetables. Or make a more elaborate presentation by arranging bowls of Smoky Salsa (page 416), Red Pepper Aïoli (page 408) and either of the tapenades alongside the vegetables.

RECOMMENDED WINE: Try a crisp, fruity Sauvignon Blanc with this dish. The herbal qualities of the wine will blend nicely with the vegetables.

2   red bell peppers
2   yellow bell peppers
4   medium Japanese eggplant
4   medium zucchini
1   small butternut squash
1   medium fennel bulb, quartered
1/2 cup olive oil

GARNISH
fresh lemon or lime juice
olive oil
assorted finely chopped fresh herbs

1. Prepare the barbecue for medium-high heat grilling. Grill the peppers approximately 4 inches from the heat until the skin is blistered and slightly charred on all sides. Always use long tongs to turn the peppers. Put the peppers in a brown paper bag and close it tightly. Let the peppers rest for 10 minutes. Remove the peppers from the bag and drain them. Peel off the charred skin with your fingers. Make a slit in each pepper and open it up. Core and cut off the stem. Scrape the seeds and ribs from the peppers. Cut the peppers into 1/2-inch wide slices.

2. Trim the stems off the zucchini and eggplants and slice them into 1/4-inch lengthwise pieces. Peel and cut the butternut squash in half. Remove the seeds. Slice it into 1/4-inch thick slices. Cut the fennel bulb into quarters.

3. Brush the eggplant and zucchini slices with oil and grill on each side for about 3 minutes or until the vegetables have grill marks and are beginning to feel soft. Repeat with the squash which may take 4 to 5 minutes on a side. Repeat again with the fennel, about 3 to 4 minutes per side.

4. Arrange the vegetables on a large platter in an attractive design. Drizzle them with olive oil, lemon or lime juice, and a sprinkle of fresh herbs. Serve with olives and dipping sauces if desired.

ADVANCE PREPARATION: Can be prepared up to 2 days ahead, covered well and refrigerated. Remove from the refrigerator 1/2 hour before serving.

ROASTED PEPPERS WITH MINT VINAIGRETTE AND GOAT CHEESE CROUTONS

SERVES 6

COLORFUL SWEET BELL peppers, available for much of the year, make a lovely first course. Fresh mint is a surprise with the sweet peppers, and goat cheese croutons add a creamy dimension. You can also serve the goat cheese croutons topped with the minted pepper mixture on a serving platter.

RECOMMENDED WINE: A steely, crisp Sauvignon Blanc is an excellent match for the peppers.

6   red or yellow bell peppers, peeled (page 287) and cut into 1/2-inch
      slices

DRESSING
2   teaspoons fresh lemon juice
3   tablespoons red wine vinegar
1   garlic clove, minced
2   tablespoons very finely chopped fresh mint
6   tablespoons olive oil
1/4 teaspoon salt
      pinch of white pepper

GARNISH
3/4 cup softened fresh goat cheese or herbed cream cheese
18 1/4-inch-thick slices of French or sourdough bread, lightly toasted
      mint sprigs

1. For the dressing, combine the lemon juice, vinegar, garlic, and mint and mix well. Slowly add the oil and whisk to combine until it is emulsified. Add salt and pepper and taste for seasoning. Place the peppers in a bowl and pour the dressing over them. Marinate for 2 hours or more.

2. To serve, drain the peppers and place them on a serving platter. Spread the softened cheese on croutons and arrange them around the outside of the platter. Garnish the peppers with mint sprigs and serve.

ADVANCE PREPARATION: The marinated peppers can be kept up to 3 days in the refrigerator. Remove from the refrigerator 2 hours before serving. Add the goat cheese croutons just before serving.

CHILLED ARTICHOKE HALVES WITH RED PEPPER AÏOLI

SERVES 6

AMERICA'S ENTIRE COMMERCIAL artichoke crop is grown on just over 9,000 acres concentrated in only five California counties—a meager harvest compared to Italy's 150,000 acres of artichokes. In recent years even fewer farmers have been growing artichokes because the demand has declined. Sadly, some artichoke enthusiasts think the decline is linked to Italian families not passing on their culinary traditions and instead opting for quicker cooking solutions. But Californians love artichokes and consume nearly 40 percent of the domestic crop.

This simple first course is a nice way to begin a small sit-down dinner party since everything can be prepared ahead. Have small bowls on the table for your guests to put the leaves in when they're finished. If you prefer a lighter sauce, reduce the mayonnaise by one quarter and make up the difference with plain nonfat yogurt.

RECOMMENDED WINE: Although artichokes are thought to be unfriendly to wine, a dry Chenin Blanc or spicy Sauvignon Blanc goes nicely with this dish.

3   large artichokes
3   slices of lemon
1   tablespoon olive oil
3/4 cup Red Pepper Aïoli (page 408)
2   tablespoons finely chopped parsley

1. Cut the sharp points off the artichoke leaves with kitchen shears. Remove the small dry outer leaves from around the base of the artichoke. Cut off the stem 1 inch from the bottom of each artichoke. Soak the artichokes in cold water for at least 15 minutes to clean them.

2. Place the artichokes upright in a pan with about 4 inches of water, the lemon slices, and the olive oil. Cook over medium heat for 30 to 45 minutes, partially covered, or until the leaves pull off easily. Bring the artichokes to room temperature and then cut them in half lengthwise.

3. Scoop out the fuzzy choke with a teaspoon and discard. Mound 2 to 3 tablespoons of Red Pepper Aïoli in the center of each half. Sprinkle with parsley just before serving.

ADVANCE PREPARATION: The artichokes can be prepared up to 1 day ahead, covered, and refrigerated. Bring to room temperature to serve.

GREEN OLIVE TAPENADE

MAKES ABOUT 1 CUP

WITH ORCHARDS OF European olive trees sprouting up throughout Napa and Sonoma counties, observers are beginning to compare today's burgeoning California olive oil industry to the Napa Valley wine industry of the 1950s. This recipe for tapenade uses California's plentiful green olives as a less pungent alternative to the traditional black Niçoise olives. Pitted French green olives also work well. Either way, be sure to rinse the olives well, since they're often packed in strong brine.

This intensely flavored olive paste is often used as a flavor enhancer, not just as a spread for crackers or interesting-flavored breads. Excellent as a dipping sauce for raw vegetables, it can also be used to flavor mayonnaise or salad dressing. Or spread it on chicken before roasting or grilling.

RECOMMENDED WINE: This tapenade goes nicely with crisp, dry sparkling wine, dry Chenin Blanc, or Sauvignon Blanc.

20 large or 30 medium pitted green olives, drained and rinsed
2   garlic cloves, minced
2   tablespoons capers, well drained and rinsed
2   canned anchovy fillets, drained
2   teaspoons Dijon mustard
2   tablespoons fresh lemon juice
2   tablespoons finely chopped fresh basil
1/4 cup finely chopped flat-leaf parsley
1/8 teaspoon cayenne pepper
1/3 cup olive oil

1. Combine all the ingredients except the oil in a food processor fitted with the metal blade. Process the ingredients until pureed, using a rubber spatula to scrape the bowl and push down the ingredients that are not getting pureed.

2. With the motor running, slowly add the olive oil until it is completely absorbed. Taste for seasoning. Transfer to an airtight container and refrigerate until needed.

ADVANCE PREPARATION: Can be prepared up to 1 week ahead and refrigerated.

SUN-DRIED TOMATO TAPENADE

MAKES ABOUT 1 CUP

CHEF GARY DANKO of the San Francisco Ritz-Carlton Hotel is known for his innovative blending of classic French cooking style with California ingredients. This rich, thick paste, a variation on Gary's recipe, is perfect to serve as a dip or as a spread on Parmesan cheese toasts or a simple cracker. I like to serve Green Olive Tapenade (page 19) alongside this one for a marvelous contrast of colors and flavors. It's fun to watch your guests decide which they prefer. You can be sure that opinions will change more than once.

RECOMMENDED WINE: Dry sparkling wine, dry Chenin Blanc, or Sauvignon Blanc is ideal.

2	garlic cloves, minced
1	8-ounce jar oil-packed sun-dried tomatoes
1/4 cup capers, well drained and rinsed	
3	canned anchovy fillets, drained
1	tablespoon finely chopped parsley
1	tablespoon finely chopped fresh basil
2	teaspoons Dijon mustard
2	teaspoons balsamic vinegar
2	tablespoons olive oil or hot water
	pinch of black pepper

1. With the motor running, mince the garlic in a food processor fitted with the metal blade. Combine all the remaining ingredients except the oil and pepper and process until pureed, using a rubber spatula to scrape the bowl and push down the ingredients that are not getting pureed. Add the oil and pepper and process until combined. Taste for seasoning. Transfer to an airtight container and refrigerate until needed.

ADVANCE PREPARATION: Can be prepared up to 1 week ahead and refrigerated.

GREEN PEA GUACAMOLE
SERVES 4 TO 6

MICHAEL ROBERTS IS an inventive Southern California chef who's always coming up with unusual variations on classic dishes. When I first tasted his green pea guacamole, I was puzzled by the unusual yet pleasing quality of the green peas he used instead of avocado. I have combined the two in this adaptation to create a refreshing, clean flavor. If you like a creamier consistency, add a bit more sour cream. Serve this with crisp tortilla chips (page 324), Griddled Quesadillas (page 29), or Grilled Flank Steak with Smoky Salsa (page 235).

RECOMMENDED WINE: A fresh, youthful Chardonnay or a dry Chenin Blanc complements the creaminess of this guacamole.

1/2 pound thawed frozen baby peas
1/2 medium or 1 small very ripe avocado, peeled, pitted, and cubed
2   tablespoons fresh lemon juice
2   tablespoons tomatillo salsa (page 414)
2   tablespoons sour cream
2   tablespoons finely chopped cilantro
1/4 teaspoon ground cumin
1/4 teaspoon salt
1   small jalapeño chile, seeded and finely chopped*

GARNISH
cilantro leaves

---

* When you're working with chiles, always wear rubber gloves. Wash the cutting surface and knife immediately.

1. In a food processor fitted with the metal blade, combine all the ingredients and process until the peas are pureed. Taste for seasoning. Spoon into a small serving bowl and garnish with cilantro leaves. Serve with crudités or yellow or blue corn chips.

ADVANCE PREPARATION: Can be prepared up to 4 hours ahead, covered, and refrigerated.

ASIAN GUACAMOLE

SERVES 4 TO 6

ALAN WONG, CHEF at the Mauna Lani Bay Hotel's Canoe House on the Big Island of Hawaii, is renowned for his intriguing twists on traditional recipes. He serves this simple but uniquely flavored guacamole with taro chips, which unfortunately are difficult to find. Substitute shrimp chips or blue or yellow corn chips for a great beginning to an informal Asian-inspired dinner. If available, use Haas avocados, which have fuller flavor than other types.

RECOMMENDED WINE: A crisp, dry Gewürztraminer will balance nicely with the spiciness of this dish.

1   serrano chile, seeded and finely chopped*
2   very ripe medium avocados, peeled, pitted, and coarsely chopped
2   tablespoons finely chopped red onion
1   small tomato, peeled, seeded, and finely chopped
    juice of 1 lime
1   tablespoon sake
1   tablespoon finely chopped cilantro
1   tablespoon finely chopped scallion, white and light green parts only
1   tablespoon finely chopped fresh ginger
1/2 teaspoon salt

1. Combine all the ingredients in a medium mixing bowl and stir. Taste for seasoning. Serve with corn chips, carrots, celery, or endive leaves.

---

* When you're working with chiles, always wear rubber gloves. Wash the cutting surface and knife immediately.

GOAT CHEESE WITH RUSTIC SALSA

SERVES 8

WHEN I WROTE *The Cuisine of California* in the early 1980s, California French-style goat cheese had just arrived on the scene. Laura Chenel was a pioneer in the California goat cheese industry, and it was with much excitement that I visited her small Sonoma factory at the inception of this cottage industry.

Cheese making is still a labor of love for Laura, but it's also become a viable business that continues to expand. Many different varieties of California goat's milk cheese are now available, from fresh to aged. The fresh cheese has a mild flavor and a soft, spreadable texture. Aged cheeses like Crottin and Taupinière boast a complex, sophisticated flavor, perfect on their own or accompanying a simple green salad. This recipe uses fresh goat cheese in a simple, colorful, and easy appetizer. If you don't have time to make the salsa, pick up a fresh store-bought one.

RECOMMENDED WINE: This offers a difficult combination of elements to match with wine. First there's the rich creaminess of the cheese, then there's the fruit and spice of the salsa. My first wine choice would be a Gamay Beaujolais or lively, youthful Zinfandel, both lightly chilled. If you must serve a white wine, a rich, oaky Chardonnay will do.

1 8-ounce log of fresh California goat cheese
1 cup Rustic Salsa (page 415) or store-bought
24 thin slices of French bread

1. Place the goat cheese log in the center of a serving platter. Spoon the salsa over it and then arrange the bread slices around the outside edge of the platter. Serve immediately.

ADVANCE PREPARATION: Can be prepared up to 4 hours ahead, covered well, and refrigerated. Add the bread just before serving.

SUN-DRIED TOMATOES

The southern Italians were the first to come up with the idea of drying tomatoes in the sun. In the dry and sunny Mediterranean summer the plump, meaty plum tomato was reduced to a leathery state, covered with olive oil, and bottled for winter use. Today California and the rest of the world seem to have gone sun-dried tomato crazy, and the first casualty in the industrialization of the product has been, of course, the sun.

On a recent visit to Sonoma County's largest dried-tomato producer, I expected to see racks of deep red tomatoes drying picturesquely in the sun. I was told, "That's the romance; dehydrators are the reality."

Drying tomatoes greatly intensifies their flavor and gives them a chewy texture, though the quality can vary widely among producers. The characteristic sunny, earthy flavor marries well with other Mediterranean ingredients such as polenta, grilled vegetables, and pasta. Dried tomatoes, along with goat cheese, have become a quintessential ingredient for California pizza and are often paired with fresh tomatoes for a deep, complex flavor.

•   Recipes that call for sun-dried tomatoes must be read carefully: are they dried, oil-packed, halves, or chopped? Halved dried tomatoes should always be reconstituted before being used. Pour boiling water over them and allow them to steep for 10 minutes. Drain them well and cover them with a good olive oil. Keep them in the refrigerator and use the oil for dressings or as a condiment.

•   Make Sun-Dried Tomato Pesto (page 404) and use it on baked potatoes, in salad dressings, in pasta sauces, and in dips.

•   Add chopped sun-dried tomatoes to a cheese torta or mix with ricotta for stuffing pasta.

•   Garnish an omelet with sour cream and chopped sun-dried tomatoes or very finely mince and add them to a soufflé mixture.

•   Make sun-dried tomato butter: Mix 2 tablespoons chopped dried tomatoes with softened butter. Form the tomato butter into a log in wax paper and freeze. Slice off the tomato butter as needed to garnish grilled steaks, poultry, or vegetables.

BAKED BRIE WITH SUN-DRIED TOMATO PESTO
SERVES 8 TO 10

SUN-DRIED TOMATO pesto contributes an earthy-sweet contrast to soft-ripened, creamy Brie. Dry-packed sun-dried tomatoes can either be softened in hot water or marinated in olive oil, which will also soften them. For a richer flavor you may need to add a bit more oil to the pesto if you choose water-softened tomatoes.

This baked cheese is perfect for a cocktail party, beautiful as well as utterly delicious. California produces soft-ripened Brie and Camembert, but for this dish I prefer a French Brie. Brie comes in a variety of sizes; just adjust the pesto quantity if you want to use a larger cheese than indicated here. Accompany the Brie with thinly sliced toasted French bread.

You can also serve this at room temperature with a few minor variations; remove the rim and top edge of the Brie carefully with a very sharp knife. Press the toasted pine nuts all around the rim. Spread the top thickly with the pesto. Place on a serving platter, bring to room temperature, and decorate with the basil. This is particularly enjoyable on warmer evenings.

RECOMMENDED WINE: Best with a red wine—serve Syrah, Merlot, Pinot Noir, or a Zinfandel. Another possibility is a chilled dry Vin Gris—a "blush" wine usually made from Pinot Noir.

1/2 cup Sun-Dried Tomato Pesto (page 404)
1   1-pound Brie

GARNISH
1/4 cup pine nuts
   fresh basil leaves

1. If the pesto is very thick, you may need to add a bit of olive oil. Place the Brie on an ovenproof dish. Make about 8 wheel-spoke cuts down into the cheese, leaving a little circle in the center uncut to hold the wheel together during baking. With a spoon, carefully push a few tablespoons of pesto down into each slit so it's flush with the top. Tie a piece of cooking string around the rim of the Brie to hold its shape.

2. Preheat the oven to 350°F. Toast the pine nuts on a baking sheet for 5 minutes or until lightly browned; reserve for garnish.

3. Place the cheese in the oven and bake for 10 to 15 minutes or until it just begins to melt. Remove from the oven, untie the string, sprinkle the pine nuts on top, and decorate with a garland of fresh basil leaves around the base of the cheese. Serve immediately with crisp crackers.

ADVANCE PREPARATION: Can be prepared up to 2 days ahead through step 2, covered, and refrigerated. Keep the pine nuts covered at room temperature. Bring the cheese to room temperature before baking.

GRIDDLED QUESADILLAS WITH CARAMELIZED ONIONS, CHICKEN, AND JACK CHEESE

SERVES 6

QUESADILLAS, THOSE PUFFY "little whims" as the Mexicans call appetizers, can be found in most Mexican restaurants in many variations. Sometimes called *empanadas*, these turnovers have evolved through the years. Traditionally, masa dough is flattened and folded over to enclose a variety of fillings.

In California we make quesadillas with either corn or flour tortillas. They can be simple, with a melted cheese center, or more complicated creations like this one. Olive oil spray on the pan or griddle keeps the outside crispy without being overly greasy. If you don't have the spray, add a tablespoon of vegetable or light-flavored olive oil to the pan and make sure it is very hot before cooking the tortillas. These small triangles are wonderful served as a first course before a Mexican-style main course like Grilled Skirt Steak with Avocado-Tomato Salsa (page 229) or as a main course for brunch or lunch.

RECOMMENDED WINE: A spicy, rich central coast Chardonnay is perfect with this flavorful appetizer.

3	cups chicken stock (page 397) and/or water
1	boneless medium chicken breast or 1-1/2 cups shredded cooked chicken breast
1	tablespoon vegetable oil
2	large red onions, thinly sliced
1/2	cup beer, a medium bodied lager
2	tablespoons balsamic vinegar
1	teaspoon sugar

1   medium jalapeño chile, seeded and finely chopped*
1   teaspoon finely chopped fresh oregano or 1/2 teaspoon dried
1/4   teaspoon salt
1/8   teaspoon pepper
     nonstick spray
3   12-inch flour tortillas
1-1/2 cups shredded Jack cheese

GARNISH
1/2   cup Green Pea Guacamole (page 22)
1/2   cup salsa of your choice
1/2   cup sour cream

1. In a deep medium skillet or a large saucepan, bring the chicken stock (or enough of a combination of chicken stock and water to cover the chicken) to a simmer. If you're using water only, add 1/2 teaspoon salt. Add the chicken breast and simmer for 10 to 12 minutes or until just tender. Cool the chicken in the stock. Drain the chicken, remove the skin, and shred it into bite-size slices.

2. Heat the oil in large nonaluminum casserole over medium-high heat. Add the onions and sauté, stirring frequently, for about 10 to 15 minutes or until well softened.

3. Add the beer, vinegar, sugar, and jalapeño to the onions and simmer over low heat until almost all of the liquid has evaporated. The onions should be very tender and slightly caramelized. Add the oregano, salt, and pepper. Taste for seasoning and let cool.

4. Lightly spray a 12-inch nonstick skillet or griddle with nonstick spray or add a tablespoon of oil and place over medium-high heat. Place a tortilla in the skillet and spoon 1/2 cup of the onion mixture evenly over one half. Sprinkle with 1/2 cup chicken and top evenly with 1/2 cup shredded cheese; fold the tortilla in half, pressing down with a spatula. Cook the quesadilla until lightly brown, then turn over and cook the other side until lightly brown. Place on a cutting board, slice into bite-size wedges, and keep warm under foil.

5. Repeat to cook the remaining quesadillas. Arrange on a large serving platter and serve immediately accompanied by Green Pea Guacamole, salsa, and sour cream.

ADVANCE PREPARATION: Can be prepared up to 1 day ahead through step 3 and refrigerated. Remove from refrigerator 1 hour before continuing.

---

* When you're working with chiles, always wear rubber gloves. Wash the cutting surface and knife immediately.

CALIFORNIA CAPONATA

MAKES ABOUT 1-1/2 CUPS TO SERVE 4 TO 6

CAPONATA, THE SICILIAN appetizer, is often served at room temperature on toasted croutons. Traditionally it includes tomatoes, eggplant, onions, and capers to produce a pronounced sweet and sour taste. In this California version there's no tomato; roasted eggplant is paired with sweet onions and pungent Italian Gorgonzola to become a fragrant, warm spread for crisp toasts or warm French bread.

RECOMMENDED WINE: Use a rich, oaky Chardonnay to balance the richness of this dish.

1   medium eggplant
1   tablespoon olive oil
1   large red onion, finely chopped
2   tablespoons balsamic vinegar
1/4 cup water
2   tablespoons finely chopped parsley
    salt and pepper to taste
1/3 pound Gorgonzola Dolcelatte or other creamy blue cheese, cut into
      small pieces

1. Preheat the oven to 400°F. Place the eggplant on a baking sheet and prick in several spots. Bake for 50 minutes or until very tender. Remove from the oven. Cool, peel, and cut into 1/2-inch cubes.

2. While the eggplant is baking, heat the olive oil in a large skillet over medium heat. Add the onion and sauté, stirring frequently, until nicely browned, about 7 to 10 minutes. Add 1 tablespoon of the vinegar and continue cooking until the onions are very soft and thinly glazed, about 5 minutes. As the onions cook and the liquid evaporates, add the water, a spoonful at a time, to keep the onions moist and prevent burning. (This takes about 30 minutes.)

3. Add the eggplant and the remaining tablespoon of balsamic vinegar to the onions. Add the parsley, salt, and pepper and taste for seasoning. Gently heat through on medium heat for about 3 to 5 minutes. Add the cheese to the eggplant mixture and cook briefly, until just melted and distributed.

4. Spoon the mixture into a 2-cup crock and serve immediately with thin slices of French or sourdough bread.

ADVANCE PREPARATION: Can be prepared up to 8 hours ahead through step 3 and refrigerated. Bring to room temperature and then reheat gently before serving.

RICOTTA CORN CAKES WITH SMOKY SALSA TOPPING

SERVES 6 TO 8

WHEN I FIRST made light and fluffy Ricotta Pancakes with Spiced Pears, I wondered how a similar mixture would go with corn. Ricotta Corn Cakes are the result. The sweet flavors of fresh corn and ricotta cheese are a perfect contrast to the smoky salsa. For an equally delicious variation, combine the salsa and sour cream and spoon it over the corn cakes. For your main course, consider Roasted Cornish Hens with Honey Tangerine Marinade (page 212) and Tricolor Vegetable Sauté (page 272).

RECOMMENDED WINE: Use a crisp, spicy Sauvignon Blanc to balance the smokiness of this dish.

4   tablespoons unsalted butter
4   scallions, white and light green parts only, thinly sliced
4   large eggs
1   cup low-fat ricotta cheese
1/3 cup all-purpose flour
1/3 cup yellow cornmeal
1   teaspoon salt
1/4 teaspoon white pepper
1   cup fresh corn kernels (about 2 medium ears)

GARNISH
1/2 cup Smoky Salsa (page 416)
1/2 cup sour cream

1. In a medium skillet over medium heat, melt 3 tablespoons of the butter, add the scallions, and sauté until softened and slightly caramelized, stirring frequently,

about 7 minutes. Add the sautéed scallions and the melted butter in the pan to a food processor fitted with a metal blade.

2. To the sautéed scallions, add the eggs, cheese, flour, cornmeal, salt, and pepper and process until you have a smooth batter. Add the corn kernels and pulse a few times, being sure not to break up the corn too much.

3. Heat the remaining tablespoon of butter in a large nonstick skillet or griddle over medium heat. Using a small ladle or measuring cup with a pouring spout, pour about 1 tablespoon of batter into the skillet for each cake (the pancakes should be the size of silver dollars). Cook for approximately 2 minutes or until they bubble and are just set. Then flip the cakes and cook for another minute.

4. To serve, place the cakes on a large serving platter and garnish each with a dollop of salsa and sour cream. Serve immediately.

ADVANCE PREPARATION: The batter can be made up to 1 day in advance, covered well, and refrigerated. The corn cakes can be made up to 2 hours ahead and kept warm in a warm oven.

TUNA TARTARE

SERVES 6

LOS ANGELES'S CHAYA Brasserie Restaurant is known for its innovative cross-cultural blending of French, Italian, and Japanese cuisine with a California point of view. The appetizers are among the best in Los Angeles. In the Chaya version of tuna tartare (which might be called a double tuna sashimi), thick slices of raw tuna and a refreshing tuna tartare sit on top of a crispy wonton square. It is important to use only the freshest top quality grade tuna since the tuna is not cooked. This simplified adaptation is best served with crackers or lightly toasted French bread.

RECOMMENDED WINE: A big, rich, oaky Chardonnay should do the trick here. It will balance nicely with the tangy cornichons and the herbs. If you want to be a bit daring, try Champagne.

1	pound fresh tuna, cut into 1/2-inch pieces
1	teaspoon grainy mustard
2	tablespoons finely chopped scallion, both white and green parts
2	tablespoons finely chopped cornichons
1/2	cup finely chopped European cucumber
1 to 2	teaspoons finely chopped fresh tarragon
1 to 2	teaspoons green peppercorns, rinsed, drained, and crushed
1/2	ripe medium avocado, peeled, pitted, and cut into 1/2-inch pieces

DRESSING

2	tablespoons Champagne vinegar
1	teaspoon fresh lemon juice
1	teaspoon grainy mustard
1/4	cup light olive oil
	salt and pepper to taste

GARNISH

1   tablespoon finely chopped scallion, both white and green parts

1. In a medium mixing bowl, combine the tuna, mustard, scallion, cornichons, cucumber, tarragon, green peppercorns, and avocado.

2. To make the dressing, blend the vinegar, lemon juice, and mustard in a small mixing bowl using a whisk. Slowly add the oil, whisking until it is completely emulsified. Add salt and pepper and taste for seasoning.

3. Combine the dressing with the tuna mixture, blending thoroughly, and spoon it into a small serving bowl. Serve with simple crackers or sliced French bread toasts. Garnish with chopped scallion.

ADVANCE PREPARATION: Can be prepared up to 2 hours ahead, covered, and refrigerated.

SPECIAL SUPER COLOSSAL: CALIFORNIA'S OLIVE INDUSTRY

Sometime around 1785 a few olive pits were planted in California's missions, and from that humble beginning the Golden State now produces 99 percent of the nation's table olives. The bland Mission olive, as it came to be known, was the only olive on the scene for many years, because Americans' taste for olives and the oil produced from them was slow to develop.

It was not until the 1920s that olive production in the state began on a serious scale, and size designations had to be made for the fledgling industry. These, of course, were based on the Mission olive: small, medium, large, and extra large. Then came the arrival of the "Queen of Olives," the Sevillano, which quickly became popular for its lack of oiliness and much larger size. This new olive necessitated a new system of size definition, giving rise to the somewhat confusing labels *giant, jumbo, colossal,* and *super colossal.*

Since the birth of the industry in this country, and even to a large extent today, demand has been only for the "black-ripe" olive. This is simply a green olive that has been allowed to ripen on the tree before harvesting, then cured in a very mild brine. To lovers of the myriad black, green, or purple, spicy, sour, and vinegary Mediterranean olives, this olive seems bland, overly rich, and much too large. The olive industry has clearly sensed this demand trend and has recently responded by producing several different green and even black olives with a more Mediterranean style. Though these olives tend to be packed in a very strong brine, they offer vastly improved flavor over the standard "black-ripe."

SOUPS

ROASTED GARLIC AND BUTTERNUT SQUASH SOUP WITH
   ANCHO CHILE CREAM 41
ROASTED VEGETABLE SOUP 43
SWEET POTATO–JALAPEÑO SOUP WITH TOMATILLO CREAM 45
BROCCOLI LEEK SOUP WITH PARMESAN CREAM 47
SPINACH, PASTA, AND FAGIOLI SOUP 49
WHITE BEAN SOUP WITH LEEKS, CARROTS, AND EGGPLANT 51
LENTIL SOUP WITH THYME AND BALSAMIC VINEGAR 55
YELLOW SPLIT PEA SOUP WITH MUSHROOMS AND SMOKED TURKEY 57
PINTO BEAN SOUP WITH GREMOLATA 59
BLACK BEAN SOUP WITH LIME CREAM 61
CHICKEN MINESTRONE WITH MIXED-HERB PESTO 63
GRILLED SEAFOOD BISQUE WITH RED PEPPER AÏOLI 65
CORN AND TOMATO SOUP 67
CUCUMBER AVOCADO GAZPACHO 69
SQUASH VICHYSSOISE 71

ROASTED GARLIC AND BUTTERNUT SQUASH SOUP WITH ANCHO CHILE CREAM

SERVES 4 TO 6

I LIKE TO serve this soup in mugs on Thanksgiving or during the holidays, when there's lots of excitement in the kitchen and a fire in the fireplace. Butternut squash is sweetest during these months and is well complemented by the spicy ancho chile cream. Roasting the garlic with the squash allows the sweet nutty flavors to develop fully. Slowly sautéed onions turn caramel brown and adds another layer of flavor. For a large crowd, this recipe can easily be doubled.

1　large butternut squash (about 4 pounds)
1　medium head of garlic, cloves separated but unpeeled
1/4 cup olive oil
1/4 cup water
2　medium onions, finely chopped
1　quart chicken stock (page 397)
1/2 teaspoon salt
1/2 teaspoon white pepper

GARNISH
1　tablespoon ancho chile paste (page 406)
1/2 cup sour cream or crème fraîche (page 425)
2　tablespoons finely chopped fresh chives

1. Preheat the oven to 350°F. Slice the squash in half lengthwise and remove the stringy pulp and seeds with a serrated spoon. Carefully slice the peel off and then cut the flesh into 1-inch-thick slices.

2. In a medium roasting pan, combine the squash and garlic. Drizzle 2 tablespoons of the olive oil over the squash and mix with a spoon until all of the ingredients are well coated. Add the water. Roast in the middle of the oven, stirring occasionally, until the squash and garlic cloves are soft and caramelized, about 50 to 60 minutes. Cool slightly.

3. While the squash is roasting, heat the remaining 2 tablespoons of olive oil in a heavy medium skillet over medium heat. Add the onions and sauté for about 20 minutes or until the onions are golden and caramelized. Reserve.

4. Spoon the roasted squash into a food processor fitted with the metal blade. Allow the garlic cloves to cool. Grasp the cloves by the root end and peel enough of the skin off so that the garlic clove will fall out; or, using a thin oven mitt, squeeze the pointed end of each garlic clove into the squash. Add the caramelized onions and puree the mixture for 1 minute or until very smooth but with tiny pieces of onion remaining. For a smoother consistency, pass the mixture through a fine strainer.

5. Pour the squash into a large saucepan. Add the stock, salt, and pepper and bring to a simmer. Taste for seasoning.

6. In a small bowl, combine the ancho chile paste with the sour cream. Blend completely.

7. When you're ready to serve, ladle the soup into individual soup bowls or mugs and place a dollop of ancho chile cream and some chives on top. Serve immediately.

ADVANCE PREPARATION: The soup and ancho chile cream can be prepared up to 3 days ahead through step 6, covered, and refrigerated. Reheat the soup gently.

GOOD GADGETS: THE HAND BLENDER

Consider this innovative kitchen tool for making soup, sauces, salad dressings, and drinks. A long and narrow handheld blender with a rotary blade at one end goes right into the pot to puree or emulsify and eliminates the extra step of transferring the mixture to a blender or food processor.

The trick here is to keep the blade at the bottom of the vessel. Occasionally lift it gently, but *never* above the surface of the liquid, so the mixture stays in the pot and doesn't splatter all over. You can use this blender in a saucepan, a pitcher, or a deep bowl—just be sure there is enough mixture to cover the blades. You'll love this gadget.

ROASTED VEGETABLE SOUP
SERVES 6 TO 8

ROASTING THE VEGETABLES adds an extra taste dimension to this soup, bringing out each vegetable's unique flavor. Use your favorite vegetables in this hearty, rustic soup. Plain nonfat yogurt gives this low-fat soup a creamy consistency while adding only a few extra calories. This is a great main-course lunch soup with toasted country sourdough bread (page 327) and Farmer's Market Chopped Salad (page 78).

2	leeks, white part only, cleaned and finely chopped
1/2	pound mushrooms, coarsely chopped
3	medium carrots, peeled and cut into 2-inch pieces
2	medium zucchini, cut into 2-inch pieces
2	large tomatoes, quartered
2	medium white potatoes, peeled and cut into 2-inch pieces
1/2	medium head of green cabbage, shredded
2	tablespoons olive oil
1/2	cup chicken stock (page 397)
	pinch of black pepper

TO FINISH
6 to 7 cups chicken stock (page 397)

2	tablespoons finely chopped mixed fresh herbs such as parsley, basil, chives, and thyme
2	tablespoons fresh lemon juice
	salt and pepper to taste

GARNISH

1/2	cup plain nonfat yogurt
2	tablespoons finely chopped mixed fresh herbs such as parsley, basil, chives, and thyme

1. Preheat the oven to 425°F. Place all vegetables in a heavy large roasting pan. Add the oil, 1/2 cup chicken stock, and a pinch of pepper and mix until all the vegetables are well coated. Roast the vegetables for 40 minutes or until soft, turning once to make sure they do not burn.

2. Place the vegetables in batches in a food processor fitted with the metal blade and process until smooth. Then transfer the puree to a large saucepan. Add 6 cups chicken stock, the herbs, and the lemon juice and mix together. Add more stock to reach the desired consistency and cook over low heat for 10 minutes to allow the flavors to blend. Add salt and pepper and taste for seasoning.

3. To serve, ladle the soup into soup bowls. Swirl in a tablespoon of yogurt and garnish with fresh herbs. Serve immediately.

ADVANCE PREPARATION: Can be prepared up to 3 days ahead through step 2, covered, and refrigerated. Reheat gently and taste for seasoning.

SWEET POTATO–JALAPEÑO SOUP WITH TOMATILLO CREAM

SERVES 6 TO 8

MOST CALIFORNIA MARKETS sell only two sweet potato varieties: moist and dry. The moist sweet potato variety is erroneously labeled *yam*. For this soup you want the reddish brown moist sweet potato, not the drier ones, which have a light brown–yellow skin and pale flesh—they are decidedly less sweet.

If you find that this soup lacks a sweet flavor, add a pinch of brown sugar for balance. Served by itself, the soup does not reach the spectacular flavor it attains when served with the garnishes. Adding sweet corn and a final squirt of lime juice brings all the flavors together harmoniously. If you're not serving sweet potatoes for Thanksgiving, begin the dinner with this soup. It is also great as a main dish on a cool autumn afternoon served with a salad and a glass of Beaujolais Nouveau.

1	tablespoon olive oil
2	medium leeks, white part only, cleaned and finely chopped
1	garlic clove, minced
1/4	teaspoon ground cumin
3	pounds moist (reddish brown–skinned) sweet potatoes (about 6 medium), peeled and cut into 2-inch pieces

6 to 7 cups chicken stock (page 397)

1	small jalapeño chile, seeded and finely chopped*
1/2	teaspoon salt
1/4	teaspoon white pepper
2	tablespoons fresh lime juice
1	teaspoon dark brown sugar (optional)
1	cup cooked fresh corn kernels (about 2 medium ears) or thawed frozen

---

* When you're working with chiles, always wear rubber gloves. Wash the cutting surface and knife immediately.

TOMATILLO CREAM AND GARNISH

1/2	cup sour cream or plain low-fat yogurt
2	tablespoons tomatillo salsa (page 414)
3	tablespoons finely chopped cilantro
1/4	teaspoon salt
	pinch of white pepper
1/2	cup cooked fresh corn kernels (about 1 medium ear) or thawed frozen
8	teaspoons fresh lime juice

1. In a 6-quart soup pot or casserole over medium-high heat, heat the oil, add the leeks, and sauté for 5 minutes or until softened. Add the garlic and cumin, lower the heat, and cook for another minute. Add the sweet potatoes, 6 cups stock, jalapeño, salt, and pepper and simmer, covered, over medium heat for 20 to 25 minutes or until sweet potatoes are very tender.

2. Puree the soup in the pan with a hand blender or in a food processor fitted with the metal blade. Add the remaining cup of chicken stock if the soup is too thick. Return the soup to the pot if necessary and bring it to a simmer. Add the lime juice, brown sugar if desired, and corn kernels and cook the soup for 3 minutes more. Taste for seasoning.

3. In a small bowl, combine the sour cream, salsa, 1 tablespoon of the cilantro, and the salt and pepper and mix together. Taste for seasoning.

4. To serve, ladle the soup into bowls and garnish with a tablespoon of tomatillo cream, a sprinkling of the corn kernels, the remaining chopped cilantro and a squeeze of fresh lime. Serve immediately.

ADVANCE PREPARATION: Can be prepared up to 3 days ahead through step 2 and refrigerated. Reheat gently.

BROCCOLI LEEK SOUP WITH PARMESAN CREAM

SERVES 4

THIS QUICK SOUP works in many roles, from an informal family dinner to an elegant starter for a dinner party. Parmesan cream is a lovely counterpoint to the distinctive bright green broccoli-leek puree. Using a hand blender saves on preparation and cleaning.

2   tablespoons olive oil
2   medium leeks, white part only, cleaned and finely chopped
1   pound red potatoes (about 2 medium), peeled and finely chopped
1-1/2 pounds broccoli flowers and stalks, trimmed and cut into 1-inch
         pieces
5   cups chicken stock (page 397)
1/2 teaspoon salt
1/4 teaspoon white pepper

PARMESAN CREAM
1/2 cup sour cream or plain nonfat yogurt
1/4 cup finely grated Parmesan
      pinch of white pepper

GARNISH
2   tablespoons finely chopped fresh chives

1. In a large soup pot over medium heat, heat the olive oil, add the leeks, and sauté for about 3 to 5 minutes or until softened. Add the potatoes and broccoli and sauté for 2 minutes, stirring frequently. Add the stock and bring to a simmer. Partially cover and simmer for about 15 to 20 minutes or until the vegetables are tender when pierced with a sharp knife.

2. Puree the soup in the pot with a hand blender or in a food processor fitted with the metal blade. Add salt and pepper and taste for seasoning.

3. To make the Parmesan cream, combine the sour cream, cheese, and pepper in a small mixing bowl and whisk until combined.

4. When you're ready to serve, ladle the soup into soup plates or bowls, spoon a dollop of the Parmesan cream on top, and garnish with chives. Serve immediately.

ADVANCE PREPARATION: The soup and cream can be prepared up to 1 day ahead through step 3, covered, and refrigerated. Gently reheat the soup and whisk the Parmesan cream before serving.

SPINACH, PASTA, AND FAGIOLI SOUP

SERVES 6

ADDING SPINACH TO this classic bean and pasta soup enriches its taste and color. Great Northern or any other white bean works nicely here.

1 cup (1/2 pound) dried white beans
2 tablespoons olive oil
2 medium onions, coarsely chopped
2 carrots, peeled and coarsely chopped
1 small bunch of spinach, cut into thin julienne
6 cups chicken stock (page 397)
2 garlic cloves, minced
2 medium tomatoes, peeled, seeded, and coarsely chopped, or 1 cup
    chopped canned tomatoes, well drained
2 tablespoons finely chopped fresh basil or 2 teaspoons dried
3/4 cup fine egg noodles or broken capellini
1 teaspoon salt or to taste
1/2 teaspoon white pepper
1/4 cup finely chopped parsley

GARNISH
6 tablespoons freshly grated Parmesan

1. Soak the beans overnight in enough cold water to cover generously or do a quick soak by bringing them to a boil in just enough water to cover, boiling for 2 minutes, then covering and letting stand for 1 hour. Drain the beans.

2. In a 6-quart soup pot over medium heat, heat the oil, add the onions, and sauté for about 5 minutes, stirring occasionally. Add the carrots and sauté for 3 minutes.

Add half of the spinach and sauté until wilted, about 2 to 3 minutes. Add the stock, beans, garlic, tomatoes, and basil and simmer for about 1 hour, partially covered, or until the beans are tender.

3. Meanwhile, cook the noodles in a medium saucepan of boiling water for 5 to 7 minutes, depending on thickness. Drain them in a colander and reserve.

4. Puree the soup in the pot with a hand blender or in a food processor fitted with the metal blade, making sure the vegetables still have some texture.

5. Return the soup to the pot if necessary, place over medium-high heat, and add the noodles and remaining spinach. Cook for about 5 minutes, then add the salt, pepper, and 2 tablespoons of the parsley and taste for seasoning.

6. To serve, ladle the soup into bowls and garnish with the remaining parsley and the Parmesan.

ADVANCE PREPARATION: Can be prepared up to 3 days ahead through step 5 and refrigerated. Reheat gently. You can also freeze the soup. Be sure to adjust the seasonings and add fresh herbs when you reheat the frozen soup.

WHITE BEAN SOUP WITH LEEKS, CARROTS, AND EGGPLANT

S E R V E S   6   T O   8

FRESH LEMON JUICE and lots of fresh herbs provide the finishing touch here. If you have access to fresh herbs, experiment with pineapple sage and lemon thyme to add an herbal, fruity flavor. Add the salt toward the end of cooking; otherwise the salt will toughen the beans and give them an inferior texture.

1   cup (1/2 pound) Great Northern or other white beans
2   tablespoons olive oil
2   large leeks, white part only, cleaned and finely chopped
2   medium carrots, peeled and coarsely chopped
1   large Japanese eggplant, peeled and coarsely chopped
3   garlic cloves, peeled
6   cups chicken stock (page 397)
1   teaspoon salt
1/4 teaspoon black pepper
1/4 cup finely chopped parsley
3   tablespoons fresh lemon juice
     pinch of cayenne pepper

GARNISH
1/4 cup finely chopped mixed fresh herbs such as chives, thyme, and
        parsley
1/4 cup freshly grated Parmesan

1. Soak the beans overnight in enough cold water to cover generously or do a quick soak by bringing them to a boil in just enough water to cover, boiling for 2 minutes, then covering and letting stand for 1 hour. Drain the beans.

2. In a 6-quart soup pot over medium heat, heat the oil, add the leeks, and sauté for about 5 minutes or until softened, stirring occasionally. Add the carrots and eggplant and sauté for 3 minutes. Add the garlic, stock, and beans. Bring to a low simmer, partially cover, and cook for about 1 hour or until the beans are tender.

3. Puree the soup in the pot with a hand blender or in a food processor fitted with the metal blade, making sure the vegetables still have some texture. Add the remaining soup ingredients and taste for seasoning.

4. To serve, garnish the soup with herbs and Parmesan and serve immediately.

ADVANCE PREPARATION: Can be prepared up to 3 days ahead through step 3, covered, and refrigerated. Reheat gently. This soup also freezes well. Be sure to adjust the seasonings and add fresh herbs when you reheat the frozen soup.

BALSAMIC VINEGAR

Think of balsamic vinegar as a cook's best friend—a flavor enhancer that brings out underlying complex flavors and sparks up simpler flavors. From pasta sauce to salad dressings, from complex meat reductions to soup enhancers, balsamic vinegar is a must ingredient in California cooking. It has, in fact, become so popular in the United States that imitations are being sold right along with the real thing. True balsamic vinegar comes from only one region of Italy, around the town of Modena in Emilia-Romagna.

There are three categories of balsamic vinegar: artisan and commercially produced balsamic vinegar, both made in the provinces of Modena and Reggio, and imitations made outside the provinces of Modena and Reggio. Balsamic vinegar is made by combining a high-quality wine vinegar, reduced grape must (the partially fermented juice and pulp of the grape), some young balsamic vinegar as a starter, and sometimes caramel. Aging takes place in a succession of wooden casks and can require from a few years up to 120.

Prices for a bottle can range from a few dollars to over $100. The really expensive artisan-produced vinegars are much too good for cooking. In Italy they are used by the drop or sometimes sipped as liqueurs.

For cooking, a commercial (*industriale*) vinegar from Modena or nearby Reggio will be fine. Look on the label for either *API MO* (referring to Modena) or *API RE* (referring to Reggio) to be sure you aren't buying an imitation from another area.

When selecting a good *industriale* balsamic, look for a refined sweet-tart balance. It shouldn't taste too acidic or too sweet—the balance is important. If you find the vinegar is too strong and tart, reduce it by half over high heat to tame the acid and give it a syrupy glaze consistency with a richer, more subtle flavor. You can keep this on hand in the refrigerator and use it as needed. Another way to help balance it is to add a pinch of dark brown sugar to each tablespoon.

As an ingredient in a marinade or as part of the acid content of a vinaigrette, balance its strength with other acids like lemon juice or other wine vinegars so that it doesn't overwhelm the dish.

Here are a few tips on using balsamic vinegar:

- Add to a vinaigrette with lemon, red wine, or rice wine vinegar.
- Add it to cooked beans or bean soups just before serving.

- Add it to roasted and caramelized onions or garlic.
- Add a teaspoon to salsas or your favorite pesto.
- Use it as a salt substitute.
- Add a teaspoon to fruit jams, roasted or grilled tomatoes, or fruit compotes.
- Drizzle it over simple grilled fish, meat, or poultry.
- Add it to sautéed vegetables.
- Drizzle it over sliced ripe tomatoes with a fresh basil garnish.
- Drizzle it over mixed grilled vegetables along with some lemon juice, extra virgin olive oil, and chopped fresh herbs.
- Drizzle it over baked potatoes or combine a bit of olive oil and balsamic and roast new potatoes in this blend.
- Add a tablespoon when you deglaze the pan before making a sauce for poultry dishes.
- Drizzle it over sliced melon.
- Drizzle it over strawberries and sprinkle with freshly ground black pepper.

LENTIL SOUP WITH THYME AND BALSAMIC VINEGAR

SERVES 6 TO 8

THIS CLASSIC MIDDLE Eastern soup has a sweet American accent: honey-cured ham. Use brown lentils, sometimes called *masoor dal*, since they cook quickly and puree well. If fresh tomatoes are not at their best, use diced well-drained, canned tomatoes.

2   tablespoons olive oil
1   large onion, finely chopped
3   carrots, peeled and coarsely chopped
2   celery ribs, finely chopped
2   cups (1 pound) brown lentils, rinsed and picked over
1/2 pound coarsely chopped honey-cured or other sweet-flavored ham
2   quarts chicken stock (page 397)
2   cups peeled, seeded, and finely chopped fresh tomatoes (about 2 large)
        or diced well-drained canned tomatoes
1/4 cup finely chopped parsley
1   teaspoon finely chopped fresh thyme leaves or 1/3 teaspoon dried
2   teaspoons balsamic vinegar
1   teaspoon salt
1/4 teaspoon finely ground black pepper

GARNISH
1   large tomato, peeled, seeded, and finely chopped
1/4 cup finely chopped parsley

1. In a 6-quart soup pot over medium heat, heat the oil, add the onion, and sauté for about 3 minutes. Add the carrots and celery and continue sautéing for about 5 minutes.

2. Add the lentils, 1/2 cup ham, the stock, tomatoes, and 2 tablespoons of the parsley. Bring to a simmer, reduce the heat to medium-low, and cook for about 30 minutes or until the lentils are tender, stirring occasionally.

3. Process the soup in the pot with a hand blender or in a food processor fitted with the metal blade, pulsing until the soup is partially pureed but still has plenty of texture.

4. Add the remaining ham, parsley, thyme, vinegar, salt, and pepper and simmer for 5 minutes more. Taste for seasoning.

5. To serve, ladle into soup bowls and garnish with the tomatoes and parsley.

ADVANCE PREPARATION: Can be prepared up to 3 days ahead through step 4 and refrigerated. This soup also freezes well. Be sure to adjust the seasonings and add fresh herbs when you reheat the frozen soup.

YELLOW SPLIT PEA SOUP WITH MUSHROOMS AND SMOKED TURKEY

SERVES 4 TO 6

THIS SIMPLE SOUP has a couple of surprises: smoked turkey instead of the usual ham and shredded sugar snap or snow peas for a garden-sweet crunch. Most of the turkey goes in right before serving so the texture is preserved. Serve with Sourdough Rye Rolls (page 330) or focaccia (page 337).

2   tablespoons olive oil
1   medium onion, finely chopped
1   celery rib, sliced
2   carrots, peeled and sliced
3/4 pound mushrooms, sliced
1   medium yellow bell pepper, coarsely chopped
1   cup (1/2 pound) yellow split peas, cleaned and picked over
1/2 pound smoked turkey breast, coarsely chopped
6   cups chicken stock (page 397)
1/4 cup finely chopped parsley
1/2 teaspoon finely chopped fresh sage or 1/4 teaspoon dried
1/2 teaspoon finely chopped fresh thyme or 1/4 teaspoon dried
1/4 teaspoon salt
1/4 teaspoon black pepper
1/4 pound sugar snap or snow peas, cleaned and thinly sliced

GARNISH
1/4 cup finely chopped parsley
    fresh thyme leaves

1. In a 6-quart soup pot, over medium heat, heat the oil, add the onion, and sauté for 3 to 5 minutes or until softened. Add the celery, carrots, mushrooms, and yellow pepper and sauté for another 2 minutes or until slightly softened.

2. Add the split peas, 1/4 cup of the smoked turkey, the stock, and the fresh herbs and bring to a simmer over medium-low heat. Partially cover and cook for about 50 to 60 minutes, until the peas are tender.

3. Coarsely puree the soup in the pan using a hand blender or in a food processor fitted with the metal blade. Add the remaining turkey, salt, and pepper, return the soup to the pan if necessary, and simmer for 5 minutes. Taste for seasoning.

4. Just before serving, add the sliced snow peas and heat through. Serve immediately, garnished with the fresh herbs.

ADVANCE PREPARATION: Can be prepared up to 3 days ahead through step 3 and refrigerated. You can also freeze the soup. Be sure to adjust the seasonings and add fresh herbs when you reheat the frozen soup.

PINTO BEAN SOUP WITH GREMOLATA

SERVES 6 TO 8

GREMOLATA, THE ITALIAN flavoring blend of lemon zest, garlic, and parsley, is traditionally used as a finishing touch for osso buco. This savory herb blend is even better as a garnish for less complicated flavors, like this pureed soup. Try using turkey bacon—it's much lower in fat but still gives the desired smoky flavor. For a satisfying lunch, follow with Grilled Steak and Potato Salad (page 100).

2 cups (1 pound) pinto beans
2 tablespoons olive oil
1 medium onion, finely chopped
1 carrot, peeled and finely chopped
2 garlic cloves, minced
7 cups chicken stock (page 397)
4 strips of bacon
   salt and pepper to taste

GREMOLATA
2 garlic cloves, minced
1/4 cup chopped parsley
   zest of 1 lemon, finely chopped

1. Soak the beans overnight in cold water to cover generously or do a quick soak by bringing them to a boil in just enough water to cover, boiling for 2 minutes, covering, and letting stand for 1 hour. Drain the beans.

2. In a 6-quart soup pot over medium heat, heat the oil, add the onion, and sauté for 3 to 5 minutes, or until softened. Add the carrot and sauté for 3 minutes. Add the garlic and sauté for another minute.

3. Add the beans, stock, and bacon and simmer for 50 to 60 minutes or until the beans are softened. Puree the mixture in the soup pot using a hand blender or in batches in a food processor fitted with the metal blade. Add salt and pepper and taste for seasoning.

4. To make the gremolata, combine the garlic, parsley, and lemon zest in a small bowl.

5. To serve, ladle the soup into bowls and garnish with gremolata.

ADVANCE PREPARATION: Can be prepared up to 3 days ahead through step 3 and refrigerated. You can also freeze the soup. Be sure to adjust the seasonings and add fresh herbs when you reheat the frozen soup.

BLACK BEAN SOUP WITH LIME CREAM

SERVES 6 TO 8

BLACK BEANS HAVE become a welcome staple in many California kitchens, where they're blended into soups, stews, pancakes, salsas, and relishes.

Credit for this inspired soup idea goes to Hugo Molina, executive chef of The Parkway Grill in Pasadena. His lime cream adds a sophisticated touch to ordinary black beans. Most black bean soups are coarse textured, but I like to puree this soup and put it through a fine strainer to achieve a velvety texture. I prefer a mild smoky flavor, so I don't add the meat from the ham bone.

Salsa makes a wonderful accompaniment—try tomatillo (page 414), spicy tomato (page 413), or your favorite store-bought salsa. Serve warm tortillas or tortilla chips on the side.

2	cups (1 pound) black beans, picked over and cleaned
2	tablespoons olive oil
2	medium onions, finely chopped
1 to 2	jalapeño chiles to taste, seeded and finely chopped*
3	garlic cloves, minced
1	small red bell pepper, finely chopped
1	teaspoon ground cumin
1	teaspoon ground coriander
2	teaspoons finely chopped fresh oregano or 1 teaspoon dried
2	quarts water
1/2	small ham hock or ham bone
2	tablespoons fresh lime juice
2	tablespoons finely chopped cilantro
	salt and pepper to taste

---

* When you're working with chiles, always wear rubber gloves. Wash the cutting surface and knife immediately.

GARNISH

1/2   cup sour cream
1 to 2 tablespoons fresh lime juice to taste
1/4   teaspoon salt
        pinch of white pepper
        cilantro sprigs
1/2   cup tomato salsa of your choice (optional)

1. Soak the beans overnight in cold water to cover generously or do a quick soak by bringing the beans to a boil in just enough water to cover, boiling for 2 minutes, covering, and letting stand for 1 hour. Drain the beans.

2. In a large soup pot or casserole over medium heat, heat the olive oil, add the onions, and sauté for 3 minutes or until softened. Add the jalapeño, garlic, red pepper, cumin, coriander, and oregano and sauté for another 10 minutes, stirring frequently.

3. Add the beans, water, and ham bone and simmer, partially covered, for 1-1/2 to 2 hours or until the beans are soft. Remove the ham bone.

4. Puree half the bean mixture in a food processor fitted with the metal blade or in a blender and return it to the soup pot or puree in the soup pot using a hand blender, leaving a bit of texture. Add the lime juice, cilantro, salt, and pepper and taste for seasoning. If the soup is too thick, thin it with water. (If you prefer a velvety texture, puree the soup well and then pour it through a fine strainer into a saucepan.)

5. To make the lime cream, combine the sour cream, lime juice, salt, and pepper in a small bowl. Taste for seasoning.

6. To serve, ladle the soup into soup bowls and garnish with lime cream, a sprig of cilantro, and a dollop of salsa if desired.

ADVANCE PREPARATION: Can be prepared up to 2 days ahead through step 4 and refrigerated. Reheat the soup gently. You can also freeze the soup. Be sure to adjust the seasonings and add fresh herbs when you reheat the frozen soup.

CHICKEN MINESTRONE WITH MIXED-HERB PESTO

SERVES 8 AS A MAIN COURSE

THIS INFORMAL ONE-DISH meal is a family favorite. Italian Arborio rice and an assertive mixed-herb pesto balance the soup in a most pleasing way. Shiitake mushrooms introduce a slightly chewy texture. Cutting all the vegetables is labor-intensive, so I make the soup in large quantities to enjoy on more than one occasion. Serve with warm Jalapeño Cheese Bread (page 334) or country sourdough bread (page 327) for a satisfying lunch or dinner.

3 quarts chicken stock (page 397) and/or water
2 medium whole chicken breasts, skinned and boned
2 tablespoons olive oil
2 medium onions, finely chopped
4 carrots, peeled and cut into 1-inch pieces
2 large zucchini, cut into 1-inch pieces
1/2 pound green beans, trimmed and cut into 1-inch pieces
1 Japanese eggplant, unpeeled and cut into 1-inch pieces
1/2 small head of green cabbage, shredded
1/4 pound mushrooms, preferably shiitake, sliced
2 garlic cloves, minced
1 cup diced drained canned tomatoes or 2 medium fresh tomatoes,
      peeled, seeded, and finely chopped
2 tablespoons finely chopped fresh basil or 1 tablespoon dried
1/4 cup Arborio rice
2 cups cooked white beans such as cannellini or 1 15-ounce can, drained
      and rinsed well
1/2 teaspoon salt
1/2 teaspoon black pepper

GARNISH
1/2 cup Mixed-Herb Pesto (page 402)

1. In a deep medium skillet or a large saucepan, bring the stock (enough to cover the chicken) to a simmer. If you're using only water, add 1/2 teaspoon salt. Add the chicken breasts and simmer for 8 to 10 minutes or until just tender. Cool the chicken in the liquid and reserve the stock. Drain the chicken and cut it into 1-inch pieces. Reserve.

2. In a 6-quart soup pot over medium heat, heat the oil, add the onions, and sauté for about 3 to 5 minutes, until onions are softened, stirring occasionally. Add the carrots, zucchini, green beans, and eggplant and sauté for about 3 minutes, stirring frequently. Add the cabbage and sauté just until softened. Add the mushrooms and sauté for 2 minutes. Add the garlic and sauté for 1 minute longer.

3. Add the tomatoes, reserved stock plus enough water to make 3 quarts, and basil and bring to a boil. Reduce the heat and simmer until all the vegetables are tender, about 15 minutes. The soup will be slightly thickened.

4. Add the rice and beans and cook for about 15 minutes or until the rice is al dente. Add the reserved cooked chicken and heat through. Add salt and pepper and taste for seasoning.

5. To serve, ladle the hot soup into soup bowls and swirl a tablespoon of pesto into each bowl.

ADVANCE PREPARATION: The soup and pesto can be prepared up to 3 days ahead and refrigerated. Bring both to room temperature, heat the soup, and serve. This soup also freezes well. Be sure to adjust the seasonings and add fresh herbs when you reheat the frozen soup.

GRILLED SEAFOOD BISQUE WITH RED PEPPER AÏOLI

S E R V E S 4 T O 6

A RICH ORANGE saffron broth with bits of tomato is paired with grilled scallops and shrimp for an unusual twist on cioppino, the seafood soup that San Franciscans made famous. Cooking seafood in broth tends to make the fish a bit rubbery, so here the fish is grilled instead, with outstanding results.

The leek-flecked tomato broth is poured into soup bowls, and grilled seafood is arranged decoratively on top. With the simple aïoli spooned over the seafood, the soup becomes a satisfying main course. You can also garnish the soup with plain toasted French bread topped with a dollop of the aïoli. Begin with California Caponata (page 31) and serve the bisque with plenty of warm country sourdough bread (page 327). For dessert, try Banana Split Ice Cream Torte (page 384).

RECOMMENDED WINE: Try a crisp, lively Sauvignon Blanc with this smoky soup.

2 tablespoons olive oil
2 medium leeks, white part only, cleaned and thinly sliced
1 carrot, peeled and finely chopped
3 garlic cloves, minced
2 cups fish stock or bottled clam juice
2 cups dry white wine such as Sauvignon Blanc
1 28-ounce can tomatoes, diced, with juice
   large pinch of saffron threads
1 2-inch-long strip of orange zest
   salt and black pepper to taste
12 large shrimp, peeled and deveined, tails left on
12 medium sea scallops

1   teaspoon black pepper
1/2 cup Red Pepper Aïoli (page 408)

GARNISH
2   tablespoons finely chopped chives

1. Heat the oil in a 4-quart nonaluminum Dutch oven or stockpot over medium heat. Add the leeks and carrot and sauté, stirring occasionally, for about 5 minutes or until slightly softened. Add the garlic and sauté for another minute. Add the fish stock, wine, tomatoes, saffron, and orange zest and simmer over medium-low heat for 20 minutes. Add salt and pepper and taste for seasoning. Remove the orange zest. With a hand blender or in a food processor fitted with a metal blade, puree the soup, leaving some texture.

2. Thread the shrimp and scallops on metal skewers. Lightly sprinkle them with black pepper. When you're ready to serve, prepare a barbecue for medium-high-heat grilling. Place the skewers on the grill, 3 to 4 inches from the heat, flat side down and grill until just cooked, about 3 to 4 minutes on each side. Remove the seafood from the skewers with a fork, place it on a plate, and keep it warm.

3. To serve, reheat the soup and ladle some bisque into each soup plate. Arrange 2 shrimp and 2 scallops on top in a decorative circular pattern. Dollop the aïoli in the center and garnish with chopped chives. Serve immediately.

ADVANCE PREPARATION: Can be prepared up to 1 day ahead through step 1 and refrigerated. Reheat gently.

CORN AND TOMATO SOUP

SERVES 8

THIS SOUP HAS won rave reviews from my students and guests alike. What makes it so special is the layering of flavors. First a simple corn and tomato soup is simmered with hints of sun-dried tomato and basil and chilled. Next a rosy, mahogany cream bursting with sun-dried tomato essence is spooned on top of crispy sun-dried tomato toasts. Finally a corn and tomato relish is garnished on the toasts. While this may sound like too much tomato, I urge you to try it. It gets my vote for best summer soup.

If you love corn and cook with it frequently, you might want to invest in a gadget that removes the corn kernels from the cob in a single swoop. If you prefer the old-fashioned method, take a very sharp chef's knife, stand the husked ear of corn in a bowl, and slice down on an angle, separating the corn from the cob and letting it fall into the bowl. Sweet white corn is particularly delicious in this soup.

2	tablespoons olive oil
4	medium leeks, white part only, cleaned and finely chopped
1	carrot, peeled and finely chopped
1	celery rib, finely chopped
6	large tomatoes, coarsely chopped
3	tablespoons all-purpose flour
3-1/2	cups corn kernels (about 7 medium ears)
2	garlic cloves, minced
6	dry-packed sun-dried tomatoes
8	fresh basil leaves
2	tablespoons tomato paste
6	cups chicken stock (page 397)
1	teaspoon salt
1/4	teaspoon pepper

RELISH

1/2	cup reserved diced tomato
1/2	cup reserved corn kernels
1	tablespoon finely chopped fresh basil
1/8	teaspoon salt
	pinch of pepper

SUN-DRIED TOMATO CREAM

1/2	cup dry-packed sun-dried tomatoes
1/2	cup sour cream
1/4	teaspoon salt
	pinch of white pepper

sun-dried tomato toasts (page 312)

1. In a large soup pot over medium heat, heat the olive oil, add the leeks, carrot, and celery, and sauté for about 5 minutes or until softened. Reserve 1/2 cup of the tomatoes for the relish, add the remaining tomatoes, and cook for 3 minutes or until slightly softened. Add the flour and stir with a wooden spoon, making sure the flour is dissolved. Continue cooking for 2 minutes.

2. Reserve 1/2 cup of the corn kernels for the relish and add the remaining corn kernels, garlic, sun-dried tomatoes, basil, tomato paste, and stock and bring to a simmer. Simmer, partially covered, for about 25 minutes. Puree the soup in the pot using a hand blender or in a food processor fitted with the metal blade. Pour the soup through a fine-mesh strainer into a large container. Add the salt and pepper and taste for seasoning. Bring to room temperature and then refrigerate for at least 2 hours.

3. For the corn relish, finely chop the reserved tomato and place in a small mixing bowl. Add the reserved corn kernels, basil, salt, and pepper. Taste for seasoning and set aside.

4. For the sun-dried tomato cream, pour boiling water over the sun-dried tomatoes and soften for about 20 minutes. Drain the tomatoes and combine them with the sour cream, salt, and pepper in a food processor fitted with the metal blade. Puree and taste for seasoning.

5. To serve, ladle some soup into a serving bowl and place a few toasts on top. Place a spoonful of tomato cream on top of the toast and then garnish each toast with a spoonful of corn-tomato relish.

ADVANCE PREPARATION: The soup, relish, and tomato cream can be prepared up to 1 day ahead and refrigerated. This soup can also be served warm if desired. Gently reheat before serving.

CUCUMBER AVOCADO GAZPACHO
SERVES 4

FOR THIS DISH, a refreshing uncooked puree of cucumber and avocado is accented by crunchy chopped cucumber and creamy diced avocado. If you don't have time to make your own salsa, use the jalapeño salsa that comes in a jar or the fresh store-bought variety, but be careful—it can be very spicy. Serve the gazpacho icy cold followed by Grilled Chicken Niçoise (page 197) with Assorted Grilled Vegetables (page 13).

BASE
1   large ripe avocado, peeled, pitted, and cut into 2-inch pieces
1   large European cucumber, cut into 2-inch pieces
1-1/2 cups chicken stock (page 397)
2   tablespoons finely chopped fresh chives
2   tablespoons finely chopped red onion
3   tablespoons fresh lemon juice
1/2   cup sour cream
2   tablespoons tomatillo salsa (page 414) or to taste
        salt and white pepper to taste

VEGETABLES
2   cups finely chopped European cucumber
1   medium avocado, peeled, pitted, and cut into 1/2-inch pieces

GARNISH
1/4   cup sour cream
4   teaspoons tomatillo salsa (page 414)
1/4   cup finely chopped fresh chives

1. In a food processor fitted with the metal blade, combine the chunks of avocado and cucumber and process until smooth. Add the stock, chives, red onion, lemon juice, sour cream, and salsa and blend until combined. Season with salt and pepper.

2. Pour into a medium bowl and add the chopped cucumber and avocado, mixing to distribute. Taste for seasoning and chill for at least 2 hours.

3. To serve, ladle the soup into glass bowls and garnish with sour cream, salsa, and chives.

ADVANCE PREPARATION: Can be prepared up to 4 hours ahead and refrigerated. Do not add lemon juice more than 1 hour before serving.

SQUASH VICHYSSOISE

SERVES 6

THIS COOL AND refreshing potato soup includes green zucchini and yellow squash for color and subtle flavor. Onions are used in place of the usual leek, and lots of fresh basil adds a fragrant garden freshness. Remember not to chop the fresh basil until just before using it or it will turn black. If you prefer a lighter soup, use plain nonfat yogurt as an alternative to sour cream. Serve this as a prelude to Grilled Lamb Chops with Cranberry-Rosemary Marinade (page 242) and Roasted Onions and Baby Potatoes (page 299).

2	tablespoons olive oil
1	medium onion, finely chopped
3	medium yellow crookneck squash, thinly sliced
3	medium zucchini, thinly sliced
3	medium White Rose potatoes (about 1 pound), peeled and thinly sliced
7	cups chicken stock (page 397)
2	tablespoons finely chopped fresh basil or 1 tablespoon dried
1-1/2	teaspoons salt
1/4	teaspoon white pepper
1	tablespoon fresh lemon juice
1/2	cup sour cream or plain nonfat yogurt

GARNISH

1/4	cup sour cream or plain nonfat yogurt
2	tablespoons finely chopped fresh basil

1. In a medium saucepan over medium heat, heat the oil, add the onion, and sauté for about 3 minutes or until softened. Add the squashes and potatoes and sauté for about 3 minutes.

2. Add the stock and basil and simmer, partially covered, for about 15 minutes or until the vegetables are tender. Add the salt and pepper.

3. Puree the soup in the pot using a hand blender or in a blender or food processor fitted with the metal blade. Bring to room temperature and refrigerate until well chilled.

4. Whisk in the lemon juice and sour cream until well combined. Taste for seasoning. To serve, ladle the soup into soup bowls and garnish with the sour cream and basil.

ADVANCE PREPARATION: Can be prepared up to 1 day ahead through step 3 and refrigerated. Add the lemon juice and sour cream just before serving.

SALADS

CAESAR SALAD WITH MIXED BABY LETTUCES AND PARMESAN TOASTS 76
FARMER'S MARKET CHOPPED SALAD 78
PEPPERY GREENS WITH GORGONZOLA AND PINE NUTS 80
CALIFORNIA SALAD 83
MIXED GREENS WITH BEETS AND PEPPERS 85
SPINACH AND MUSHROOM SALAD WITH WARM TOMATO-BACON
    VINAIGRETTE 87
BLOOD ORANGE, MUSHROOM, AND AVOCADO SALAD 89
LA SCALA CHOPPED SALAD 92
WHEATBERRY VEGETABLE SALAD 94
LONG-GRAIN AND WILD RICE SALAD WITH CORN AND SALMON 96
PASTA SALAD WITH PARMESAN DRESSING 98
GRILLED STEAK AND POTATO SALAD 100
GRILLED CHICKEN, BLACK BEAN, AND CORN SALAD
    WITH SALSA DRESSING 103
WARM GRILLED CHICKEN SALAD WITH PESTO 105
CHICKEN SALAD WITH CHINESE NOODLES 107
WINE COUNTRY CHICKEN SALAD 109
WARM GRILLED VEGETABLE AND SHRIMP SALAD 111
SPRINGTIME SALMON SALAD 113

HAIL, CAESAR

There are many stories about how Caesar salad came into being. One legend has it that on July 4, 1924, Tijuana restaurateur Caesar Cardini found himself in a bit of a pickle. He was running low on food during this particular holiday weekend, but he was stocked up with the staple ingredients for this salad—garlic, bread, romaine lettuce, and Parmesan. From these humble ingredients sprang the first Caesar salad, prepared and served tableside. The salad was a lifesaver for Mr. Cardini on that Fourth of July weekend; he later moved to California, and since 1948 his family has bottled Cardini's Caesar Salad Dressing.

CAESAR SALAD WITH MIXED BABY LETTUCES AND PARMESAN TOASTS

S E R V E S 4 T O 6

CAESAR SALAD IS a favorite of mine, but the undercooked egg in the traditional version—actually it's a coddled egg—is out of the question in the age of salmonella scares. Giving up Caesar salad seems equally out of the question.

But there's an alternative. Cook the egg completely and then blend it into the dressing. The result is a particularly creamy dressing. In this version thin, crispy oven-baked Parmesan toasts replace the overused fried crouton. The usual romaine lettuce is mixed with radicchio and butter lettuce. And though it's far from traditional, I like to garnish the salad with ripe, juicy chopped tomatoes.

24   Parmesan toasts (page 311)

DRESSING
1   large egg
3   garlic cloves
1/4   cup fresh lemon juice
1 to 2   teaspoons anchovy paste to taste
1/4   teaspoon black pepper
1/2   cup olive oil
1/2   cup freshly grated Parmesan

SALAD
1   medium head of radicchio, torn into bite-size pieces
1   medium head of butter lettuce, torn into bite-size pieces
1   medium head of romaine lettuce, heart only, torn into bite-size
       pieces

GARNISH

1/2   pound tomato (1 large), peeled, seeded, and finely chopped

1. To make the toasts, preheat the oven to 375°F, place the bread slices on a cookie sheet, and toast for 5 minutes. Brush each toast with butter. Place the Parmesan on a flat plate and press each buttered bread side evenly into the cheese. Return the toasts to the baking sheet and bake for about 5 to 7 minutes or until the cheese is melted but not browned. Watch carefully. Remove from the oven and cool. Place in an airtight container and use as needed.

2. To make the dressing, immerse the egg in a small pan of boiling water. Remove the pan from the heat and cover it for 10 minutes. Remove the egg from the water and let it cool for 10 minutes.

3. Mince the garlic in a food processor fitted with the metal blade. While the motor is running, add the lemon juice, anchovy paste, and pepper and process to combine. Crack the egg, then spoon it out of the shell into the food processor. Pulse the egg with the other ingredients until combined. Add the oil in a steady stream until emulsified. Whisk in 1/4 cup of the Parmesan. Taste for seasoning.

4. In a large salad bowl, combine the mixed lettuces and toss with the dressing and remaining cheese. Add 12 toasts, breaking them into smaller bite-sized pieces, and toss again. Place the salad on individual plates and garnish the center of each with chopped tomatoes and the remaining toasts.

ADVANCE PREPARATION: The toasts can be prepared up to 1 week ahead and stored in an airtight container. The dressing can be prepared up to 1 day ahead and refrigerated.

FARMER'S MARKET CHOPPED SALAD

SERVES 2 TO 3 AS A MAIN COURSE OR 4 TO 6 AS A FIRST COURSE

GROWING UP IN Los Angeles, I had the opportunity to enjoy just about every version of the famous Brown Derby Cobb salad that was offered. You can still find the original Cobb salad, named after Bob Cobb, the owner of the Brown Derby, at any number of California restaurants. Chopped iceberg lettuce was the basic ingredient, with blue cheese, cooked chicken, crumbled crisp bacon, diced avocado, and tomato garnishes.

I've reinterpreted this salad by adding a mix of more flavorful greens, including arugula and watercress, and blending in raw corn and shreds of imported Parmesan. I often forgo the chicken and serve this as a first course. While the old standards of blue cheese, avocado, and bacon are delicious, this lighter version is a welcome change.

RECOMMENDED WINE: This fresh garden salad requires a crisp, dry white wine to balance its creamy dressing. Try a bone-dry Sauvignon Blanc or Riesling.

CREAMY BALSAMIC YOGURT DRESSING

1	medium shallot, finely chopped
1-1/2	tablespoons balsamic vinegar
2	teaspoons fresh lemon juice
1	teaspoon Dijon mustard
3	tablespoons olive oil
2	tablespoons plain nonfat yogurt
1/4	teaspoon salt
	pinch of black pepper

SALAD

1	medium head of romaine lettuce, light green and white leaves only, finely chopped
1	bunch of arugula, coarsely chopped
1	bunch of watercress, leaves only, coarsely chopped
1	skinless medium whole chicken breast, cooked and diced into 1/4-inch pieces
1/2	medium red bell pepper, diced into 1/4-inch pieces
1/4	European cucumber, diced into 1/4-inch pieces
1	ear of white or sweet yellow corn, husked and shucked
1/4	cup coarsely shredded Parmesan (use a shredder or peeler)

1. In a small mixing bowl, combine the shallot, vinegar, lemon juice, and mustard and whisk to combine. Slowly add the oil, whisking to incorporate. Add the yogurt, salt, and pepper and blend well. Taste for seasoning.

2. Combine all the salad ingredients in a large salad bowl. Add the dressing and toss until all the vegetables are well coated. Sprinkle freshly ground pepper on the salad if desired and serve.

ADVANCE PREPARATION: The dressing can be prepared up to 1 day ahead and refrigerated. Whisk the dressing well before using. The salad can be prepared up to 2 hours ahead and refrigerated. (Since the salad is chopped with a metal knife, the lettuce may begin to brown after 2 hours.)

PEPPERY GREENS WITH GORGONZOLA AND PINE NUTS

SERVES 4 TO 6

TANGY SOFT GORGONZOLA and rich toasted pine nuts are the perfect complement to a bed of peppery greens. There are a number of varieties of Gorgonzola cheese, Italy's oldest blue cheese. Ask to taste the cheese at the market to make sure it's the right strength for you. If you're looking for a mild version, specify Dolcelatte, also called *sweet Gorgonzola*, which is younger and much less pungent than regular Gorgonzola.

Use a good-quality sherry vinegar for best results. Since this salad is richer than a simple dinner salad, follow it with a simple grilled or roasted main course like Grilled Lamb Chops with Cranberry-Rosemary Marinade (page 242) or Grilled Orange Mustard Chicken (page 195).

1/4 cup pine nuts

VINAIGRETTE
1   medium shallot, finely chopped
1   teaspoon Dijon mustard
2   tablespoons sherry wine vinegar
1/4 cup olive oil
     salt and pepper to taste

SALAD
1   bunch of watercress, leaves only
1   head of butter lettuce, torn into bite-size pieces
1   small head of radicchio, torn into bite-size pieces
1   bunch of arugula, torn into bite-size pieces
1/4 cup crumbled Italian Gorgonzola, preferably Dolcelatte

GARNISH

10 red or yellow cherry tomatoes or a mixture, sliced in half

1. Preheat the oven to 350°F. Toast the pine nuts on a baking sheet for 5 to 7 minutes or until lightly browned or place them in a skillet and toast over medium heat for a few minutes, shaking constantly to keep them from burning. Watch carefully. Reserve.

2. To prepare the vinaigrette, whisk the shallot, mustard, and vinegar together in a small bowl and then slowly whisk in the oil until it is incorporated. Add salt and pepper and taste for seasoning.

3. Place all of the greens in a salad bowl. Toss with the vinaigrette. Add the pine nuts and Gorgonzola and toss again. Arrange on salad plates and garnish with the cherry tomato halves.

ADVANCE PREPARATION: The dressing can be prepared up to 3 days ahead, covered and refrigerated. The salad can be arranged up to 4 hours ahead and refrigerated.

OLIVE OIL

Which olive oil is right for cooking? There's no single answer, because you really need more than one olive oil. Not unlike wines, olive oils differ dramatically depending on where and how the olives are grown. Each olive oil has its own distinctive signature based on the olive variety, the climate and soil of the grove, and how much processing the olives have undergone.

Extra virgin olive oils are not heated when processed and are very rich and full-flavored. Pure olive oils, which have been heated and pressed to extract the last bit of oil, are much milder in flavor. A cold-pressed extra virgin oil is usually fruity, green, and redolent of olives. Used unheated in a salad dressing, drizzled over sliced tomatoes or a crusty piece of bread, or simply served as a condiment, it's heavenly.

Sautéing with a heavy fruity olive oil, however, can often overwhelm the delicate flavors of a particular dish—it's better to use a lighter-style oil. Ultimately your decision should be based on what you like and what works with what you're cooking. Just remember the oil should be a flavoring agent and not overwhelm the taste of a dish.

For many years California olive oils were considered inferior. But the industry has developed into a serious business that is fast becoming competitive with its Mediterranean counterpart. Unfortunately, California producers of unrefined oil are permitted to label their oils any way they choose. As of this writing there is no legislation to regulate labeling, so there is no sure way to identify the quality of the oil you are buying. The only sure way to judge a particular oil is to taste it.

A few northern California entrepreneurs have begun importing and planting Italian olive trees, bringing over the latest technology for milling and pressing the olives and then filtering the oil in consultation with Italy's experts. California chefs are also experimenting with blending their own private oils, using a combination of the Mission olive and the manzanillo olive. These new endeavors hold great promise for the fledgling domestic olive oil industry.

CALIFORNIA SALAD

SERVES 6

THIS SALAD SOUNDS like all the California culinary buzzwords wrapped into one, but it's truly outstanding. Roasted garlic adds a nutty-rich character to the dressing. You can prepare the dressing several days ahead so that the salad can be assembled quickly at the last minute. Spokes of red pepper and crumbled fresh goat cheese add a pretty California touch. Serve this as a prelude to Roast Crispy Fish with Warm Lentils (page 172) or Grilled Chicken Niçoise (page 197).

DRESSING
1   medium head of garlic
1/4 cup fresh lemon juice
1   teaspoon Dijon mustard
2   teaspoons finely chopped parsley
2   teaspoons finely chopped peeled red bell pepper (page 287)
2   teaspoons finely chopped fresh chives
1/4 teaspoon salt
1/8 teaspoon black pepper
1/2 cup olive oil

SALAD
1   medium head of butter lettuce, torn into bite-size pieces
1   small head of radicchio, torn into bite-size pieces
4   medium heads of Belgian endive
1   medium yellow bell pepper, peeled (page 287) and thinly sliced
1   medium red bell pepper, peeled and thinly sliced (page 287)
1/4 pound goat cheese, crumbled

1. For the dressing, preheat the oven to 425°F. With a sharp knife, cut off the top of the whole head of garlic, then score gently, cutting through just a few layers of the papery skin, all around the diameter. Pull off the loose skin from the top half, trying not to remove every shred. (This will make it easier to squeeze out the cooked cloves later.) Wrap the garlic head tightly in a piece of aluminum foil. Place on a baking sheet and bake for 45 to 60 minutes or until the garlic is soft when pierced with a knife. Remove from the oven and cool. Using your fingers, squeeze the soft garlic pulp into a small bowl.

2. Combine the garlic pulp, lemon juice, mustard, parsley, peeled red pepper, chives, salt, and pepper in a food processor fitted with the metal blade and puree the ingredients. Slowly add the oil until completely incorporated. Taste for seasoning.

3. Arrange the butter lettuce and radicchio in a shallow salad bowl. Slice 2 endive heads into 1/4-inch slices (use a stainless-steel knife) and scatter them on top of the lettuce. Separate the other endive leaves and arrange on the outside edge of the salad bowl. Arrange the pepper slices in a spokelike fashion around the salad and sprinkle the crumbled goat cheese on top.

4. When you're ready to serve, pour enough dressing over the top to coat the salad lightly, then toss and serve.

ADVANCE PREPARATION: The dressing can be prepared up to 3 days ahead, covered, and refrigerated. The salad can be arranged up to 4 hours ahead and refrigerated.

MIXED GREENS WITH BEETS AND PEPPERS

S E R V E S   6

LAWRY'S RESTAURANT IN Los Angeles specializes in prime rib and is renowned for the salad carts that servers bring tableside. As a child I loved to watch that salad bowl spin as the servers theatrically poured the sweet sherry dressing over it. This first-course salad is a contemporary version of that childhood favorite with the traditional beets and chopped egg but updated with roasted peppers and a zingy lemon balsamic dressing. Follow the salad with Grilled Steaks with Olivada and Port Wine Sauce (page 240) and Potatoes Vaugirard (page 294).

DRESSING
1   medium shallot, finely chopped
1   tablespoon grainy mustard
2   tablespoons fresh lemon juice
2   tablespoons balsamic vinegar
3/4 cup olive oil
1/2 teaspoon salt
1/4 teaspoon black pepper
2   tablespoons finely chopped parsley

SALAD
2   large eggs
2   medium beets, tops removed
2   medium heads of butter lettuce, torn into bite-size pieces
1   small head of radicchio, torn into bite-size pieces
1   bunch of arugula or watercress, torn into bite-size pieces
2   heads of Belgian endive, thinly sliced
1   medium yellow bell pepper, peeled (page 287) and thinly sliced
1   medium red bell pepper, peeled (page 287) and thinly sliced

1. For the dressing, combine the shallot, mustard, lemon juice, and vinegar in a medium mixing bowl. Slowly add the oil, whisking until completely blended. Add the salt, pepper, and parsley and taste for seasoning.

2. Place the eggs in a pan of cold water to cover and bring to a rolling boil. Turn off the heat and cover the pan for 12 minutes. Cool the eggs under cold running water. Peel and finely chop. Reserve.

3. In a medium saucepan, bring water to a boil. Immerse the beets and cook them until tender but slightly resistant, about 25 minutes. Peel and let them cool. When the beets are cool, finely chop them and reserve.

4. In a large mixing bowl, combine the lettuce, radicchio, arugula, and endive and toss with half the dressing. Place some lettuce on each serving plate and then decorate with the beets and peppers and finish with the chopped egg. Serve the remaining dressing on the side.

ADVANCE PREPARATION: Can be prepared up to 8 hours in advance through step 3 and refrigerated. Let the dressing come to room temperature before serving.

SPINACH AND MUSHROOM SALAD WITH WARM TOMATO-BACON VINAIGRETTE

SERVES 2 AS A MAIN COURSE OR 4 AS A FIRST COURSE

WARM SPINACH SALADS were popular back in the 1960s and '70s. Most versions had one thing in common: bacon grease was the foundation of the salad dressing. In this contemporary version a warm vinaigrette, enhanced by finely chopped fresh tomatoes and crisp bacon, is an updated healthful and flavorful adaptation. Golden egg yolks and bright red tomatoes set off the dark green spinach leaves and make a pleasing presentation. To reduce the fat even more, use turkey bacon. This is a nice prelude to Grilled Chicken with Pesto Bean Sauce (page 199) or Roast Crispy Fish with Warm Lentils (page 172). I also like to serve this as a brunch dish since it contains all the components for breakfast and lunch.

RECOMMENDED WINE: A smoky and crisp Sauvignon Blanc works really well with this salad.

SALAD
2   medium bunches of baby spinach, leaves only, cleaned, well dried, and torn into bite-size pieces

1/2 pound mushrooms, thinly sliced

4   large eggs

8   strips of bacon, cut into 1-inch pieces

DRESSING

6   tablespoons olive oil
2   medium shallots, finely chopped
1/4 cup sherry vinegar or red wine vinegar
1/8 teaspoon coarsely cracked black pepper
1   medium tomato, peeled, seeded, and finely chopped

1. Place the spinach and mushrooms in a large salad bowl. Set aside.

2. Place the eggs in a medium saucepan and cover by 1 inch with cold water. Bring the water to a boil over high heat. Immediately remove the pan from the heat, cover, and let sit for 10 minutes. Cool the eggs under cold running water. Peel and quarter the eggs lengthwise. Set aside.

3. In a medium skillet over medium-high heat, sauté the bacon until crisp. Remove the bacon from the pan and drain it on a paper towel. Set aside. Discard the bacon grease.

4. Add the oil to the skillet and turn the heat down to medium. Add the shallots and sauté for about 2 minutes or until just softened. Add the vinegar and pepper and boil for another minute. Taste for seasoning. Add the tomatoes and all but 2 tablespoons of the bacon to the dressing and heat through for another minute.

5. Pour the hot dressing over the spinach and toss to coat all the leaves.

6. Arrange the spinach and mushroom mixture on serving plates. Arrange the egg quarters on the outside edge of the plates. Garnish with the remaining bacon. Serve immediately.

ADVANCE PREPARATION: Can be prepared up to 4 hours ahead through step 3 and kept at room temperature.

BLOOD ORANGE, MUSHROOM, AND AVOCADO SALAD

SERVES 4 TO 6

THIS FIRST-COURSE salad is best in the winter and early spring months, when the vivid maroon-colored blood oranges, now grown commercially in California, make their appearance. Blood oranges have a distinctively rich orange flavor with raspberry overtones that has been featured in Mediterranean cooking for centuries.

This update on the classic grapefruit and avocado combination includes thinly sliced white mushrooms, which offer a pleasant textural contrast. Serve this as a prelude to Roast Crispy Fish with Warm Lentils (page 172) and Home Ranch Butternut Squash (page 279).

DRESSING
1   medium shallot, finely chopped
     juice of 1 medium blood orange (about 1/3 cup)
1   tablespoon balsamic vinegar
1/2 cup olive oil
1/2 teaspoon salt
1/4 teaspoon black pepper

SALAD
2   medium heads of butter lettuce, torn into bite-size pieces
2   blood oranges, peeled and cut into 1-inch pieces
6   medium mushrooms, thinly sliced
1   ripe medium avocado, peeled, pitted, and sliced into 1/4-inch slices

1. For the dressing, finely chop the shallot in a food processor fitted with the metal blade and with the motor running add the orange juice and vinegar. Slowly add the oil until it is completely incorporated. Add the salt and pepper. Taste for seasoning.

2. Arrange the butter lettuce in a shallow salad bowl. Place the orange pieces and mushrooms on top of the lettuce in an attractive pattern, in order to make a pretty presentation before tossing.

3. When you're ready to serve, arrange the avocado slices around the outside edge of the bowl. Toss the salad with the dressing and serve.

ADVANCE PREPARATION: Can be arranged up to 4 hours ahead through step 2, covered, and refrigerated. The dressing can be prepared up to 2 days ahead, covered, and refrigerated.

AVOCADOS

Guacamole is only the first step in appreciating avocados; try them in omelets, chilled soups, salads, salsas, or even to replace the mayonnaise in a sandwich. Here are a few avocado facts to help you enjoy them:

• Eighty percent of California avocado production is the Haas variety, with its characteristic knobbly skin and pale green creamy flesh. Available most of the year, the Haas is considered the best avocado, but during the few winter months when it's out of season, look for the smooth-skinned but less full-flavored Fuerte.

• To test for ripeness, squeeze the fruit gently; it should just yield to pressure. Haas avocados change from green to purple-black as they ripen, but the Fuerte remains green even when completely ripe. To speed up ripening, place the avocados in a paper bag at room temperature for a few days. When ripe, avocados can be stored in the refrigerator for up to five days.

• Ideally, don't peel the avocado until just before serving, but do sprinkle all cut surfaces with lemon or lime juice to help prevent discoloration. For mashed or cubed avocado, be sure there is lemon juice in the mixture if the dish is to be held in the refrigerator for any length of time—and cover it tightly.

• Avocado oil (extracted from the fruit, not the pit of the avocado) is a healthy choice for cooking because it's high in monounsaturated fatty acids. It also has a high smoking point, which makes it a nice option for sautéing. Because it's light in both flavor and aroma, avocado oil is versatile enough to use in any dish.

LA SCALA CHOPPED SALAD

SERVES 4

LA SCALA RESTAURANT, opened in 1957 in Beverly Hills, catered to Hollywood celebrities and politicians. Today there are boutique La Scala branches all over Los Angeles, where this salad of enduring popularity is still the number-one seller.

There is much disagreement about the value of iceberg lettuce in terms of both nutrition and flavor. While it's true that iceberg doesn't have the panache of the so-called designer greens, there are times when I prefer its simple flavor and crunchy character. The creators of this salad were obviously aware of these attributes when La Scala first introduced its chopped salad more than 30 years ago.

To separate the core from the lettuce easily, hit the core against a hard surface. Use a stainless-steel or ceramic knife to cut the lettuce to slow the browning of the cut edges. Vary the salad, adding olives and mushrooms as you like. Begin with Roasted Vegetable Soup (page 43) and serve with warm crusty country sourdough bread (page 327).

RECOMMENDED WINE: Serve a ripe, oaky Chardonnay or an oak-aged Sauvignon Blanc with this full-flavored salad.

1   medium head of iceberg lettuce, cleaned, cored, and finely chopped
1/2 pound Italian fontina or Jarlsberg cheese, finely chopped
1/2 pound salami or fresh turkey breast, finely chopped
1   cup well-drained cooked garbanzo beans (chick peas)
1   red bell pepper, peeled (page 287) and finely chopped

1   large tomato, peeled, seeded, and finely chopped
1/3 cup basic vinaigrette (page 410)
2   tablespoons finely chopped parsley
1/4 teaspoon freshly ground black pepper

1. In a medium salad bowl, combine the lettuce, cheese, salami, beans, red pepper and tomato. Add the dressing, parsley, and pepper and toss. Taste for seasoning and serve immediately. (This is best made just before serving to retain the individual texture of the ingredients.)

WHEATBERRY VEGETABLE SALAD
SERVES 4 TO 6

THIS IS A variation on tabouli, the Middle Eastern cracked wheat salad traditionally made with olive oil, lemon, mint, tomato, and loads of parsley. Wheatberries, which are actually unprocessed whole wheat kernels, must be soaked before cooking and will have a distinctive al dente crunchiness to them. You can find wheatberries in a health food store. In this recipe mint and tomatoes are replaced by chopped cucumber, radishes, and fresh goat or feta cheese. Serve this with White Bean Soup with Leeks, Carrots, and Eggplant (page 51) for a satisfying lunch or supper.

1	cup wheatberries
3-1/2	cups water
1/2	teaspoon salt
2	tablespoons finely chopped red onion
1/2	cup finely diced European cucumber
3/4	cup finely diced radishes
3/4	cup peeled and finely diced carrots
2	tablespoons finely chopped parsley
2	tablespoons finely chopped fresh chives
3	tablespoons finely chopped cilantro
1/2	cup basic vinaigrette (page 410)
2	tablespoons fresh lemon juice
	salt and pepper to taste
1/2	pound goat or feta cheese, crumbled

GARNISH
cilantro leaves

1. Soak the wheatberries overnight in cold water to cover generously or do a quick soak by bringing them to a boil in water to cover, boiling for 2 minutes, covering, and letting stand for 1 hour. Drain the wheatberries.

2. Put the wheatberries in a 3-quart pot with enough water to cover by 2 inches, add salt, and bring to a boil. Cover, reduce the heat, and simmer for 40 minutes or until most of the liquid is absorbed. Uncover and cook for 10 minutes longer to remove excess liquid. Drain wheatberries well and place in a serving bowl. Cool to room temperature.

3. Add the onion, cucumber, radishes, and carrots. Mix with a two-pronged fork, adding the parsley, chives, and cilantro.

4. To make the dressing, combine the vinaigrette, lemon juice, salt, and pepper in a medium bowl and whisk until incorporated. Taste for seasoning.

5. Pour the dressing over the wheatberries and mix with a fork. Carefully add the goat or feta cheese. Taste for seasoning and garnish with cilantro leaves.

ADVANCE PREPARATION: Can be prepared 4 hours ahead, covered, and refrigerated until serving.

LONG-GRAIN AND WILD RICE SALAD WITH CORN AND SALMON

Serves 4 to 6

THIS COLORFUL SALAD, tinged with yellow and pink, is beautiful on a buffet table. I like to shuck just-picked corn and put it in the salad immediately for a garden-to-table flavor. If the corn is a bit older, drop it into boiling water for a minute and then cool it before adding it to the salad.

For a smart luncheon menu, begin with Broccoli Leek Soup (page 47) and serve this salad as a light main course. For dessert, try Orange, Almond, and Olive Oil Cake (page 353). Or serve this on a buffet table along with other cold salads.

RECOMMENDED WINE: A full-bodied Sauvignon Blanc is very effective with this salad. If you are serving it as a main course, Pinot Noir will also perform nicely.

1   6-ounce box long-grain and wild rice
1   pound salmon fillet

DRESSING
3   tablespoons fresh lemon juice
1   teaspoon Dijon mustard
6   tablespoons olive oil
1/2 teaspoon salt
     pinch of white pepper

1   cup fresh corn kernels (about 2 medium ears)
3   tablespoons finely chopped fresh chives
3   tablespoons finely chopped fresh dill

GARNISH
fresh dill sprigs

1. Cook the rice according to box directions. Allow it to cool to room temperature.

2. Prepare a barbecue for medium-heat grilling. Wrap the salmon tightly in aluminum foil or place it directly on the barbecue 3 inches from the heat. Grill for 5 or 6 minutes per side, depending on the thickness. (You can also roast it in a preheated 425°F oven in a roasting pan for about 12 to 15 minutes.) Cool the salmon for 15 minutes. Remove the skin and brown part of the flesh and break the rest into 1-inch pieces. Refrigerate.

3. In a small mixing bowl, combine the lemon juice and mustard. Slowly whisk in the oil until it's emulsified. Add the salt and pepper and taste for seasoning.

4. Combine the corn, herbs, rice, and dressing in a deep serving bowl and toss. Taste for seasoning. Just before serving, add the salmon and toss, being sure not to break up the salmon pieces. Taste for seasoning and garnish with dill sprigs. If you're serving on individual plates, line the plate with pretty lettuce leaves and place a mound of the rice salad on top. Garnish with dill sprigs.

ADVANCE PREPARATION: This gets better if it sits for a day, so you can prepare it up to 1 day ahead and refrigerate until serving. Adjust the seasoning just before serving.

PASTA SALAD WITH PARMESAN DRESSING

SERVES 6

PASTA SALADS HAVE become a standard dish for lunch or even dinner in the last few years. This vegetarian recipe, filled with colorful vegetables and two cheeses, is vastly different from the macaroni salad of my youth. The dressing has enough body and flavor to stand up to the inherent blandness of chilled pasta.

Pick your favorite vegetables and make sure that once they have been cooked they retain some crunch. Include contrasting colors and cut all the vegetables into the same-size pieces. You can also add some shredded chicken, turkey, or even seafood.

SALAD

2   tablespoons oil
1   teaspoon salt
1   pound dried pasta wheels, fusilli, or small shells
4   cups vegetables—any combination of carrots, zucchini, broccoli, asparagus, red or yellow bell peppers—cut into 1-inch pieces, about the same size as the pasta
1   pound whole-milk mozzarella cheese, cut into 1-inch pieces

DRESSING

1/4 cup grainy mustard
2   garlic cloves, minced
1/4 cup fresh lemon juice
2   tablespoons sherry vinegar or red wine vinegar
1/4 teaspoon salt
1/4 teaspoon pepper
1/2 cup olive oil

1/2 cup freshly grated Parmesan

1   tablespoon sour cream or plain nonfat yogurt

1/2 cup finely chopped fresh basil

1. Add 1 tablespoon of the oil and the salt to a large pot of boiling water. Add the pasta and cook over high heat for 10 minutes or until al dente. Drain and transfer to a bowl of ice water mixed with the remaining tablespoon of oil until cool. Drain thoroughly.

2. Immerse the vegetables in a large pan of boiling water and boil until barely tender. Drain and pour cold water over the vegetables to stop the cooking. Drain thoroughly.

3. Combine the mustard, garlic, lemon juice, vinegar, salt, and pepper in a small bowl. Slowly whisk in the olive oil until blended. Add 1/4 cup of the Parmesan and the sour cream and continue whisking until well blended. Taste for seasoning.

4. In a medium serving bowl, combine the drained pasta, vegetables, and mozzarella with the dressing. Add the basil and remaining Parmesan. Taste for seasoning. Refrigerate for 1 hour before serving.

ADVANCE PREPARATION: Can be prepared up to 8 hours ahead and refrigerated. Do not add the basil until immediately before serving. Remove from the refrigerator 1/2 hour before serving.

GRILLED STEAK AND POTATO SALAD

SERVES 4 AS A MAIN COURSE OR 6 TO 8 ON A BUFFET

THE FAVORITE AMERICAN combination of steak and potatoes is reinterpreted here in a hearty salad. I like to leave the peel on the red-skinned potatoes for extra texture and color. If you have any dressing left over, save it and use it for other marinades or on a simple green salad. Begin with Corn and Tomato Soup (page 67) and serve warm country sourdough bread (page 327) or French bread with the salad. For dessert, try Glazed Lemon Sour Cream Cake (page 355).

RECOMMENDED WINE: Serve a hearty red wine with this main-course salad. Best would be Pinot Noir, Zinfandel, or Syrah, although Cabernet Sauvignon would work too.

MARINADE AND DRESSING

2   garlic cloves, minced
2   teaspoons Dijon mustard
2   tablespoons finely chopped fresh chervil or basil
2/3   cup fresh lemon juice
1   cup extra virgin olive oil
1/2   teaspoon salt
1/4   teaspoon pepper

SALAD

1-1/4 pounds triangle tip (bottom sirloin) roast
1   pound red-skinned potatoes (about 3 medium)
1/2   pound green beans, cleaned and cut into 1-1/2-inch pieces
3   celery ribs, thinly sliced on a diagonal
1   small red onion, thinly sliced and cut into 1-1/2-inch pieces

2   tablespoons capers, well drained and rinsed
2   tablespoons finely chopped fresh chervil or basil
1/4 teaspoon black pepper

GARNISH
3   hard-cooked eggs, quartered
1   pint yellow or red cherry tomatoes, halved
     fresh chervil sprigs or basil leaves and basil flowers

1. For the marinade and dressing, combine the garlic, mustard, chervil, and lemon juice in a small bowl. Slowly whisk in the oil until it's thoroughly incorporated. Add the salt and pepper and taste for seasoning.

2. Place the meat in a nonaluminum shallow dish and spoon over 1/2 cup of the marinade, reserving the rest for the salad dressing. Rub the marinade all over the meat and marinate for 2 to 4 hours, covered in the refrigerator.

3. In a large pot of boiling water, cook the potatoes for 20 to 30 minutes or until tender but slightly resistant when pierced with a fork. Drain and cool. When cool, cut into thick matchstick pieces. Place in a large bowl.

4. In a medium saucepan, bring water to boil. Immerse the green beans in the water and cook for about 5 to 7 minutes or until tender but slightly resistant when pierced with a fork. Drain them and place in ice water to stop the cooking. When cool, drain them well and place them in a bowl with the potatoes.

5. Add the celery, onion, capers, chervil, and pepper to the vegetable mixture and stir to combine.

6. Prepare a barbecue for medium-heat grilling. Remove the beef from the marinade and place it on the grill about 3 inches from the heat. Sear each side for about 3 minutes. Cover the barbecue and grill each side for about 10 minutes more or until the internal temperature is 135°F (you can use an instant-read thermometer). Or preheat the oven to 425°F and roast the meat for 30 minutes in a roasting pan. Remove from the heat and let cool. When the meat has cooled, slice it into thick matchstick pieces and add it to the vegetable mixture.

7. When you're ready to serve, combine just enough dressing with the steak salad to moisten it. Stir carefully to combine, being sure not to break up the capers. Taste for seasoning.

8. Arrange the steak salad in a large shallow bowl, mounding it high. Alternate the egg wedges and cherry tomato halves around the outside edge. Garnish with the herbs and serve. Serve extra dressing on the side.

ADVANCE PREPARATION: Can be prepared up to 1 day in advance through step 6. Refrigerate the salad, making sure the potatoes are on the bottom of the bowl, and cover well. The dressing can be left at room temperature. The salad can be made completely, including the garnish, up to 2 hours ahead. Cover well and refrigerate.

GRILLED CHICKEN, BLACK BEAN, AND CORN SALAD WITH SALSA DRESSING

SERVES 4 TO 6

BLACK BEANS AND corn often appear together on the California table in salsas, soups, salads, and vegetable dishes. In this salad grilled marinated chicken is combined with corn and beans for a substantial and satisfying main course.

The black bean has a slightly earthy mushroom flavor that gives a distinctive dimension to this Mexican-style grilled chicken salad. If you're in a hurry, use canned black beans, rinsed and well drained. You can serve this either warm or chilled. Begin with Sweet Potato–Jalapeño Soup with Tomatillo Cream (page 45).

RECOMMENDED WINE: A lively red wine is the answer here. Try Cabernet Sauvignon or Merlot to bring out the earthiness of the salad flavors.

DRESSING
1/4 cup fresh lemon juice
1 tablespoon grainy mustard
1/2 cup olive oil
2 tablespoons spicy tomato salsa (page 413) or mild or spicy store-bought
1/4 teaspoon salt
    pinch of pepper

SALAD
2 large whole chicken breasts, boned, halved, and skinned
2 medium or 1 large head of romaine lettuce, light green and white parts only, torn into bite-size pieces

2   medium carrots, peeled and thinly sliced
1/2 European cucumber, thinly sliced
2   cups cooked black beans
1   cup cooked fresh corn kernels (about 2 medium ears) or thawed
      frozen
1   ripe medium avocado, peeled, pitted, and cut into 1/2-inch pieces

GARNISH
blue or yellow corn tortilla chips
additional tomato salsa

1. Prepare the dressing by mixing the lemon juice and mustard together. Slowly whisk in the oil until it's incorporated. Add the salsa and salt and pepper and taste for seasoning.

2. Marinate the chicken breasts with 1/3 cup of the dressing in a shallow medium nonaluminum dish for at least 1/2 hour and no more than 2 hours, covered in the refrigerator.

3. Arrange the lettuce in a large salad bowl. Place the carrots, cucumbers, beans, corn, and avocado on top of the greens.

4. Prepare a barbecue for medium-heat grilling. Grill the chicken breasts 3 inches from the heat for about 7 to 10 minutes on each side, depending on their thickness. Transfer to a carving board and cut on a diagonal into 1/2-inch slices. Place the chicken on top of the salad.

5. To serve, pour over enough dressing to moisten the salad, toss, and garnish with the tortilla chips. Drizzle salsa decoratively on top. Serve the remaining dressing on the side.

ADVANCE PREPARATION: Can be prepared 4 hours ahead through step 3, but add the avocado just before serving. Refrigerate until you're ready to grill the chicken breasts.

WARM GRILLED CHICKEN SALAD WITH PESTO

S E R V E S 6 A S A M A I N C O U R S E

THIS UNUSUAL CHICKEN salad always wins raves from guests and works either for a luncheon or as the main course for a picnic under the stars. Warm grilled chicken salads are a satisfying solution to summer dining when you're not in the mood for a heavy meal. This is very easy to assemble and can be served cold with equally satisfying results. If you're in a hurry, use your favorite store-bought pesto. Begin with Pinto Bean Soup with Gremolata (page 59) and serve the salad with country sourdough bread (page 327). For dessert, try a plate of Chocolate Truffle Brownies (page 386).

RECOMMENDED WINE: A bright and lively red wine is the answer here. Serve Zinfandel, Pinot Noir, Gamay, Beaujolais, or Syrah.

1/4 cup pine nuts

DRESSING
1/3 cup fresh lemon juice
2/3 cup olive oil
1/4 cup pesto (page 403) or store-bought
     salt and white pepper to taste

SALAD
3   medium whole chicken breasts, boned, halved, and skinned
2   heads of romaine lettuce, light green and white parts only, torn into
     bite-size pieces
3   medium carrots, peeled and shredded

1/2 pound jícama, peeled and cut into julienne
1/4 pound mushrooms, thinly sliced
2   medium tomatoes, thinly sliced or cut into eighths

1. Preheat the oven to 350°F. Toast the pine nuts on a baking sheet for 5 to 7 minutes or until lightly browned. Watch carefully. Remove the pine nuts from the oven and cool.

2. Prepare the dressing by mixing the lemon juice, olive oil, and pesto together. Slowly whisk until incorporated. Add salt and pepper and taste for seasoning.

3. Arrange the chicken breasts in a shallow large nonaluminum dish and pour 1/4 cup of the dressing over them. Marinate for at least 1/2 hour and up to 4 hours, covered and refrigerated.

4. Arrange the salad greens in a large salad bowl. Arrange the carrots, jícama, and mushrooms on top of the lettuce. Arrange the sliced tomatoes on the outside in a ring design.

5. Prepare a barbecue for medium-heat grilling. Grill the chicken breasts 3 inches from the heat for about 6 to 8 minutes per side, depending on their thickness. Transfer the chicken to a carving board and cut on a diagonal into 1/2-inch slices.

6. Arrange the warm strips of chicken on top of the salad. Scatter the pine nuts on top, pour over enough dressing to moisten, toss, and serve. Serve the remaining dressing on the side.

ADVANCE PREPARATION: Can be prepared up to 4 hours ahead through step 4 and refrigerated until you're ready to grill the chicken breasts.

CHICKEN SALAD WITH CHINESE NOODLES
SERVES 6

REMEMBER TO USE a thick noodle that can stand up to the concentrated peanut-tahini dressing in this recipe. I like the sturdier wheat and egg noodle that you can find at a Chinese grocery, or you can substitute fettuccine if you can't find the Chinese noodle. The spicy-sweet peanut sauce, crunchy peanuts, and refreshing carrot and cucumber garnish offset the comforting but bland noodles. Serve this as a main-course luncheon dish. To start, consider Squash Vichyssoise (page 71). The salad also goes well with other vegetable salads on a buffet.

RECOMMENDED WINE: A robust and ripe Chardonnay balances nicely with this spicy salad, or, if you're feeling a bit daring, try a crisp, off-dry Gewürztraminer.

3	cups chicken stock (page 397) and/or water
2	medium whole chicken breasts, boned
1	pound Chinese-style noodles or your favorite thick noodles
2	tablespoons dark sesame oil

DRESSING

1	tablespoon vegetable oil
6	tablespoons peanut butter
1/4	cup water
5	tablespoons soy sauce
6	tablespoons tahini (sesame paste)
2	tablespoons dry sherry
1/4	cup rice wine vinegar
1/4	cup honey
3	garlic cloves, minced
1	tablespoon minced fresh ginger

1 to 2 teaspoons hot pepper oil (page 412)
1/2   cup very hot water

1   medium carrot, peeled and cut into julienne
1/2   European cucumber, seeded and cut into julienne
2   scallions, white and light green parts only, thinly sliced

GARNISH
1   carrot, peeled, cut in half lengthwise, and shaved with a vegetable
        peeler
1/2   medium European cucumber, cut in half lengthwise, seeded, and
        shaved with a vegetable peeler
2   scallions, finely sliced
1/2   cup roasted peanuts, coarsely chopped

1. In a deep medium skillet or a large saucepan, bring the stock to a simmer. If you're using water only, add 1/2 teaspoon salt. Add the chicken breasts and simmer for 10 to 12 minutes or until just tender.

2. Cool the chicken in the liquid. Drain the chicken and remove the skin. Shred the chicken by tearing the meat into long, 1/2-inch-thick pieces (or slice it with a knife). Reserve in a medium mixing bowl.

3. Cook the noodles in a large pot of boiling water over medium heat for about 2-1/2 to 3 minutes or until barely tender and still firm. Drain the noodles immediately and rinse them with cold water until cooled. Drain them well, place in a large serving bowl, and toss with the sesame oil so they don't stick together.

4. For the dressing, combine all the ingredients except the hot water in a blender or a food processor fitted with the metal blade and blend until smooth. Thin with hot water to the consistency of heavy cream.

5. Combine the chicken and vegetables with the noodles and add enough dressing to coat the noodles generously. Place the noodles in a serving bowl and garnish them with the carrots, cucumber, scallions, and peanuts. Refrigerate for 1/2 hour before serving.

ADVANCE PREPARATION: Can be prepared up to 1 day ahead through step 4 and refrigerated. Bring the dressing to room temperature before tossing. Extra dressing will keep for up to 1 month in the refrigerator and is great as a sauce with lamb.

WINE COUNTRY CHICKEN SALAD

SERVES 4

ANNIE ROBERTS, THE gifted chef at the Robert Mondavi Winery in the Napa Valley, prepared this lovely main-course salad for me at the winery. Sitting outside overlooking the vines and mountains and enjoying the perfect weather, I thought about how this salad represents the best of California's fresh, lively flavors.

This salad is perfect for a hot summer day or evening since it can be prepared well ahead of time. Begin with California Caponata (page 31) on French bread. Finish with sliced fresh seasonal fruit and White Chocolate and Pistachio Cookies (page 387).

RECOMMENDED WINE: An oak-aged Sauvignon Blanc (such as Mondavi's Fumé Blanc) or a crisp, medium-weight Chardonnay is a perfect foil for this lively salad.

SALAD
3   cups chicken stock (page 397) and/or water
2   medium whole chicken breasts, boned
1/2 pound pencil-thin asparagus, trimmed and cut into 2-inch lengths
1/2 cup Niçoise olives, pitted
10 cherry tomatoes, quartered
2   tablespoons capers, drained and rinsed
2   tablespoons finely chopped fresh chervil or basil
1/4 teaspoon black pepper

DRESSING
1   medium shallot, minced
2   teaspoons finely chopped fresh thyme

1   tablespoon finely chopped parsley
1/4 cup fresh lemon juice (1 medium lemon)
1/2 cup extra virgin olive oil
1/2 teaspoon salt
1/4 teaspoon pepper

GARNISH
butter lettuce leaves
fresh chervil sprigs or basil leaves

1. In a deep medium skillet or a large saucepan, bring the stock to a simmer. If you're using only water, add 1/2 teaspoon salt. Add the chicken and simmer for 10 to 12 minutes or until just tender.

2. Cool the chicken in the liquid, drain, and remove the skin. Shred the chicken by tearing it into long, thin pieces (or slice with a knife). Reserve in a large bowl.

3. In a medium skillet of boiling water, cook the asparagus for 3 to 4 minutes or until tender but slightly resistant when pierced with a fork. Drain and cool under running water. Place in the bowl with the chicken.

4. Add the olives, tomatoes, capers, chervil, and pepper to the chicken and stir to combine.

5. For the dressing, combine the shallot, thyme, parsley, and lemon juice in a small bowl. Slowly whisk in the oil until it's thoroughly incorporated. Add the salt and pepper and taste for seasoning.

6. When you're ready to serve, add enough dressing to the chicken salad to moisten it. Stir carefully to combine, being sure not to break up the capers. Taste for seasoning.

7. Arrange the chicken salad on a bed of butter lettuce. Garnish with the herbs and serve. Serve extra dressing on the side.

ADVANCE PREPARATION: Can be prepared up to 6 hours ahead through step 5. Cover and refrigerate the salad. The dressing can be left at room temperature. The salad can be made completely up to 2 hours ahead, covered well, and refrigerated.

WARM GRILLED VEGETABLE AND SHRIMP SALAD

SERVES 6 TO 8

PICTURE THE SMOKY-VIBRANT colors of grilled shrimp, asparagus, scallions, corn, and fresh lettuce. In this quintessential California salad, the shrimp and all accompanying ingredients are grilled and slightly charred, chopped, and combined in a lightly smoked medley.

This salad is fun to prepare for guests because you can chat with them as the vegetables and shrimp are grilling. For a lighter beginning to your meal, serve the salad without the shrimp. For a main course, begin with Goat Cheese with Rustic Salsa (page 25) and sliced country sourdough bread (page 327) or French bread.

RECOMMENDED WINE: A crisp, spicy Sauvignon Blanc or a dry Chenin Blanc offers an attractive contrast to the richness of the shrimp.

1   pound large shrimp, shelled and deveined
3/4 cup basic vinaigrette (page 410)
1   teaspoon Dijon mustard
3   medium zucchini, cut lengthwise into 1/4-inch slices
16 asparagus, trimmed
8   scallions, white and light green parts only
2   ears of corn, husked
2   medium heads of Belgian endive
2   medium heads of radicchio
2   medium heads of butter lettuce
1   ripe medium avocado, peeled, pitted, and diced
2   tablespoons finely chopped fresh herbs: any combination of basil, parsley, dill, and chives

1. Thread the shrimp on metal or bamboo skewers (soak bamboo in cold water for 1/2 hour before grilling) and lay them flat in a shallow nonaluminum dish. In a small bowl, combine the vinaigrette and mustard. Pour 1/4 cup of the vinaigrette over the shrimp and marinate for 1/2 hour in the refrigerator, turning once or twice.

2. Prepare a barbecue for medium-heat grilling. Place the zucchini, asparagus, and scallions on the grill 3 inches from the heat and barbecue for about 4 minutes per side or until slightly charred. Remove the vegetables from the grill and coarsely chop them into 1-inch pieces. Transfer to a salad bowl. Place the corn on the barbecue and grill, turning as it just begins to darken. Remove from the grill and, when cool enough, shuck the corn kernels with a sharp knife into the salad bowl.

3. Place the endive, radicchio, and lettuce on the grill and barbecue for about 3 minutes a side, turning to cook evenly. Remove them from the grill and coarsely chop. Place them in the salad bowl.

4. Place the skewered shrimp flat on the grill. Baste each side with the vinaigrette marinade and grill until just cooked, about 3 to 4 minutes per side. Remove the shrimp from the grill, withdraw the skewers, and coarsely chop the shrimp into 1-inch pieces. Place in the salad bowl.

5. Add the avocado and herbs and then drizzle on the remaining dressing. Toss and serve immediately.

ADVANCE PREPARATION: Can be prepared up to 1 day ahead through step 4 and served cold.

SPRINGTIME SALMON SALAD
SERVES 4

SALMON AND ASPARAGUS are at their peak in the spring. I love this salad for its piquant herbed dressing, which perfectly accents the vegetables and salmon. Buttery Yellow Finn or Yukon Gold potatoes give the salad a superb flavor. Serve with Sourdough Rye Rolls (page 330).

RECOMMENDED WINE: A rich, nicely oaked Chardonnay does well with this hearty salad. A chilled Gamay Beaujolais or light Pinot Noir is a more daring choice.

SALAD
1   pound salmon fillet
1   pound yellow or White Rose potatoes, peeled
1   pound thin asparagus
2   large eggs

DRESSING
1/4 cup fresh lemon juice
1   garlic clove, minced
1   tablespoon capers, well drained and rinsed
3   tablespoons finely chopped fresh dill
2   tablespoons finely chopped parsley
1   teaspoon finely chopped lemon zest
1/4 teaspoon salt
1/8 teaspoon pepper
1/2 cup olive oil

GARNISH
1   head of red leaf lettuce, cleaned and torn into 2-inch pieces
    red and yellow teardrop cherry tomatoes

1. Bring enough water to cover the salmon to a simmer in a medium sauté pan. Poach the salmon over medium heat for about 10 to 12 minutes, depending on the thickness. Remove the salmon from the heat and let it cool in the liquid. When the salmon is cool, remove the skin and break it up into 1-1/2-inch pieces.

2. In a medium saucepan of boiling water, cook the potatoes until tender but slightly resistant when pierced with a fork, 20 to 30 minutes. Drain and cool, then cut into 1-1/2-inch strips.

3. Peel the asparagus and trim the tough ends off. Cut into 1-1/2-inch pieces. Bring a large sauté pan of salted water to a boil and cook the asparagus for about 3 to 5 minutes or until just tender. Drain and cool.

4. Place the eggs in a pan of cold water to cover and bring to a rolling boil. Turn off the heat and cover the pan for 12 minutes. Cool the eggs under cold running water. Peel and cut into quarters. Reserve.

5. For the dressing, combine all the ingredients in a blender or a food processor fitted with the metal blade and blend until creamy. Taste for seasoning.

6. Combine the salmon, potatoes, and asparagus in a medium mixing bowl and add 1/3 cup of dressing. Toss to combine. Taste for seasoning.

7. To serve, arrange lettuce leaves on each serving plate. Place some salmon salad on top and then garnish with alternating egg quarters and red and yellow cherry tomato halves. Serve the remaining dressing on the side.

ADVANCE PREPARATION: Can be prepared up to 4 hours ahead through step 5, covered, and refrigerated.

PASTA, PIZZA, POLENTA, RISOTTO, AND EGGS

GOLDEN FRITTATA WITH TOMATILLO SALSA 117
PUFFED APPLE-ORANGE OVEN PANCAKE 119
SCRAMBLED EGGS WITH ASPARAGUS AND SMOKED SALMON 120
HERBED SCRAMBLED EGGS WITH GOAT CHEESE 122
RICOTTA PANCAKES WITH SAUTÉED SPICED PEARS 124
PASTA WITH ANCHO CHILE AND TOMATO CREAM 126
INDIAN SUMMER PASTA 128
BAKED VEGETABLE RIGATONI WITH TOMATOES AND PROVOLONE 130
PASTA WITH TOMATOES, BASIL, AND BALSAMIC VINAIGRETTE 132
WONTON BUTTERNUT SQUASH RAVIOLI WITH SPINACH PESTO 134
HOLIDAY LASAGNE WITH ROASTED VEGETABLES AND PESTO 137
RISOTTO WITH LEEKS, TOMATOES, AND NIÇOISE OLIVES 141
GARDEN RISOTTO 143
TWO-MUSHROOM BARLEY RISOTTO 145
SOFT POLENTA WITH SUN-DRIED TOMATO PESTO 147
GRILLED POLENTA WITH CONFIT OF RED ONIONS AND PROSCIUTTO 149
GRILLED INSTANT POLENTA 149
GRILLED POLENTA USING YELLOW CORNMEAL 151
CONFIT OF RED ONIONS AND PROSCIUTTO 153
JEWISH BREAKFAST PIZZA 154
BARBECUED PIZZA WITH LEEKS, MOZZARELLA, TOMATOES,
    AND PANCETTA 156

GOLDEN FRITTATA WITH TOMATILLO SALSA

SERVES 4 TO 6

THIS LARGE GOLDEN pancake-style omelet looks like an egg pizza. Select your favorite sautéed vegetables, such as onions, zucchini, yellow squash, or broccoli, for this main-course brunch favorite. A nonstick skillet makes it easy to invert the frittata onto a serving platter. Begin with a sliced seasonal fruit platter and serve with a sampling of Ciji's Scones with Currants (page 315), Orange–Poppy Seed Bread (page 317), and Fresh Pear Bread (page 318). Grilled Chicken and Apple Sausage (page 223) or crisp bacon makes a nice accompaniment.

RECOMMENDED WINE: A light, fresh Chardonnay or a dry Chenin Blanc works well with the flavors of this frittata.

2	tablespoons olive oil
2	medium leeks, white part only, cleaned and finely chopped
1	pound mushrooms, thinly sliced
1	medium yellow bell pepper, thinly sliced
1	garlic clove, minced
1/2	teaspoon salt
1/4	teaspoon pepper
12	large eggs
1-1/2 cups shredded Swiss Gruyère or sharp cheddar cheese	

GARNISH
1/2	cup sour cream
1/2	cup tomatillo salsa (page 414)

1. In a 12-inch nonstick skillet with an ovenproof handle or a shallow paella pan over medium-high heat, heat the oil, add the leeks, and sauté until soft but not

brown, about 3 minutes. Add the mushrooms and sauté for 2 minutes, then add the yellow pepper. Cook for a few more minutes, until the peppers are slightly soft. Add the garlic and cook for another minute. Season with salt and pepper.

2. Preheat the oven to 425°F. Whisk the eggs until well blended. Stir in 1-1/4 cups of the shredded cheese. Pour the egg mixture over the vegetables in the skillet and cook over medium-low heat, stirring occasionally, until the bottom of the mixture is lightly browned, about 5 minutes. Sprinkle with the remaining cheese.

3. Transfer the skillet to the middle rack in the oven and bake until the frittata is puffed and brown, about 10 to 15 minutes. Remove it from the oven and invert it onto a plate. Invert it again onto a serving platter, so the browned top faces up. Arrange a large dollop of sour cream in the middle and then spoon on the salsa in an attractive pattern. Serve immediately. (You can also serve the frittata right out of the pan if you prefer.)

ADVANCE PREPARATION: Can be prepared up to 4 hours ahead through step 1, covered, and kept at room temperature. Although it will be a heavier texture, the frittata can be made 1 day ahead, refrigerated, and served at room temperature.

PUFFED APPLE-ORANGE OVEN PANCAKE

SERVES 2

LIKE A POPOVER, this giant vanilla-scented pancake magically puffs up into a light yet satisfying breakfast or brunch main course. Serve this pancake with grilled assorted sausages and big cups of cappuccino.

RECOMMENDED WINE: Serve a crisp, slightly off-dry Johannisberg Riesling with this fruity pancake.

3/4 cup milk
1/2 cup all-purpose flour
2 large eggs
2 tablespoons sugar
1 teaspoon vanilla extract
1 teaspoon finely chopped orange zest
1 small Pippin, Granny Smith, or Golden Delicious apple, peeled, cored, and finely chopped (about 1 cup)
2 tablespoons unsalted butter

GARNISH
powdered sugar

1. Preheat the oven to 450°F. Combine the milk, flour, eggs, sugar, vanilla, and orange zest in a food processor fitted with the metal blade, a blender, or a bowl and whisk or process until smooth. Add the apple pieces and stir to combine.

2. Place the butter in a 10-inch pie plate or ovenproof skillet and put it in the oven to melt. Brush the inside of the pan to coat it evenly with butter.

3. Pour the batter into the pan and bake for 15 minutes. Reduce the heat to 350°F and bake for 15 minutes longer or until the pancake is nicely browned, cooked in the center, and well puffed. Remove from the oven and sprinkle powdered sugar generously on top. Serve immediately.

SCRAMBLED EGGS WITH ASPARAGUS AND SMOKED SALMON

SERVES 4 TO 6

SCRAMBLED EGGS ARE particularly appealing paired with crisp, green asparagus and delicate pink smoked salmon. Try this recipe with toasted country sourdough bread (page 327) and fresh fruit salad.

RECOMMENDED WINE: A smoky Sauvignon Blanc is just right with the smokiness of the salmon here.

1   pound asparagus
1/8 pound smoked salmon
2   tablespoons unsalted butter
12 large eggs
1/4 teaspoon salt
    pinch of white pepper

1. Peel, trim, and rinse the asparagus. Cut off the asparagus tips and reserve. Slice the asparagus stalks into 1-1/2-inch pieces.

2. Dice all but 1 slice of the salmon. Cut the remaining slice into strips and reserve for garnish.

3. Add the asparagus pieces to a pan of boiling salted water and boil for 3 minutes or until barely tender. Drain thoroughly.

4. Melt the butter in a medium saucepan over medium heat. Add the asparagus pieces and cook, stirring, for 2 minutes.

5. Meanwhile, cook the asparagus tips in a large pan of boiling salted water for about 3 minutes or until they're bright green and barely tender. Drain and cover to keep them warm.

6. Whisk the eggs with the salt and pepper. Add the eggs to the saucepan containing the asparagus pieces and cook over low heat, stirring constantly, until the egg mixture becomes thick but not dry, about 4 to 5 minutes. Stir in the diced smoked salmon and remove from the heat. Taste for seasoning.

7. Transfer the egg mixture to a serving bowl. Arrange the asparagus tips facing outward around the scrambled eggs and then sprinkle with the reserved smoked salmon strips. Serve immediately.

ADVANCE PREPARATION: Can be prepared up to 2 hours ahead through step 3 and kept at room temperature.

HERBED SCRAMBLED EGGS WITH GOAT CHEESE

SERVES 4 TO 6

GOAT CHEESE HAS become a staple in California cooking and is readily available in local supermarkets. The fresh soft variety is used here to give the eggs a fluffy texture. Check the freshness of the goat cheese; there should be no ammonia scent.

California or other American goat cheeses are generally fresher than imported ones, which have traveled a long way to reach you. Fresh goat cheese should have a tangy lively flavor; as it ages it unfortunately develops a sharper, more bitter, and sometimes chalky flavor, so check the date on the package.

This is a sensational Sunday brunch dish accompanied by sautéed or grilled Chicken and Apple Sausage (page 223) and crispy roasted potatoes. Serve Mixed Exotic Fruit Gazpacho (page 349) with Orange, Almond, and Olive Oil Cake (page 353) for dessert.

RECOMMENDED WINE: A slightly chilled Gamay Beaujolais or a Pinot Noir underlines the richness and creaminess of the cheese.

12 large eggs
1/2 teaspoon salt
1/4 teaspoon pepper
2   tablespoons unsalted butter
1   cup crumbled fresh goat cheese
3   tablespoons finely chopped mixed fresh herbs such as parsley, chives, basil, thyme, and burnet

GARNISH
fresh herb sprigs such as parsley, chives, basil, burnet, or thyme

1. Whisk the eggs with the salt and pepper.

2. Melt the butter in a heavy medium saucepan. Add the egg mixture and cook over low heat, whisking constantly, until the mixture becomes thick but not dry, about 4 to 5 minutes. Remove from the heat. Carefully stir in the goat cheese and fresh herbs so they blend in well. Taste for seasoning.

3. Transfer the egg mixture to a serving bowl. Garnish with fresh herb sprigs. Serve immediately.

RICOTTA PANCAKES WITH SAUTÉED SPICED PEARS

SERVES 4

ON A TRIP to the Sonoma wine country I spent the evening at a charming bed-and-breakfast called the George Alexander House in the little town of Healdsburg. I awoke the next morning to find a version of these heavenly, fluffy pancakes awaiting me in the cozy country dining room. Those pancakes were flavored with lemon extract and lemon zest, but I like the addition of orange with the pear topping. Some crisp bacon and fresh fruit juice are all you need to make this a breakfast or brunch you won't soon forget. Serve these on a lazy Sunday morning with caffe latte.

RECOMMENDED WINE: Accompany these pancakes with a crisp, fruity Johannisberg Riesling or a spicy Gewürztraminer.

PEAR TOPPING
2   tablespoons unsalted butter
3   large Bosc or Anjou pears, peeled, cored, and cut into 1-inch dice
2   tablespoons sugar
1/4 teaspoon ground ginger
1/4 teaspoon ground cinnamon
1   tablespoon fresh orange juice
1   teaspoon vanilla extract

PANCAKES
4   large eggs, separated
1   cup low-fat ricotta cheese
2   tablespoons sugar

1   tablespoon finely chopped orange zest
1/2 cup all-purpose flour
    pinch of salt

4   tablespoons unsalted butter for cooking the pancakes

1. For the pear topping, melt the butter in a large sauté pan over medium-high heat. Add the pears and sauté for about 5 minutes or until the pears are softened. Add the sugar and continue cooking until the pears are soft and the sauce is slightly caramelized, about 3 minutes. Add the ginger, cinnamon, orange juice, and vanilla and cook for another minute. Cover and set aside, keeping warm.

2. For the pancakes, combine the egg yolks, ricotta, sugar, orange zest, and flour in a medium mixing bowl and whisk until well combined.

3. In a large bowl with an electric mixer, combine the egg whites and a pinch of salt and beat on medium speed until the egg whites are stiff but not dry. Add one third of the egg whites to the pancake mixture and fold them in gently. Fold in the remaining egg whites, making sure no white streaks are left in the batter.

4. To cook the pancakes, heat 2 tablespoons of the butter in a large griddle or sauté pan over medium heat. Pour in about 1/4 cup batter for each pancake and cook for about 2 to 3 minutes on each side or until lightly browned. Add more butter as necessary.

5. Serve the pancakes immediately with a large dollop of pear topping. You can also serve these with some warm maple syrup if you like.

ADVANCE PREPARATION: Can be prepared up to 1 day ahead through step 1 and refrigerated. Reheat gently to serve.

PASTA WITH ANCHO CHILE AND TOMATO CREAM

SERVES 4 TO 6

ANCHO CHILE HAS a smoky rich flavor that brings a southwestern touch to this typical Italian dish. The addition of Sun-Dried Tomato Pesto provides a subtle, sweet undertone to the sauce. This twist on pasta with pesto becomes particularly colorful with bright green peas and crisp mahogany brown pancetta.

I like to make the Ancho Chile Paste and Sun-Dried Tomato Pesto in advance and keep them in my refrigerator for future use. I find these versatile condiments useful in ways I never would have imagined had they not been readily available for experimentation. (If you don't have time to make the chile paste or pesto, you can buy the packaged supermarket versions.)

Adding chicken stock to the sauce gives it both flavor and lightness so less cream is required. I like to serve this for lunch or dinner as a main course. Start with Farmer's Market Chopped Salad (page 78) and finish with Peach Melba Buckle (page 359).

RECOMMENDED WINE: A crisp, medium-weight Chardonnay is a good companion to this rich dish.

1/2 pound pancetta or other bacon, thinly sliced
1/2 cup Ancho Chile Paste (page 406)
1/2 cup Sun-Dried Tomato Pesto (page 404)
2 cups chicken stock (page 397)
1/2 cup whipping cream
1/4 teaspoon finely ground pepper
1 tablespoon olive oil
1 teaspoon salt
1 pound dried fusilli or small pasta shells
1 cup thawed frozen baby peas or fresh baby peas cooked until tender

GARNISH

1/2 cup freshly grated Parmesan

1. For the sauce, cook the pancetta in a medium skillet over medium heat, turning it occasionally until crisp and brown, about 4 to 5 minutes. Drain on paper towels and crumble into bite-size pieces. Reserve.

2. Combine the chile paste, pesto, stock, cream, and pepper in a medium saucepan over medium heat and bring to a simmer. Whisk to blend the ingredients and cook for 5 minutes. Taste for seasoning.

3. Add the oil and salt to a large pot of boiling water. Add the pasta and cook over high heat until al dente, about 7 to 10 minutes. Drain well. Place in a large pasta bowl. Add the sauce to the pasta and then carefully add the peas and pancetta, tossing to combine. Taste for seasoning. Serve immediately with Parmesan.

ADVANCE PREPARATION: Can be prepared up to 4 hours ahead through step 2 and refrigerated. Gently reheat the sauce.

VARIATIONS: Substitute julienned cooked chicken, shrimp, or scallops for the pancetta or let cool and mix with 1/2 cup basic vinaigrette (page 410) for a pasta salad.

INDIAN SUMMER PASTA

SERVES 6 TO 8

EVERY YEAR I look forward to the time when summer drifts away into the cool, crisp days of autumn. From a cook's point of view, I can recognize the signals. The tomatoes, corn, fresh herbs, and summer fruits are slowly being replaced in the markets by sturdier produce fit for fall weather. Just before this change of season occurs, I have a compelling desire to enjoy all the tastes of summer one last time. That's how this dish came into being.

As I stood at the produce stand eyeing the possibilities, I wondered how to reinterpret these ingredients. This light, simple sauce takes into account a broad array of seasonal vegetables and includes your choice of grilled sausages for a substantial main course. If you have any left over, refrigerate it and add some vinaigrette to make it into a pasta salad. Begin with Squash Vichyssoise (page 71) and serve a simple dessert of Baked Pears in Burgundy and Port Glaze (page 345).

RECOMMENDED WINE: This dish will be best with a fruity red wine that will balance its strong flavors. Try a Zinfandel, Gamay Beaujolais, or Rhône variety.

1-1/2 pounds assorted sausages: sweet, hot, or Turkey Sausages with Sun-Dried Tomatoes (page 225)

SAUCE
3   tablespoons olive oil
2   garlic cloves, minced
3/4   pound green beans, yellow wax beans, or sugar snap peas, cut into 2-inch pieces and cooked until crisp-tender
2-1/2 pounds peeled, seeded, and coarsely chopped red and, if available, yellow tomatoes
1   cup corn kernels (about 2 medium ears)

1/4   cup finely chopped fresh basil
1   tablespoon finely chopped parsley
1   teaspoon salt
1/2   teaspoon finely ground white pepper

PASTA

1   tablespoon olive oil
1   teaspoon salt
1   pound small pasta shells

GARNISH

1   tablespoon finely chopped fresh basil
1   cup freshly grated Parmesan

1. Prepare a barbecue for medium-high-heat grilling. Place the sausages on the barbecue and grill 3 inches from the heat for about 20 minutes, rotating them on all sides until the fat runs clear. Or place them on a microwave-safe plate and cook at 100 percent power for 4 minutes or until the fat runs clear. Transfer to a platter and cool. When cool, slice into 1/4-inch pieces or crumble if desired.

2. In a deep large skillet over medium heat, heat the oil, add the garlic, and cook for 1 minute, making sure it does not burn. Add the beans and cook for 2 minutes. Add the tomatoes and cook for 5 minutes, stirring occasionally until some of the liquid has evaporated. Add the corn and cook for 2 minutes. Add the basil, parsley, salt, and pepper and taste for seasoning. Add the sausages to the sauce.

3. Add the oil and salt to a large pot of boiling water. Add the pasta and cook over high heat until al dente, about 7 to 10 minutes. Drain well.

4. Place the pasta in a large serving bowl. Pour the sauce over the pasta and mix well. Garnish with the basil and a few tablespoons of the Parmesan. Pass the remaining Parmesan separately. Serve immediately.

ADVANCE PREPARATION: Can be prepared up to 8 hours ahead through step 2, covered, and refrigerated. Remove from the refrigerator 1/2 hour before reheating. Gently reheat the sauce.

BAKED VEGETABLE RIGATONI WITH TOMATOES AND PROVOLONE

SERVES 6

I PARTICULARLY LIKE this great party dish because it won't overwhelm whatever else I might serve with it. Roasting the vegetables before baking them with the pasta brings a rustic, rich flavor to this dish. You can add zucchini, leeks, or other peppers for a more complex flavor. The melted smoky provolone adds a comforting touch.

Try this for a party when you don't want to prepare a sit-down dinner. Choose simple roast chicken breasts with herbs, sliced roast leg of lamb, or tenderloin of beef to complete the menu.

RECOMMENDED WINE: A medium-weight, fruity red wine is an excellent match for this dish. The acidic nature of the eggplant and tomatoes pairs nicely with Gamay Beaujolais, Zinfandel, or Pinot Noir.

2	tablespoons olive oil
1	small onion, finely chopped
8	medium Japanese eggplants or 1 large eggplant, cut into 1-inch slices
1-1/4	pounds medium mushrooms, cleaned and quartered
2	large red bell peppers, cut into 1-inch pieces
1	teaspoon salt
1/2	teaspoon pepper

PASTA

1	tablespoon olive oil
1	teaspoon salt
1	pound dried rigatoni

4   cups Double-Tomato Herb Sauce (page 400) or your favorite cooked
        tomato sauce
2   tablespoons finely chopped fresh basil
1/2   pound provolone, cut into 1/2-inch pieces
3/4   cup freshly grated Parmesan

1. Preheat the oven to 425°F. In a large roasting pan, combine the oil, onion, eggplants, mushrooms, and red peppers and mix to coat all the ingredients. Roast the vegetables until softened, about 40 to 45 minutes, turning them occasionally to keep them from sticking. Remove from the oven, cool, and season with salt and pepper.

2. Add the oil and salt to a large pot of boiling water. Add the pasta and cook over high heat until al dente, about 12 minutes. Drain well.

3. Place the pasta in a large mixing bowl. Pour 3-1/2 cups of the tomato sauce over the pasta and mix well. Add the basil, provolone, 1/4 cup of the Parmesan, and the roasted vegetables and mix well. Taste for seasoning.

4. Grease a 9- by 13-inch ovenproof baking dish. Spoon the pasta mixture into the dish and dot the top with the remaining 1/2 cup tomato sauce. Sprinkle the remaining Parmesan on top.

5. When you're ready to serve, preheat the oven to 400°F. Bake the pasta for 20 minutes or until bubbling hot. Serve immediately.

ADVANCE PREPARATION: Can be prepared up to 1 day ahead through step 4, covered, and refrigerated. Remove from the refrigerator 1/2 hour before baking.

PASTA WITH TOMATOES, BASIL, AND BALSAMIC VINAIGRETTE

SERVES 4 TO 6

BALSAMIC VINEGAR IS the vital ingredient in this no-cook pasta sauce. Light and refreshing, this is a great side dish for any simple grilled entrée. You can also serve it as a main course for lunch.

RECOMMENDED WINE: Pairing wine with vinegar is always a problem, but the sweetness in the balsamic vinegar takes the edge off its volatile acidity. Pour a rich, complex Chardonnay with this dish.

SAUCE

2   pounds Italian plum or Roma tomatoes, peeled, seeded, and finely
      chopped
1   medium bunch of basil, finely chopped
4   garlic cloves, minced
1/4 cup olive oil
2   tablespoons balsamic vinegar
1/2 teaspoon salt
1/4 teaspoon black pepper
1/2 cup freshly shaved Parmesan

PASTA

1   tablespoon oil
1   teaspoon salt
1   pound dried capellini or linguine

GARNISH
fresh basil leaves

1. In a medium pasta serving bowl, combine all the sauce ingredients, reserving 1/4 cup of the Parmesan.

2. Add the oil and salt to a large pot of boiling water. Add the pasta and cook over high heat until al dente, about 5 to 8 minutes. Drain well. Arrange the pasta over the sauce. Mix to combine. Garnish the bowl with fresh basil leaves and pass the remaining Parmesan. Serve immediately.

ADVANCE PREPARATION: The sauce can be prepared up to 4 hours ahead, covered, and left at room temperature.

WONTON BUTTERNUT SQUASH RAVIOLI WITH SPINACH PESTO

MAKES ABOUT 38 RAVIOLI TO SERVE 6 TO 8

IF YOU'VE NEVER made ravioli with wonton skins instead of pasta, you'll be amazed at how easy and how good they are. These plump pasta bundles signal the arrival of autumn for me. Pumpkin is sometimes used in this ravioli, but I find butternut squash has a better texture and flavor.

Spinach pesto heightens the sweetness of the squash, and its emerald-green color looks particularly pretty with the bright orange ravioli triangles. You can serve these either in individual bowls with a drizzle of pesto on top or in a large serving bowl—gently toss the ravioli with the pesto sauce.

These ravioli make a wonderful beginning to an Italian-inspired menu or a main course followed by Essencia Zabaglione with Fresh Fruit Compote (page 347).

RECOMMENDED WINE: The flavors of this dish lend themselves to both Chardonnay and Pinot Noir. A Rhône variety would also do the trick.

FILLING
2   pounds butternut squash
2   tablespoons olive oil
1/4 cup water
2   medium shallots, minced
1/4 cup freshly grated Parmesan
1/8 teaspoon freshly grated nutmeg
1/8 teaspoon ground sage
1/4 teaspoon salt
1/8 teaspoon white pepper
1/4 teaspoon minced fresh sage

38 3- by 3-1/2-inch wonton wrappers
1 large egg white, beaten

SPINACH PESTO
2 garlic cloves, peeled
2 cups well-packed fresh spinach leaves
1 cup well-packed fresh basil leaves
1/2 cup olive oil
1/4 teaspoon black pepper
2/3 cup freshly grated Parmesan

GARNISH
2 tablespoons freshly grated Parmesan

1. Preheat the oven to 350°F. Cut the squash in half lengthwise and rub 1 tablespoon of oil evenly over the cut sides. Place the squash halves in a roasting pan, add the water, and bake for about 1 hour or until tender, adding a little more water if it evaporates during cooking. Or microwave the squash by placing the halves flat side down in a glass dish, covering with plastic wrap, cooking on 100 percent power for 6 minutes, removing the plastic, and cooking for 6 minutes longer. Cool the squash and remove the seeds. Spoon out the flesh and place in a food processor fitted with the metal blade. Process until completely pureed. Drain any accumulated juices. Place in a medium mixing bowl.

2. In a small skillet over medium heat, heat the remaining oil, add the shallots, and sauté for 3 to 5 minutes or until softened. Add the shallots and remaining filling ingredients to the squash and mix to combine. Taste for seasoning. The filling should be firm enough to hold together. Refrigerate the filling until needed.

3. For each ravioli, place a wrapper on a work surface. Put 1 rounded teaspoon of filling in the center. Brush the edges with egg white and then fold over to make a triangle, pressing the edges together firmly so that the squash will not leak. Place the finished ravioli on a floured baking sheet and cover with a very damp kitchen towel.

4. To make the pesto, add the garlic cloves to the food processor fitted with the metal blade with the motor running. Process until minced. Add the spinach and basil and process until finely chopped. Slowly pour in the olive oil in a fine stream. Add the pepper. Add the Parmesan and process until well blended. Taste for seasoning.

5. Bring a deep large skillet of water to a simmer. Cook half the ravioli until they're hot in the center and float to the top, about 3 minutes. Use a slotted spoon to turn them. When cooked, spoon them into a large serving bowl or individual shallow soup plates. Repeat to cook the remaining ravioli.

6. To serve, pour on just enough pesto to coat the ravioli, mixing very gently so they don't break. Drizzle with a little extra pesto and sprinkle with the Parmesan. Serve immediately.

ADVANCE PREPARATION: Can be prepared up to 6 hours ahead through step 3 and refrigerated. The pesto can be prepared 2 days ahead, covered, and refrigerated. Bring it to room temperature before serving. Refrigerate any remaining pesto in a tightly covered container.

HOLIDAY LASAGNE WITH ROASTED VEGETABLES AND PESTO

SERVES 8 TO 10

THIS ONE-DISH PASTA recipe evolved with the help of my dear friend Laurie Burrows Grad. One of our first cooking days together was spent making Ed Giobbi's delectable lasagne recipe, which took the two of us 10 hours to put together.

This streamlined interpretation is meatless, lighter than the original, and will win raves from your guests. I like to serve this for holiday buffet dinners. Accompany the lasagne with a mixed green salad and some warm crusty bread. For dessert, try Orange, Almond, and Olive Oil Cake (page 353) and a bowl of fresh berries.

RECOMMENDED WINE: This dish works well with Sauvignon Blanc or a bright and lively Chardonnay. A tangy Gamay Beaujolais or a Pinot Noir would also be a good choice.

ROASTED VEGETABLES
2	tablespoons olive oil
6	medium zucchini (1-1/2 pounds), cleaned and sliced into 1/2-inch rounds
2	large red bell peppers, cut into 1-inch pieces
2	large leeks, white and light green parts only, cleaned and thinly sliced

1-1/4 pounds medium mushrooms, cleaned and quartered
salt and pepper to taste

1/2	cup pesto, Mixed-Herb Pesto, or Sun-Dried Tomato Pesto (pages 402–4)

WHITE SAUCE

3	tablespoons unsalted butter
3	tablespoons all-purpose flour
2	cups hot whole milk
	salt and white pepper to taste
1/4	teaspoon freshly grated nutmeg

RICOTTA-CHEESE LAYER

1-1/2 pounds ricotta cheese

3	large eggs
1	cup freshly grated Parmesan
2	tablespoons finely chopped parsley
	salt and white pepper to taste

1	pound fresh or dried green or white lasagne noodles
3/4	pound thinly sliced Muenster cheese, diced
1/3	cup freshly grated Parmesan

1. To roast the vegetables, preheat the oven to 450°F. In a large roasting pan, combine the oil, zucchini, peppers, leeks, and mushrooms and toss to coat all the ingredients. Roast the vegetables until softened, about 45 to 50 minutes, turning occasionally to keep them from sticking. (Note: If water accumulates in the pan during cooking, pour off the excess and continue to roast.) Transfer the vegetables to a mixing bowl, cool, and season with salt and pepper. Gently toss the vegetables with the pesto, taste for seasoning, and set aside.

2. To prepare the white sauce, melt the butter in a heavy medium saucepan over medium heat. Off the heat, whisk in the flour until blended. Return the pan to the heat and cook the flour for 2 minutes, whisking continuously, until it is bubbling but the mixture has not changed color. Remove from the heat and gradually whisk in the hot milk, beating to prevent lumps from forming. Return to the heat and bring to a boil. Reduce the heat to low and whisk until thickened, about 10 minutes. Season with salt, pepper, and nutmeg and taste for seasoning. Cover with plastic wrap. Set aside.

3. To prepare the ricotta-cheese layer, combine the ricotta, eggs, Parmesan, parsley, salt, and pepper in a medium mixing bowl and mix well.

4. To prepare the noodles, cook in a large pot of salted boiling water (10 minutes if dried, 3 to 4 minutes if fresh), until just al dente. Drain and place the pasta in a mixing bowl; cover with lukewarm water. When the noodles are tepid, lay

them in a single layer on paper towels to dry. Blot the pasta dry and set aside.

5. Preheat the oven to 375°F. To assemble the lasagne, spread half of the white sauce in the bottom of a deep 13-inch-long ovenproof lasagne pan. Top the sauce with one third of the noodles, then half of the vegetable pesto mixture, then half the ricotta-cheese mixture. On top of the ricotta-cheese mixture, place half of the Muenster. Continue building the lasagne with the second third of noodles, the remaining white sauce, the remaining vegetables, and the last third of the noodles. Add the second half of the ricotta-cheese mixture, the remaining Muenster, and then sprinkle the 1/3 cup Parmesan evenly on top. With a serrated knife, cut the lasagne into equal squares, which will help when you serve it.

6. Bake the lasagne for about 45 minutes or until piping hot and bubbling throughout. Cut into squares and serve immediately.

ADVANCE PREPARATION: Can be prepared up to 2 days ahead through step 5, sealed in plastic wrap or aluminum foil, and refrigerated. Bring to room temperature and continue step 6. It can also be frozen. Bake the lasagne without defrosting for 1 hour at 375°F or until piping hot in the center.

LAYERING ORDER

If you get as confused as I do with all the separate layers in this dish, here's the sequence:

- 1/2 white sauce
- 1/3 lasagne noodles
- 1/2 roasted vegetables with pesto
- 1/2 ricotta-cheese mixture
- 1/2 Muenster
- 1/3 lasagne noodles
- the rest of the white sauce
- the rest of the roasted vegetables with pesto
- the rest of the lasagne noodles
- the rest of the ricotta-cheese mixture
- the rest of the Muenster
- a sprinkling of Parmesan

PARMESAN CHEESE

The true Italian Parmigiano-Reggiano comes from an area of Emilia-Romagna where it is strictly licensed and has been produced in much the same way for almost 700 years. The 80-pound wheels were exported to enthusiasts from England to Constantinople as early as the 17th century, and today some of the cheeses are so valuable that they are aged in special "cheese banks."

Once you've tasted an aged block of Parmigiano-Reggiano, it's difficult to settle for anything less. The cheese should be straw yellow in color and have a crumbly but moist texture. Look for the words *Parmigiano-Reggiano* stamped on the rind of the cheese to be sure it's authentic.

In Sonoma, California Vella Cheese Factory produces a dry Jack cheese that is aged for nine months. It has a buttery nutty quality similar to Parmesan but less piquant and grainy. It is excellent grated for pasta or shaved for salads or vegetables.

Tips:

- Store the cheese in plastic wrap in the refrigerator for up to three weeks. If it becomes dry, wrap it in moist cheesecloth and leave it in the refrigerator for a few hours. Then rewrap it in plastic.
- It's best to grate the Parmesan when needed for the best flavor since the cheese begins to lose its punch and texture soon after it's grated.
- Parmesan can also be shaved with a swivel-blade peeler into long or short curls on whatever is to be garnished.
- Remember that pasta dishes containing fish don't require Parmesan.
- Try shaved pieces of Parmesan with sliced apple or pear for dessert.

RISOTTO WITH LEEKS, TOMATOES, AND NIÇOISE OLIVES

SERVES 6

CALIFORNIANS HAVE BEEN making risotto for decades. Both *Helen Brown's West Coast Cook Book* (1952) and Genevieve Callahan's *The California Cook Book* (1946) refer to risotto but never mention the crucial ingredient—Arborio rice—that is vital to the authentic creamy and slightly al dente consistency.

Now that Arborio rice is widely available in supermarkets and specialty food stores, the traditional risotto has become commonplace on California-style restaurant menus. A key to making this dish taste so good without using excessive fat is a trio of Mediterranean flavoring agents—tomatoes, leeks, and olives—that offset the blandness of the rice.

But the real secret ingredient in this dish is the olives. You don't need a lot of them—a little goes a long way with the pungent Niçoise variety. I've tried using other types of olives with less success. Pitting olives can be tedious; you can press down on the olive with your thumb or you can use an olive pitter. Either way, try to keep the olive meat in coarse pieces. I like to serve this dish before Rack of Lamb with Mint Crust (page 244).

RECOMMENDED WINE: When this is served as an appetizer, a ripe Chardonnay is the wine to serve since it leads logically to the next wine, a red of some sort. If this is served as a main course, the Chardonnay will be fine, but so will a Zinfandel or Pinot Noir.

3	tablespoons olive oil
1	large leek, white part only, cleaned and finely chopped
2	medium tomatoes, peeled, seeded, and finely chopped
1/4	teaspoon salt
	pinch of black pepper
5	cups chicken stock (page 397)
1-1/2	cups Arborio rice

1/4   cup pitted and coarsely chopped Niçoise olives
2   tablespoons finely chopped parsley
1/2   cup freshly grated Parmesan

1. In a medium sauté pan over medium heat, heat 1 tablespoon of the olive oil, add the leek, and sauté until softened, about 5 to 7 minutes. Add the tomatoes and cook for about 4 minutes, turning up the heat to reduce the excess tomato juice. Season with salt and pepper and set aside.

2. In a medium saucepan over medium-high heat, bring the stock to a simmer. In a heavy 4-quart saucepan over medium heat, heat the remaining olive oil. Add the rice and stir, making sure all the grains are well coated. Pour in 1/2 cup of the hot stock and stir, using a wooden spoon, until all of the stock is absorbed. Continue adding the stock 1/2 cup at a time, making sure the rice has absorbed the previous stock and always stirring to prevent burning or sticking. The rice should have a very creamy consistency as you continue to add the stock.

3. Reserve the last 1/4 cup of stock and add it with the leek and tomato mixture to the rice. Cook over low heat for 2 minutes. Turn off the heat, add the olives, parsley, and Parmesan, and stir well to combine evenly with the rice. Serve immediately.

RISOTTO TIPS

- Look for superfino Arborio rice from Italy, a small oval variety high in amylopectin starch. This starch lends a creaminess to the finished risotto that is accentuated by the slow addition of liquid and constant stirring. Another unique feature of Arborio rice is the firm central core it retains when cooked, giving it a distinctive al dente texture. Other Italian rices for risotto are Carnaroli and Vialone Nano, but they're a bit more difficult to find.
- Never wash the rice; you'll be washing away the starch that gives risotto its creamy character.
- Use a heavy pot with a handle so you can mix the risotto with one hand while holding the pot with the other.
- Use a wooden spoon for stirring.
- Keep the rice at a very low boil so that it cooks evenly and retains a creamy yet firm quality.
- Serve the risotto immediately in warm shallow bowls.

GARDEN RISOTTO

SERVES 6

I FIRST TASTED a version of this dish at Campanile Restaurant in Los Angeles. Each vegetable had an individual character that was preserved in a fresh clean way. The vegetables were picked that day at Chino Ranch in Rancho Santa Fe, just north of San Diego. Chino Ranch (or, as the retail stand is called, The Vegetable Shop) specializes in unusual produce for Chez Panisse in Berkeley and select Southern California restaurants like Spago and Campanile. The tender sweet peas, carrots, and squash were truly memorable for their straight-from-the-garden flavor.

Don't worry if you can't pick vegetables from your garden; what's important is to select the freshest available. Feel free to alter this basic recipe to include what's freshest; for instance, asparagus, fresh exotic mushrooms, peas, and summer squash all make delectable variations. For an informal dinner, begin with Blood Orange, Mushroom, and Avocado Salad (page 89). Try Tiramisu with Toasted Hazelnuts and Chocolate (page 369) for dessert.

RECOMMENDED WINE: This is a classic match for a rich, creamy Chardonnay. The wine enhances the flavors of the vegetables.

3	tablespoons olive oil
1	large leek, white part only, cleaned and finely chopped
1	cup chopped mushrooms in 1/2-inch pieces
1	small carrot, peeled and chopped into 1/2-inch pieces
1/2	cup sugar snap peas, cut into 1/2-inch pieces
1/2	medium red bell pepper, roasted and peeled (page 287) and cut into 1/2-inch pieces
1/4	teaspoon salt
	pinch of black pepper
5	cups chicken stock (page 397)

1/2   cup dry white wine
1-1/2 cups Arborio rice
2   tablespoons finely chopped parsley
1/2   cup freshly grated Parmesan
       additional Parmesan for passing

1. In a medium sauté pan over medium heat, heat 1 tablespoon of the olive oil, add the leek, and sauté until softened, about 5 to 7 minutes. Add the mushrooms and cook for about 3 minutes. Add the carrot and peas and sauté for 2 minutes. Add the roasted pepper and cook for another minute. Season with salt and pepper and set aside.

2. In a medium saucepan over medium-high heat, bring the stock and wine to a simmer. In a heavy 4-quart saucepan over medium heat, heat the remaining olive oil, add the rice, and stir well, making sure all the grains are well coated. Pour in 1/2 cup of the hot stock and stir, using a wooden spoon, until all of the stock is absorbed. Continue adding the stock 1/2 cup at a time, making sure the rice has absorbed the previous stock and always stirring to prevent burning or sticking. The rice should have a very creamy consistency as you continue to add the stock.

3. Reserve the last 1/4 cup of stock and add it with the vegetable mixture, cooking over low heat for another 2 minutes. Turn off the heat, add the parsley and Parmesan, and stir well to combine evenly with the rice. Serve immediately. Pass the additional Parmesan separately.

TWO-MUSHROOM BARLEY RISOTTO

SERVES 4 TO 6

MOST OF US think of barley as a hearty ingredient in soup or as a side dish with meat. Here the creamy texture and sophisticated taste of barley are a complete surprise.

Use dried shiitake or other earthy-flavored mushrooms and freshly grated good-quality Parmesan. Adding the strained shiitake liquid to the barley intensifies the mushroom flavor. Pearl barley, available in most markets, will take less time to cook and require a bit less liquid. The barley should not be cooked until soft all the way through but should have a nutty, slightly crunchy center.

This takeoff on risotto is best served as a main course in shallow soup bowls. Begin with Farmer's Market Chopped Salad (page 78) and serve Banana Split Ice Cream Torte (page 384) for dessert.

RECOMMENDED WINE: The earthy flavors of this dish blend well with a young Cabernet Sauvignon or Merlot.

3/4	cup dried shiitake mushrooms
3	cups simmering chicken stock (page 397)
2	tablespoons olive oil
1	large onion, finely chopped
1	pound fresh white mushrooms, coarsely chopped
1	garlic clove, minced
1-1/2	cups pearl barley
1	cup dry white wine
2	tablespoons Marsala
1	teaspoon salt

1/4   teaspoon pepper
3   tablespoons finely chopped parsley
1/2   cup finely grated Parmesan

1. Place the dried mushrooms in a medium bowl and cover with boiling water. Let soften for at least 1/2 hour, remove the mushrooms from the water, cut off and discard the tough stems, and coarsely chop. Strain the soaking liquid and add it to the simmering stock.

2. In a large saucepan over medium-high heat, heat the olive oil, add the onion, and sauté for 3 to 5 minutes or until softened. Add the fresh mushrooms and sauté for 3 minutes. Add the garlic and sauté for another minute. Add the barley and stir to coat completely with the onion-mushroom mixture.

3. Turn down the heat to medium and stir in 1 cup of the hot stock, stirring frequently, until all the liquid has been absorbed, about 7 to 10 minutes. Stir in another cup of stock and continue cooking, stirring frequently, until all the liquid has been absorbed, about 7 to 10 minutes. Add the wine and continue cooking, stirring frequently, until all the liquid has been absorbed, about 7 to 10 minutes.

4. Add the remaining stock and Marsala and continue to cook until the barley is tender. (If you like it al dente, watch carefully.) Increase the heat and continue cooking the barley if there is excess liquid. (Total cooking time should be about 35 minutes.) Add the salt, pepper, and parsley and mix to combine. Spoon into shallow pasta or soup bowls, sprinkle on the Parmesan, and serve immediately.

ADVANCE PREPARATION: Can be prepared up to 4 hours ahead through step 2, covered, and kept at room temperature.

SOFT POLENTA WITH SUN-DRIED TOMATO PESTO

SERVES 6 TO 8

I REMEMBER THE first time I tasted a warm bowl of this thick cornmeal porridge on a cold summer day in an Italian mountain village. I wondered how this creamy, soul-satisfying dish would taste in a California climate. Little did I know that years later it would become an adopted dish of chefs and home cooks alike, with as many variations as one can imagine.

Traditional polenta takes at least 30 minutes of cooking in a copper pot over low heat with constant stirring. Fortunately, an imported instant (precooked) polenta with a finer texture has become available nationwide. This fine-grained polenta yields an excellent flavor as well as texture.

Here the polenta is served with a big dollop of Sun-Dried Tomato Pesto on top and sprinkled with freshly grated Parmesan. You can also top it with a soft goat cheese or Gorgonzola Dolcelatte. This dish is good as a first course or as an accompaniment to Crispy Roast Chicken (page 208) or grilled veal or lamb chops (pages 254 or 242).

RECOMMENDED WINE: This dish is particularly good with young, fruity red wines such as Zinfandel, Sangiovese, and Rhône varieties. If it's a first course, a ripe, full-bodied Chardonnay will be quite pleasant.

    double recipe of Sun-Dried Tomato Pesto (page 404)
2   **tablespoons olive oil if needed**

POLENTA
2   **tablespoons olive oil**
1   **medium onion, very finely chopped**
2   **garlic cloves, minced**

7   cups chicken stock (page 397)
2   cups instant polenta (1 13-ounce box imported instant)
3/4 cup freshly grated Parmesan or Pecorino Romano

1. If the pesto is very thick, you may need to add a bit of olive oil. In a large saucepan over medium heat, heat the oil, add the onion, and sauté for 5 to 7 minutes or until softened and just beginning to caramelize. Add the garlic and sauté for 1 minute, making sure not to brown it. Add the stock and bring to a rolling boil. Very slowly, in a thin stream (I use a liquid measuring cup), add the cornmeal, stirring constantly with a wooden spoon. Lower the heat and continue cooking for about 5 minutes or until it is very thick, smooth, and creamy. Add 1/2 cup of the Parmesan and stir to combine until the cheese has melted into the polenta.

2. Spoon the polenta into shallow soup bowls and spoon on a large dollop of pesto and a sprinkling of the remaining cheese. Serve immediately.

ADVANCE PREPARATION: The pesto can be made 1 week ahead, covered, and refrigerated. Bring to room temperature before serving.

GRILLED POLENTA WITH CONFIT OF RED ONIONS AND PROSCIUTTO

SERVES 8

HERE ARE TWO versions of polenta, each with its own virtue. If time is a factor, use instant polenta. What you give up in texture is compensated for in preparation speed. Yellow cornmeal takes 15 to 20 minutes longer to cook but offers a superior coarse texture. The addition of garlic, onions, chicken stock, and Parmesan makes for a surprising improvement in flavor over the traditional cornmeal-and-water mixture. Make sure in both versions to cook the polenta until it is very stiff so it will hold up when grilled.

Two overlapping slices of grilled polenta make a wonderful accompaniment to other grilled dishes like grilled Turkey Sausages with Sun-Dried Tomatoes (page 225), Grilled Veal Chops with Zucchini-Corn Relish (page 254), or Grilled Chicken Niçoise (page 197).

Grilled Instant Polenta

1	tablespoon olive oil
1/2	small onion, very finely chopped
1	garlic clove, minced
1/2	teaspoon salt
3-1/2 cups chicken stock (page 397)	
1	cup instant polenta
2	tablespoons freshly grated Parmesan

FOR GRILLING

2   tablespoons olive oil
     black pepper to taste

1. In a deep large saucepan over medium heat, heat the oil, add the onion, and sauté for 5 to 7 minutes or until softened. Add the garlic and sauté for 1 minute, being sure not to brown it. Add the salt and stock and bring to a rolling boil. In a thin stream (I use a liquid measuring cup), very slowly add the instant polenta, stirring constantly with a wooden spoon.

2. Lower the heat and continue cooking for about 5 minutes, stirring almost constantly to be sure it doesn't stick, until it is very smooth and stiff. Stir in the Parmesan and then quickly pour the polenta into an 8-inch nonstick square pan that has been rinsed out with cold water, smoothing the top with a spatula if necessary. Allow the polenta to rest for 2 hours, covered.

3. With a round-bladed knife (a pizza wheel works well), cut the polenta into nine 2-inch squares. With a sharp chef's knife, carefully cut each of the squares crosswise to make eighteen 2- by 2- by 1/2-inch squares.

4. Prepare a barbecue for medium-heat grilling. Brush the polenta squares with olive oil and sprinkle with a little black pepper. Grill the squares for 6 to 7 minutes on each side, until brown and crispy but not blackened. Use 2 flat spatulas to turn the squares.

5. Place overlapping slices on individual serving plates or a platter and garnish with warm Confit of Red Onions and Prosciutto (page 153). Serve immediately.

ADVANCE PREPARATION: Can be prepared up to 6 hours ahead through step 2, covered, and kept at room temperature.

Grilled Polenta Using Yellow Cornmeal

SPRINKLE THE CORNMEAL very gradually over the simmering chicken stock, stirring all the time, to prevent lumps from forming.

1   tablespoon olive oil
1/2 small onion, very finely chopped
1   garlic clove, minced
1/2 teaspoon salt
1   quart chicken stock (page 397)
1   cup coarse yellow cornmeal
2   tablespoons freshly grated Parmesan

FOR GRILLING
2   tablespoons olive oil
     black pepper to taste

1. In a deep large saucepan over medium heat, heat the oil, add the onion, and sauté for 5 to 7 minutes or until softened. Add the garlic and sauté for 1 minute, being sure not to brown it. Add the salt and stock and bring to a rolling boil. In a thin stream (I use a liquid measuring cup), very slowly add the cornmeal, stirring constantly with a wooden spoon. Lower the heat and continue cooking for about 15 to 20 minutes, stirring almost constantly to be sure it doesn't stick, until it is very smooth and stiff. Stir in the Parmesan and then quickly pour the polenta into an 8-inch nonstick square pan that has been rinsed out with cold water, smoothing the top with a spatula if necessary. Allow the polenta to rest for 2 hours, covered.

2. With a round-bladed knife (a pizza wheel works well), cut the polenta into nine 2-inch squares. With a sharp chef's knife, carefully cut each of the squares crosswise to make eighteen 2- by 2- by 1/2-inch squares.

3. Prepare a barbecue for medium-heat grilling. Brush the polenta squares with olive oil and sprinkle with a little black pepper. Grill the squares for 6 to 7 minutes on each side, until brown and crispy but not blackened. Use 2 flat spatulas to turn the squares.

4. Place overlapping slices on individual serving plates or a platter and garnish with warm Confit of Red Onions and Prosciutto (page 153). Serve immediately.

ADVANCE PREPARATION: Can be prepared up to 6 hours ahead through step 1, covered, and kept at room temperature.

POLENTA: INSTANT VS. TRADITIONAL

Many enthusiastic cooks have stopped making polenta because of the long, labor-intensive cooking. The arrival on the scene of instant polenta (a finer-grained cornmeal) has changed all that, and unless you are a purist, there is very little difference in the final result except in the texture. Traditional polenta is simply coarse yellow cornmeal added to boiling water with salt and stirred, *constantly*, for 30 to 40 minutes. Instant polenta, which has long been used in Italy, takes only 5 minutes to prepare, after which you can serve it immediately or cool and slice it for grilling. Substituting chicken stock for part or all of the water called for in the recipe will produce a more flavorful result, but polenta is really a foil, like pasta or pizza, for its topping.

CONFIT OF RED ONIONS AND PROSCIUTTO

MAKES ABOUT 1/2 CUP

THIS TOPPING FOR grilled polenta is also an excellent flavor enhancer for scrambled eggs, omelet fillings, stir-fries, or pasta or as a topping for pizza or focaccia.

2 tablespoons olive oil
2 large red onions, coarsely chopped
3/4 cup dry red wine
1/4 cup balsamic vinegar
2 teaspoons sugar
1/4 cup finely chopped prosciutto (about 2 ounces)
2 tablespoons finely chopped fresh basil or 1 tablespoon dried
1/4 teaspoon salt
1/4 teaspoon black pepper
1/4 cup chicken stock (page 397), approximately

1. In a large skillet over medium-low heat, heat the olive oil, add the red onions, and sauté for 20 minutes, until very soft. Add the wine, vinegar, and sugar and continue to cook until almost all of the liquid has evaporated. The onions should be very tender and slightly caramelized. Stir in the prosciutto, basil, salt, pepper, and enough of the stock to give the mixture a thick saucelike consistency. Taste for seasoning.

ADVANCE PREPARATION: Can be prepared up to 5 days ahead and refrigerated. Reheat gently, adding more chicken stock to achieve a thick saucelike consistency.

JEWISH BREAKFAST PIZZA

S E R V E S   2

AFTER A BUSY morning in downtown San Francisco, I stopped into Wolfgang Puck's Postrio restaurant for a version of this combination deli dish/pizza. It's a wonderful main course for an early lunch or a weekend late-morning breakfast.

The objective here is to have a slightly bready center. To accomplish this, let the dough sit after it has baked to collect a bit of moisture. Then turn it over so the bottom is crisp and the top has a nice texture for topping. Be sure to buy mild, not too salty, smoked salmon. If you like extra color, add different-colored fish eggs. Start with a simple mixed green salad and serve a fresh fruit compote (page 347) for dessert.

RECOMMENDED WINE: A crisp, dry sparkling wine makes this pizza appropriately festive. A lively Sauvignon Blanc is a good alternative.

1/2 recipe pizza dough (page 340)

CREAM SPREAD
2   tablespoons sour cream
1   teaspoon very finely chopped red onion
1   teaspoon finely chopped fresh chives
    pinch of salt
    pinch of white pepper

FILLING
4   large eggs
1/8 teaspoon pepper
1   tablespoon unsalted butter
1   ounce smoked salmon, coarsely chopped

GARNISH

2 tablespoons sour cream
1 ounce smoked salmon, cut into thin strips
1 teaspoon finely chopped fresh chives
1 ounce golden caviar

1. Preheat the oven to 475°F. Press the prepared dough into a 9-inch round on a lightly oiled baking sheet and poke the dough all over with your finger to give it a dimpled effect. Bake for 20 minutes or until puffed and golden. Remove and let cool on the baking sheet for 10 minutes. (This will allow the bottom to become soft enough to use as the top for filling the pizza.) Turn upside down and place on a serving plate.

2. For the cream spread, combine the sour cream, onion, chives, salt, and pepper in a small bowl.

3. For the filling, whisk the eggs with the pepper in a small bowl. Melt the butter in a heavy medium saucepan. Add the whisked eggs and cook over low heat, stirring constantly, until the mixture becomes thick but not dry. Remove from the heat. Carefully stir in the smoked salmon so that it blends in well. Taste for seasoning.

4. Spread the pizza shell evenly with the sour cream mixture and then spoon on the egg mixture. Place a dollop of sour cream in the center. Garnish with smoked salmon, chives, and caviar. Serve immediately.

ADVANCE PREPARATION: Can be prepared up to 2 hours ahead through step 2. Bring the cream spread to room temperature. The pizza crust can be refrigerated.

BARBECUED PIZZA WITH LEEKS, MOZZARELLA, TOMATOES, AND PANCETTA

MAKES 2 MEDIUM PIZZAS TO SERVE 2 TO 4
AS A MAIN COURSE OR 6 TO 8 AS AN
APPETIZER

I FIRST MADE this recipe for my last book, *The Taste of Summer*, and it's still my favorite pizza with its delightful smoky taste and crispy grill-marked crust. A grill with a lid works best so the cheese will melt. If pancetta, the Italian cured bacon, isn't available, substitute thick-sliced bacon. If you're in the mood to experiment, try your hand at one of the other toppings on page 158.

RECOMMENDED WINE: Try a fruity, red wine like a Rhône variety that will balance this pizza's strong complex flavors. Or consider a full-bodied beer.

1/2	pound plum or Roma tomatoes
7	tablespoons olive oil
3	medium leeks, white and light green parts only, cleaned and thinly sliced
1/4	teaspoon salt
1/8	teaspoon pepper
1/2	pound pancetta, cut into 1-inch pieces
1	recipe pizza dough (page 340)
1-1/2	cups shredded mozzarella cheese
1/4	cup finely chopped fresh basil

1. Slice the tomatoes crosswise into 1/4-inch slices. Put the slices in a colander and leave for 1/2 hour to drain excess liquid.

2. In a deep sauté pan over very low heat, heat 3 tablespoons of the olive oil, add the leeks, and mix thoroughly. Cover and cook, stirring often, for about 20 minutes or until tender. If liquid remains in pan, uncover and continue cooking, stirring often, until it evaporates. Add the salt and pepper and taste for seasoning.

3. In a medium skillet over medium-low heat, cook the pancetta until crisp and slightly brown, about 4 to 5 minutes. Transfer it to paper towels and drain.

4. When you're ready to barbecue, prepare the barbecue for medium-high-heat grilling. Make sure your barbecue has a lid.

5. Oil 2 round baking sheets or pizza pans. Knead the dough again briefly and divide it into 2 equal parts. Put each on a baking sheet. With oiled hands, pat each piece of dough out to a 9-inch circle. Or use a rolling pin to roll out the dough on a floured surface and transfer it to baking sheets.

6. Brush the top of the pizzas with 2 tablespoons of the remaining olive oil. Using a spatula, transfer the pizzas to the center of the grill grate and grill for about 2 minutes or until the dough begins to puff and there are grill marks on the bottom.

7. Using a large spatula, turn the pizzas over and move them to the coolest part of the grill. Brush the grilled pizza top with the remaining 2 tablespoons of olive oil. Divide the leek mixture between the pizzas, spreading it evenly, and then sprinkle 3/4 cup of the mozzarella over each pizza. Divide and arrange the pancetta on top. Divide and overlap the tomatoes in an attractive pattern. Sprinkle with basil.

8. Move the pizzas to the center of the grill and cover the barbecue for 3 minutes. Check the pizzas and rotate them. Cover the grill and cook for another 2 to 3 minutes. Watch carefully so that they do not burn on the bottom. The cheese should be completely melted. (If you want them hotter on top, you can place them under your preheated broiler for a minute or two.) They should be slightly charred. Place on platters and cut into pieces with a pizza wheel. Serve immediately.

PIZZA TOPPINGS

Thinking up toppings for pizza is a lot of fun—and the possibilities are almost endless. I tend to prefer simple combinations, but every now and then I want one with "the works" like the Mexican-inspired pizza. Here are some of my favorites:

- Italian Roma tomato, mozzarella, basil
- Mixed-Herb Pesto (page 402), Italian fontina, and cooked scallops or shrimp
- Green Olive and Sun-Dried Tomato Tapenades (pages 19–21) with goat cheese
- grilled eggplant and zucchini, tomato, Parmesan cheese, and thyme
- Mexican style: sautéed onion, roasted chiles, tomatoes, cheddar cheese, and cilantro. Top with avocado and sour cream
- mascarpone, smoked salmon, and caviar
- Confit of Red Onions and Prosciutto (page 153) with Niçoise olives
- yellow and red cherry tomatoes, red onion, sliced cooked sweet and hot sausage, and Parmesan cheese
- grilled mixed vegetables with Gorgonzola Dolcelatte

SEAFOOD

TOMATILLO GRILLED SHRIMP   161

ROASTED SEA BASS WITH MUSTARD SALSA   163

GRILLED SEA BASS WITH CAPONATA   165

GRILLED SALMON FILLET WITH AVOCADO, CUCUMBER, AND DILL SALSA 167

BAKED SALMON WITH RED ONION SAUCE   169

ROAST CRISPY FISH WITH WARM LENTILS   172

GRILLED HALIBUT WITH RED PEPPER–MINT SAUCE   174

GLAZED HALIBUT WITH ORANGE-CHIVE SAUCE   176

GRILLED SWORDFISH ON A BED OF CUCUMBER PASTA
    WITH ASIAN SALSA   178

BROILED ORANGE ROUGHY WITH SALSA GLAZE   181

WEST COAST CRAB CAKES WITH GRAPEFRUIT SAUCE   183

GRILLED TUNA WITH VEGETABLE AND WHITE BEAN SALSA   186

GRILLED SCALLOP BROCHETTES WITH ALMOND CAPER RELISH   190

TOMATILLO GRILLED SHRIMP
SERVES 4

A SATISFYING SPICY flavor and quick preparation time are two good reasons to make this dish. Shrimp benefits from the tangy, hot flavors of tomatillo salsa.

Arrange the skewers on a platter with the sauce in the center and let your guests help themselves. This works nicely for a buffet. Accompany the dish with Confetti Rice Pilaf (page 305) and warm corn tortillas.

RECOMMENDED WINE: The shrimp go equally well with a crisp, spicy Sauvignon Blanc or a lively, well-balanced Chardonnay.

MARINADE
1/2 cup tomatillo salsa (page 414)
1   tablespoon fresh lime juice
1   tablespoon olive oil
2   tablespoons finely chopped cilantro

1   pound large shrimp or 4 to 6 per person, shelled and deveined with tail left on

SAUCE
1/2 cup sour cream
1/4 cup tomatillo salsa (page 414)
2   tablespoons finely chopped cilantro
1   teaspoon fresh lime juice
1/4 teaspoon salt
    pinch of white pepper

1   head of red leaf lettuce

1. Combine the salsa, lime juice, olive oil, and cilantro in a small mixing bowl. Whisk until combined. Taste for seasoning.

2. Thread the shrimp on metal or bamboo skewers (soak bamboo in cold water for 1/2 hour before grilling). Make sure the shrimp is divided evenly and then lay them flat in a nonaluminum shallow dish. Pour the marinade over the shrimp and marinate for 1/2 hour, covered and refrigerated, turning once or twice.

3. In a small glass serving dish, combine the sour cream, salsa, cilantro, lime juice, salt, and pepper and taste for seasoning.

4. When you're ready to serve, prepare a barbecue for medium-high-heat grilling and place the skewered shrimp flat on the grill, three inches from the heat. Baste each side with shrimp marinade and cook for about 3 minutes on each side or until just cooked through.

5. Place the lettuce on a 12-inch platter, put the glass bowl of sauce in the middle, and then place the skewered grilled shrimp on the edge of the platter and let your guests help themselves. (You can also remove the shrimp from the skewers and serve them on a platter with a fork.)

ADVANCE PREPARATION: The marinade and sauce may be made 1 day ahead and refrigerated.

ROASTED SEA BASS WITH MUSTARD SALSA

SERVES 4 TO 6

OVEN-ROASTING FISH IN individual foil or parchment packets is quick and keeps the fish moist. The sauce, a low-calorie mix of salsa and Dijon mustard, takes only a minute to assemble. You can use any fresh white sea bass or halibut for this recipe. Serve with Cauliflower Puree with Two Cheeses (page 273) and simple steamed green beans.

RECOMMENDED WINE: A smoky, well-balanced Sauvignon Blanc.

SAUCE

2/3	cup spicy tomato salsa (page 413) or fresh store-bought
1/3	cup Dijon mustard
1	tablespoon olive oil
2	tablespoons finely chopped cilantro or parsley
1	tablespoon fresh lemon juice

4 to 6 pieces of sea bass fillets, 1/3 to 1/2 pound each and no more than 1 inch thick

1. Combine the salsa, mustard, oil, cilantro, and lemon juice in a medium mixing bowl.

2. Cut 4 to 6 pieces of parchment or foil into heart or rectangular shapes large enough to overlap the fish.

3. Arrange each fish piece in the center of a piece of foil. Spoon a good tablespoon or so of sauce over the fish. Fold the paper in half over the fish. Overlap the edges,

holding down the creased edges with one index finger, using the other thumb and index finger to pinch and fold. Tuck under the excess and place the packets on a baking sheet. Two packets will fit on one baking sheet.

4. Preheat the oven to 425°F. Roast for 8 to 10 minutes, depending on the thickness of the fish. The fish should be very moist. Place the packets on serving dishes, open the packets, and serve immediately. Serve the remaining sauce separately.

ADVANCE PREPARATION: Can be prepared up to 4 hours ahead through step 3 and refrigerated.

GRILLED SEA BASS WITH CAPONATA

SERVES 4

CAPONATA IS USUALLY served as a spread or an appetizer. This zesty relish, a traditional Sicilian dish, also works well as a topping on grilled sea bass. Since eggplant soaks up oil like a sponge when sautéed, it's better to grill or broil it.

While I recommend grilling the fish, you can also poach or broil it. Select Chilean sea bass for its rich, delicate flavor if it's available. Serve this with Roasted Onions and Baby Potatoes (page 299) or Crispy Potato Pancakes with Vegetables (page 296).

RECOMMENDED WINE: The intensity of the flavors in this dish demands a wine with depth and staying power. A ripe, rich Chardonnay or an oak-aged Sauvignon Blanc does very well with the multiple flavors of this sea bass creation.

MARINADE
1   tablespoon finely chopped fresh basil
1   garlic clove, minced
2   tablespoons dry white wine
2   tablespoons olive oil

4   sea bass fillets or steaks, 1/3 to 1/2 pound each

CAPONATA
2   tablespoons olive oil
1   medium eggplant, sliced lengthwise into 1/4-inch-thick slices
6   scallions, white and light green parts only, thinly sliced
2   garlic cloves, minced
2   large tomatoes, peeled, seeded, and finely chopped
1/2 cup chicken stock (page 397)

1/2 cup Merlot or other full-bodied red wine
1   tablespoon balsamic vinegar
1   teaspoon dark brown sugar
     pinch of hot red pepper flakes
1/3 cup thinly sliced pitted green olives, well rinsed
1   tablespoon capers, well drained and rinsed
1/2 teaspoon salt
     pinch of white pepper

GARNISH
fresh basil leaves (optional)

1. In a small bowl, combine the marinade ingredients. Arrange the fish pieces in a shallow large nonaluminum dish. Coat the fish with the marinade. Cover, refrigerate, and marinate for 30 minutes to 2 hours.

2. For the sauce, prepare a barbecue for medium-high-heat grilling. Brush 1 tablespoon of the olive oil on the eggplant slices and grill the eggplant about 3 minutes per side, or until grill marks appear and the eggplant is very tender. Cut them into 1/4-inch pieces and set aside.

3. Heat the remaining tablespoon of olive oil in a large sauté pan over medium heat and sauté the scallions for 3 minutes or until slightly softened. Add the garlic and cook for a minute. Add the tomatoes, stock, wine, vinegar, brown sugar, and red pepper flakes and bring to a simmer. Reduce the heat and cook, covered, for 10 minutes. Add the eggplant, olives, capers, salt, and pepper and cook for 3 minutes. Taste for seasoning.

4. Prepare a barbecue for medium-high-heat grilling. Grill the sea bass about 3 inches from the heat for 5 to 7 minutes on each side or until done to taste. Arrange the fish on serving plates and spoon some sauce over it. Garnish the fish with fresh basil leaves if desired. Serve immediately.

ADVANCE PREPARATION: The sauce can be prepared up to 1 day ahead through step 3 and refrigerated. Reheat the caponata gently.

GRILLED SALMON FILLET WITH AVOCADO, CUCUMBER, AND DILL SALSA

SERVES 4

THIS SAUCE IS lighter and more refreshing than the traditional creamy mayonnaise-based one. It tastes more like a crunchy relish. I prefer to use European cucumber because you don't have to peel it and the dark green skin is pretty mixed with the lighter green avocado. Serve this with Confetti Rice Pilaf (page 305) and a simple steamed vegetable like asparagus or green beans.

RECOMMENDED WINE: A well-balanced Sauvignon Blanc that has spent some aging time in oak is a good match for this dish of textural and flavor contrasts.

SALSA
1   medium European cucumber, cut into 1/4-inch pieces
2   tablespoons finely chopped fresh dill
2   tablespoons olive oil
2   tablespoons rice wine vinegar
1   tablespoon fresh lemon juice
1/2 teaspoon salt
1/2 teaspoon sugar
1   ripe small avocado, peeled, pitted, and cut into 1/4-inch pieces

2   pounds salmon fillet or 4 1/2-pound pieces
1   tablespoon fresh lemon juice
1   tablespoon finely chopped fresh dill

GARNISH
lemon slices
fresh dill sprigs

1. Combine all the salsa ingredients in a medium mixing bowl and taste for seasoning. Set aside.

2. Place the salmon fillets on wax paper and sprinkle them evenly with the lemon juice and chopped dill. Prepare a barbecue for medium-high-heat grilling. Grill the salmon fillets about 3 inches from the heat for 7 to 10 minutes on each side, depending on their thickness and size.

3. Remove the salmon from the grill, slice into serving pieces if it's one large piece, and place the pieces on serving plates. Spoon the salsa over the salmon and garnish with the lemon and dill. Serve immediately.

ADVANCE PREPARATION: Can be prepared up to 4 hours ahead through step 1 and refrigerated.

BAKED SALMON WITH RED ONION SAUCE

SERVES 6

FISH WITH A red sauce? They go together perfectly here. An assertive sweet yet slightly tart sauce takes this salmon dish to new heights. The balsamic vinegar is important for its full-bodied acidic-sweet character. This is an excellent dinner party dish because the sauce can be prepared hours ahead. Begin with White Bean Soup with Leeks, Carrots, and Eggplant (page 51) or Peppery Greens with Gorgonzola and Pine Nuts (page 80). Sautéed Green and Yellow Beans with Garlic and Basil (page 271) make a colorful accompaniment.

RECOMMENDED WINE: A crisp and youthful red such as a Gamay Beaujolais, Pinot Noir, or Syrah is very effective with this dish.

SAUCE

2	tablespoons olive oil
2	large red onions, very finely chopped
1	cup full-bodied red wine
2	tablespoons balsamic vinegar
1-1/2	cups chicken stock (page 397)
3	tablespoons whipping cream
1/8	teaspoon cayenne pepper
1/4	teaspoon salt
3	pounds salmon fillet or 6 1/2-pound pieces

GARNISH

2	tablespoons finely chopped parsley

1. In a large skillet over medium heat, heat the olive oil, add the onions, and sauté slowly until completely softened and beginning to caramelize, about 15 to 20 minutes, reducing the heat if they begin to burn. Add the wine and vinegar and turn up the heat. Reduce the mixture until it becomes a syrupy glaze, about 5 to 7 minutes.

2. Place the onion mixture in a food processor fitted with the metal blade or in the cup that comes with a hand blender. Process the onion mixture until you have a fine puree.

3. Return the onion mixture to the skillet and add the stock. Bring to a boil. Simmer for about 5 minutes or until the liquid is reduced by a third.

4. Place the onion mixture in a strainer set over a medium saucepan. With a wooden spoon, push the onion mixture through the strainer, being sure to get out as much of the onion as possible. With a rubber spatula, scrape off the solids on the underside of the strainer into the saucepan.

5. Add the cream and return the pan to high heat. Reduce for about 3 to 5 minutes or until the sauce becomes a nice glaze. Add the cayenne pepper and salt and cook for another minute. Taste for seasoning.

6. Preheat the oven to 450°F. Place the salmon fillets on an oiled baking sheet and bake for about 12 minutes, depending on their thickness and size.

7. Remove the salmon from the oven and cut it into serving pieces if it is in one large piece. Place the salmon pieces on serving plates. Spoon the sauce over it, garnish with parsley, and serve immediately.

ADVANCE PREPARATION: Can be prepared up to 6 hours ahead through step 4, covered, and refrigerated. Reheat gently.

LENTILS

California cooks have rediscovered this diminutive bean, which is technically in the family of pulses. Lentils now appear not only in soups but also in salads, as a side dish, or as a bed for seafood. Lentils don't require soaking, and they cook quickly.

Most chefs and many home cooks prefer the plumper slate-colored French Le Puy lentils, which are more expensive but have a firmer texture and a light, peppery flavor. Other lentils, like the brown Masoor Dal, cook faster and break down into a puree quickly, making them ideal for soups and purees. If you want your lentils to hold their shape, for a salad or as a bed for fish or chicken, use the French green lentils. They'll take just a little longer to cook.

Red lentils, whether domestic or imported, have a milder flavor than the brown ones and turn a sort of dull gold after cooking. They break down into a puree quickly and can be mixed with other varieties that take longer to reach a puree, giving a soft, creamy background to the whole lentils.

ROAST CRISPY FISH WITH WARM LENTILS

SERVES 4

THIS UNUSUAL COMBINATION tastes wonderful. After the lentils are braised, part of the mixture is pureed to become a sauce for the fish. The simple, clear flavors of lemon, parsley, and basil are well suited to the lentil mixture. Spraying the fish rather than brushing it with olive oil gives the fish a crunchy coating without the oily aftertaste. Begin with California Salad (page 83) as a first course.

RECOMMENDED WINE: The earthy flavors of this dish are best combined with a Syrah or a Sangiovese among reds; if you want to pour a white, an oaky Chardonnay does very nicely.

1   cup (1/2 pound) brown lentils, cleaned and picked over
3   cups chicken stock (page 397)
3   tablespoons olive oil
1   medium red onion, finely chopped
1   medium celery rib, finely diced
1   medium carrot, peeled and finely diced
1   small red bell pepper, finely diced
3   tablespoons fresh lemon juice
2   tablespoons finely chopped parsley
2   tablespoons finely chopped fresh basil or 1 tablespoon dried
1   teaspoon salt
1/4 teaspoon black pepper

2   pounds sea bass or halibut fillet, about 1/2 inch thick
2   tablespoons fresh lemon juice
3   tablespoons dried bread crumbs
      olive oil cooking spray

GARNISH
fresh parsley or basil leaves

1. Place the lentils in a medium saucepan. Add 2 cups of the stock and bring it to a boil. Turn down the heat and let simmer for about 20 minutes, partially covered, or until tender but not mushy. Drain.

2. In a medium skillet over medium heat, heat 2 tablespoons of the oil, add the onion, and sauté until soft, about 5 to 7 minutes. Add the celery and carrot and continue cooking for about 5 minutes. Add the red pepper and cook for 2 minutes.

3. Add the lentils to the vegetables in the skillet and cook for 2 minutes over medium heat. Add the lemon juice, the remaining tablespoon of olive oil, the parsley, basil, salt, and pepper and mix. Transfer 1 cup of the lentil mixture to a food processor fitted with the metal blade. Add 3/4 to 1 cup of the remaining stock or enough to make it a saucelike consistency. Puree, return the puree to the whole lentils, mix well, and taste for seasoning. Cover to keep warm while you cook the fish.

4. Preheat the oven to 450°F. Place the fish in an oiled roasting pan and sprinkle on the lemon juice and then the bread crumbs in an even layer. Spray with a thin, even coating of olive oil spray. Roast the fish for 10 to 15 minutes or until it's brown and crispy.

5. To serve: Slice the fish into 4 pieces. Place a portion of lentils on each serving plate and place a piece of fish on top of the lentils. Garnish with the herbs and serve immediately.

ADVANCE PREPARATION: Can be prepared up to 4 hours ahead through step 3 and kept covered at room temperature. Gently reheat the lentils.

GRILLED HALIBUT WITH RED PEPPER–MINT SAUCE

SERVES 6

SWEET PEPPERS SEASONED with fresh mint are the foundation for this sauce. Fortunately, you don't need to roast and peel the peppers. Think about preparing this dish whenever red peppers are plentiful in the market. The sauce is also perfect with grilled chicken or shrimp. Begin with Green Olive Tapenade (page 19) with Parmesan Toasts (page 311) and serve the fish with Home Ranch Butternut Squash (page 279) or Spinach Rice Timbales (page 307).

RECOMMENDED WINE: This is a difficult dish to match with wine. The herbal flavors of mint and bell peppers can be contrasted with a spicy, crisp Sauvignon Blanc or augmented by a youthful Cabernet Sauvignon. The Sauvignon Blanc is the safer choice, but the Cabernet will certainly provoke conversation.

MARINADE
1	tablespoon finely chopped fresh mint
1	garlic clove, minced
2	tablespoons balsamic vinegar
2	tablespoons olive oil
6	halibut fillets or steaks, 1/3 to 1/2 pound each

SAUCE
1	tablespoon olive oil
2	garlic cloves, minced
4	red bell peppers, finely chopped
2	tablespoons finely chopped fresh mint
1	tablespoon balsamic vinegar

1-1/4 cups dry white wine

3   tablespoons whipping cream
1/2   teaspoon salt
      pinch of white pepper

GARNISH
fresh mint leaves
roasted red pepper slices (optional)

1. In a small bowl, combine the marinade ingredients. Arrange the fish pieces in a shallow large nonaluminum dish. Coat the fish with the marinade. Cover, refrigerate, and marinate for 30 minutes to 2 hours.

2. For the sauce, heat the olive oil in a large saucepan over low heat, add the garlic, and sauté for 30 seconds. Turn up the heat to medium, add the red pepper and mint, and sauté for 5 minutes, stirring frequently. Add the vinegar and cook the peppers until glazed, about 1 to 2 minutes.

3. Add the wine, cover, and simmer over low heat for about 15 minutes or until the peppers are softened. Puree the mixture in the pan with a hand blender or in a food processor fitted with the metal blade.

4. Pour the pepper mixture into a strainer set over a medium saucepan. With a wooden spoon, push the pepper mixture through the strainer, being sure to get out as much of the pulp as possible. With a rubber spatula, scrape off the solids on the underside of the strainer into the saucepan.

5. Add the cream, salt, and pepper and return to high heat. Reduce for about 3 to 5 minutes or until the sauce just coats a spoon. Taste for seasoning. Keep the sauce warm while you cook the fish.

6. Prepare a barbecue for medium-high-heat grilling. Grill the fish about 3 inches from the heat for 5 to 7 minutes on each side or until done to taste. Arrange the fish on serving plates and spoon some sauce over it. Garnish with fresh mint leaves and roasted pepper slices if desired. Serve immediately.

ADVANCE PREPARATION: Can be prepared up to 2 hours ahead through step 5. Refrigerate the fish and sauce. Gently reheat the sauce.

GLAZED HALIBUT WITH ORANGE-CHIVE SAUCE

SERVES 4

THIS SIMPLE RECIPE brings out the fine texture and flavor of halibut. The yogurt gives the creamy citrus sauce extra tang. Be sure to sprinkle with more fresh chives just before serving because the chives in the cooked sauce will have darkened. Serve this with Oven-Roasted Potatoes with Parmesan (page 298) and steamed asparagus.

RECOMMENDED WINE: The citrus flavors in this dish suggest a dry Riesling or a tangy, bright Chardonnay with lots of lively acidity.

SAUCE
1   tablespoon fresh orange juice
1   teaspoon finely chopped orange zest
2   garlic cloves, minced
1   tablespoon finely chopped fresh chives
1/2 cup mayonnaise (low-fat if desired)
2   tablespoons plain nonfat yogurt

4   halibut fillets, 1/3 to 1/2 pound each

GARNISH
2   tablespoons chopped fresh chives

1. In a small bowl, combine the sauce ingredients and mix.

2. Preheat the oven to broil. Place the fillets on an oiled broiler pan and spread a tablespoon of the sauce on top of the fish. Broil the fish about 3 inches from the heat for 3 to 5 minutes or until nicely browned. Turn the fish over carefully with a spatula and spread with another tablespoon of the sauce. Return the fish to the

broiler and broil it for 3 to 5 more minutes or until it is bubbly and well browned. Be careful not to let it burn. Place the fish on serving dishes, garnish with chives, and serve with the remaining sauce.

ADVANCE PREPARATION: Can be prepared up to 1 day ahead through step 1 and refrigerated.

GRILLED SWORDFISH ON A BED OF CUCUMBER PASTA WITH ASIAN SALSA

SERVES 6

SWORDFISH IS A meaty, substantial fish that benefits from an intensely flavored marinade. This light and refreshing entrée brings together flavors of Italy and Asia with tomatoes, ginger, and sesame oil in the sauce. The cucumber should not be cut more than an hour before serving, or it will become soft and mushy. Begin your dinner with Asian Guacamole (page 24) and serve the fish with Tricolor Vegetable Sauté (page 272).

RECOMMENDED WINE: Match this dish with a crisp Graves-like Sauvignon Blanc.

MARINADE

2   garlic cloves, minced
1   tablespoon finely chopped fresh ginger
3   tablespoons fresh lime juice
1   tablespoon dark sesame oil
2   tablespoons olive oil
1/4 teaspoon salt
1/8 teaspoon black pepper

6   swordfish steaks, 1/3 to 1/2 pound each

SALSA

3   medium tomatoes, peeled, seeded, and finely chopped
2   garlic cloves, minced
2   teaspoons finely chopped fresh ginger
2   tablespoons finely chopped scallion
2   tablespoons rice wine vinegar

2   teaspoons dark sesame oil
1/2 teaspoon salt
1/8 teaspoon black pepper

CUCUMBER PASTA
2   medium European cucumbers, halved lengthwise and seeded
2   tablespoons olive oil
2   tablespoons rice wine vinegar
1/4 teaspoon salt
     pinch of pepper

1. Combine the garlic, ginger, and lime juice in a small mixing bowl. Add the sesame and olive oils and blend completely. Add the salt and pepper and taste for seasoning.

2. Arrange the swordfish pieces in a shallow large nonaluminum dish. Pour the marinade over the fish, making sure the pieces are evenly coated. Cover and refrigerate for 30 minutes to 2 hours.

3. To prepare the salsa, place all the ingredients in a medium mixing bowl and stir until combined. Taste for seasoning.

4. Just before serving, shred the cucumber with a mandoline or in a food processor fitted with a thin julienne blade. *Do not do this more than 1 hour before serving.* Put the cucumber in a paper-towel-lined bowl and refrigerate.

5. Prepare a barbecue for medium-high-heat grilling. Remove the fish from the marinade and grill about 3 inches from the heat for 5 to 6 minutes on each side or until done to taste.

6. To serve, remove the paper towel from the bowl of cucumbers (discard all extra moisture) and add the oil, vinegar, salt, and pepper. Stir the cucumbers with a fork to coat them evenly. Taste for seasoning. Arrange a few tablespoons of cucumber on a plate, place the swordfish on top, and spoon the salsa over it. Serve immediately.

ADVANCE PREPARATION: The salsa can be prepared up to 4 hours ahead, covered, and refrigerated. The fish can be marinated 2 hours ahead and refrigerated.

SALSA—A CALIFORNIA TRADITION

It may seem surprising that salsa has been a California tradition since the rancho days of the late 1800s. According to Jacqueline Higuera McMahan, *California Rancho Cooking* (The Olive Press, 1988), it was known as "sarsa" and was made from fresh ingredients grown on the ranchos. Salsa was served at the table to accompany barbecued meats, to spoon over beans, or to spread over big hunks of French bread.

Today the field is wide open for you to create your own signature salsa with a vast array of fruits and vegetables. Just remember that salsa is a way to heighten simple grilled fish, poultry, meat, and vegetables, so think of complementary flavors. Here are a few ideas to get you thinking:

- cucumbers or avocados combined with fresh tomato salsa
- oranges and grapefruit with scallions, chiles, and mint
- blood oranges, green or black olives, and fresh lemon juice
- papaya, mango, and pineapple with chiles and lemon
- mixed fresh and dried chiles with tomatoes, red onions, vinegar, and cilantro
- grilled corn, red onion, and tomato salsa
- pineapple peach salsa with balsamic vinegar, brown sugar, chiles, and orange zest
- corn, black beans, garlic, and roasted red bell pepper
- yellow and red cherry tomato salsa with roasted red and yellow bell peppers, basil, olive oil, and lemon

BROILED ORANGE ROUGHY WITH SALSA GLAZE

SERVES 6

IN THE EARLY 1980s orange roughy, a delicate-textured fish, was just a funny name for inexpensive frozen fish. Now it is available fresh nine months of the year, flown in from Australia and New Zealand. One fish salesman told me he thought the reason for the high demand for orange roughy is that home cooks have discovered it is difficult to overcook.

If you can't find fresh orange roughy, consider snapper, sole, or lingcod as substitutes. This last-minute dish relies on a zippy salsa glaze to elevate the simple flavors of the fish into a casually elegant main course. Serve with Orange-Glazed Beets (page 276) and Roasted Onions and Baby Potatoes (page 299).

RECOMMENDED WINE: This spicy dish is charming with an oak-aged Sauvignon Blanc.

GLAZE

1   tablespoon fresh lime juice
2   tablespoons spicy tomato salsa (page 413) or store-bought
1/2 cup mayonnaise (low-fat if desired)
2   tablespoons plain nonfat yogurt

6   fresh orange roughy fillets, 1/3 to 1/2 pound each

GARNISH
2   tablespoons chopped parsley

1. Preheat the oven to broil. In a small bowl, combine the glaze ingredients and mix. Taste for seasoning.

2. Place the fillets on a broiler pan and spread half the glaze mixture on top. Broil the fish about 3 inches from the heat for 3 minutes or until nicely browned. Turn

the fish over carefully, using a spatula, and spread with the remaining glaze mixture. Return to the broiler and broil about 3 more minutes until bubbly and well browned. Be careful not to let the fish burn. Using a large spatula, remove the fish from the broiler pan, taking care not to break the pieces. Place the fish on serving dishes. Garnish with parsley and serve immediately.

ADVANCE PREPARATION: Can be prepared up to 1 day ahead through step 1, covered, and refrigerated.

WEST COAST CRAB CAKES WITH GRAPEFRUIT SAUCE

MAKES 8 CRAB CAKES TO SERVE 8 AS A FIRST COURSE OR 4 AS A MAIN COURSE

THESE CRAB CAKES are full of chunky crab pieces with a bare minimum of bread to bind them together. Juicy grapefruit accents the crab flavor and cuts the richness of the butter sauce. Pink grapefruit makes a pretty presentation.

Dungeness crab, also called *West Coast crab,* is named after a small town in Washington State even though it is caught from the California waters all the way up the coast to Alaska. Compared to other varieties, Dungeness has a naturally sweet, buttery flavor that is well suited to this dish. Fresh Dungeness crab is available from early December through August.

Alaskan king crab would work here too, but it's difficult to find fresh since it's usually cooked and frozen right after it's caught. It's expensive but worthwhile to buy fresh crabmeat from a reputable fish market. Whatever you do, don't substitute finely shredded crab or imitation crab (surimi) in this recipe.

These crab cakes cook best when the mixture is given a short time to chill before being sautéed. Chilling the crab cakes allows the binding to absorb some of the extra moisture so that the cakes will hold together well. Serve these crab cakes with a simple mixed green salad dressed with a light vinaigrette.

RECOMMENDED WINE: Pour a crisp, lively Chardonnay with this dish—it will highlight the interesting citrus flavors.

CRAB CAKES
1 large egg
1 tablespoon whipping cream
1 teaspoon Dijon mustard

1/4 teaspoon salt
    pinch of cayenne pepper
1   tablespoon finely chopped fresh chives
1   pound fresh Dungeness crabmeat, pulled apart into 1/2-inch chunks,
      not completely shredded
1/2 cup fine fresh bread crumbs
1/2 cup dried bread crumbs

GRAPEFRUIT SAUCE
1/2 cup fresh grapefruit juice
2   tablespoons white wine vinegar
2   medium shallots, minced
1/2 teaspoon salt
1/4 teaspoon white pepper
3/4 cup cold unsalted butter, cut into cubes

GARNISH
2   whole pink grapefruits, peeled and sectioned

FOR SAUTEEING
2   tablespoons unsalted butter
2   tablespoons vegetable oil

1. Beat the egg in a medium mixing bowl. Add the cream, mustard, salt, cayenne pepper, and chives and mix to incorporate. Add the crabmeat and fresh bread crumbs. Mix well to incorporate.

2. Spread the dried bread crumbs on a cookie sheet. Divide the crab mixture into 8 crab cakes, shaping them into patties about 3/4 inch thick and 3 inches in diameter. (Squeeze well to remove any excess liquid.) Roll the crab cakes in the dried bread crumbs using a spatula and then arrange them on a large plate. Cover the crab cakes with plastic wrap and refrigerate for at least 1 hour.

3. While the crab cakes are chilling, prepare the sauce: In a heavy saucepan, boil the grapefruit juice, vinegar, and shallots until about 2 tablespoons of liquid remain. Add the salt and pepper.

4. Over low heat, begin adding the cubes of butter, 1 or 2 at a time, to the shallot mixture, whisking constantly. Wait until they're absorbed before adding more. The sauce should thicken, but the butter should not melt. If the pan begins to get very hot, remove it from the heat and add some of the butter cubes off the heat so the sauce cools slightly. Remove the sauce from the heat as soon as the last butter cube is added.

5. Strain the sauce if a smoother consistency is desired. Taste for seasoning. Keep the sauce warm in a double boiler or thermos and serve as soon as possible.

6. Coarsely chop the sections of 1 grapefruit. Reserve the chopped grapefruit and whole sections for garnish.

7. Heat 1 tablespoon of the butter and 1 tablespoon of the oil in a medium nonstick skillet or griddle over medium-high heat. Cook 4 crab cakes at a time for about 3 to 4 minutes on each side. Be careful when turning them so they stay together. They should be golden brown on both sides. Place the crab cakes on a baking sheet in a 300°F oven to keep them warm. Add the remaining butter and oil and sauté the rest of the crab cakes until golden brown.

8. To serve, place a dollop of chopped grapefruit in the center of each individual serving plate and arrange 1 or 2 crab cakes on top, slightly overlapping if serving more than one. Spoon some sauce on top and around the cakes. Garnish with whole grapefruit sections around the perimeter of each plate and serve immediately.

ADVANCE PREPARATION: Can be prepared up to 4 hours ahead through step 2 and kept refrigerated.

GRILLED TUNA WITH VEGETABLE AND WHITE BEAN SALSA

SERVES 6

IN THE EARLY 1980s Zuni Cafe opened in San Francisco and was immediately recognized as one of the leaders in contemporary California cooking. Ten years later Zuni is still going strong. On any given day you can find the best chefs from other San Francisco restaurants dining there. Chef Judy Rodgers turns out her own brand of California cooking using Mediterranean products.

This recipe is based on one of Chef Rodgers's signatures, grilled fish with unusual light salsas. The fresh flavors are allowed to speak for themselves, calling to mind the old adage that less is more. Here a simple salsa is created using cooked white beans, earthy Niçoise olives, and a hint of mint. The salsa is spooned over a rare grilled ahi tuna steak. Ask for the center cut of the tuna loin, which will be less oily. To determine the freshness of the tuna, look for a deep red color. Begin with Assorted Grilled Vegetables (page 13) and serve this with a simple pasta or rice.

RECOMMENDED WINE: The beefiness of the tuna and the richness of the beans combine very nicely with a young Cabernet Sauvignon or Merlot. A Syrah or Rhône blend also does very nicely here.

MARINADE

2   medium shallots, minced
6   tablespoons fresh lemon juice
1   teaspoon finely chopped lemon zest
1/4 cup olive oil
1/4 teaspoon salt
     pinch of black pepper

6   tuna steaks, 1/3 to 1/2 pound each and cut from the center with no
     bone

SALSA

1 large shallot, minced
1 cup cooked white beans such as canned cannellini
1/2 cup coarsely chopped European cucumber
4 small red radishes, thinly sliced and cut in half again
2 tablespoons finely chopped fresh mint
1/4 cup Niçoise olives, pitted and cut in half
3 tablespoons olive oil
3 tablespoons fresh lemon juice
1/2 teaspoon salt
1/4 teaspoon black pepper

1. To make the marinade, whisk the ingredients together in a small bowl. Arrange the tuna in a shallow large nonaluminum dish. Pour the marinade over the tuna, making sure the steaks are coated evenly. Cover and refrigerate for 1/2 to 1 hour. (The citrus in the marinade will begin to "cook" the tuna and will change the texture if left longer.)

2. To prepare the salsa, combine all the ingredients in a small mixing bowl. Taste for seasoning.

3. Prepare a barbecue for medium-high-heat grilling. Remove the fish from the marinade and grill it about 3 inches from the heat for about 5 minutes on each side. (The tuna should be rare.)

4. Place the tuna on serving plates and garnish with a large dollop of salsa. Serve immediately.

ADVANCE PREPARATION: The salsa can be prepared up to 4 hours ahead and kept refrigerated.

GRILLING TIPS

When Is the Fire Ready?

Knowing just when to put your food on the fire is crucial to successful grilling. A fire that's too hot will char the outside of the food while leaving the center raw. If the fire is too cool, the food just won't cook properly.

Charcoal and wood fires are ready 30 to 45 minutes after the initial lighting. For most foods the fuel should have a layer of gray ash. If there is a high flame, the fire is not quite ready.

Medium-high-heat grilling: The fire should have red-hot coals with just a thin layer of gray ash and an occasional flare-up. You can test the heat by holding your hand about six inches from the grid. You should be able to keep it there for only a few seconds. Medium-high-heat grilling is excellent for boneless chicken breasts or thin pieces of seafood, poultry, or meat.

Medium-heat grilling: The coals should be covered with a thick layer of gray ash, and there should be no flames. This is a good way to cook thicker pieces of meat or poultry. You may want to use the cover on your grill for this lower-temperature cooking.

Grilling in Foil

While grilling in foil may not have the same smoky-grilled flavor of other grilled foods, this method works well for individual pieces of delicate-textured fish like sea bass, salmon, and halibut that may fall apart on the grill. Season the fish and then enclose it in aluminum foil, making sure the edges are sealed. Grill over medium-high heat until the fish reaches the desired texture and then remove it from the heat and let it rest for a few minutes before opening the foil.

Grilling Times and Temperatures

These basic guidelines will tell you how long and at what temperature to cook the food, but remember that the food will continue to cook off the grill, so remove it a minute or so before it is perfectly done.

Fish: Fish steaks and fillets are best cooked on an open grill over medium-high heat since they do not require long cooking. Brush the fish liberally with oil before placing it on the grill to prevent sticking. A hinged basket is useful for grilling a whole fish because you can turn the fish without breaking it. It's best to cook whole fish over medium heat with a cover. Cooking times will vary according to the type of fish and its thickness. Prod the fish with a fork to see if it's done. It should just begin to flake. Avoid overcooking the fish, because it will change not only the texture but also the flavor.

Poultry: Most poultry is best cooked on a covered grill over medium heat because it requires a longer and slower cooking time. Boned chicken breasts and turkey slices are the exception. They take medium-high heat and quick grilling. Boneless chicken breasts require 6 to 8 minutes per side, while chicken pieces require 8 to 14 minutes per side. Use these times as a guideline for other types of poultry.

If you don't have a covered grill, baste the poultry often to retain moisture and allow a slightly longer cooking time. Make sure there's a heavy layer of gray ash on the coals before you begin cooking to ensure an even cooking temperature.

Meats: An instant-read thermometer is handy when grilling large pieces of meat. Here are general guideline temperatures for meat: beef and lamb—130–135°F for rare, 135–145°F for medium-rare, and 150°F for medium. Pork roasts should have an internal temperature of 160°F—more than that and they tend to be very dry.

Steaks and chops can be cooked according to the thickness of the cut. Sear them on each side for 30 seconds and then cook as suggested. The lower number indicates the time for rare and the higher number for well done. These times are for each side: 1 inch, 3 to 6 minutes; 1-1/2 inches, 4 to 9 minutes; 2 inches, 6 to 10 minutes. Season the meat with salt and pepper after it has cooked.

Vegetables: Clean the vegetables and slice them for the grill. Certain vegetables, like pearl onions and summer squash, should be blanched in boiling water for just a minute to eliminate the raw taste that quick grilling might not remove. Brush the vegetables with olive oil or avocado oil and place them on the grill with whatever else you're grilling. Sear over medium-high heat to seal in their juices and then move them to the edges of the grill to finish cooking. Thinly sliced vegetables will take 6 to 10 minutes on each side to cook. Vegetables such as tomatoes or onions, which fall apart easily, should be placed in a grilling basket. All vegetables can be threaded on metal or bamboo skewers if desired. Remember to soak the bamboo skewers in cold water for at least 30 minutes before grilling.

GRILLED SCALLOP BROCHETTES WITH ALMOND CAPER RELISH

SERVES 6

THE LARGER SEA scallops work better for this recipe because they grill evenly and don't dry out as quickly as bay scallops. The light citrus relish includes blanched almonds, which give the salsa a crunchy, toasty flavor. You'll need about six limes for this dish. Scallop Brochettes go nicely with Confetti Rice Pilaf (page 305) and Sautéed Green and Yellow Beans with Garlic and Basil (page 271).

RECOMMENDED WINE: A crisp, lively Graves-style Sauvignon Blanc is a bright contrast to the sweetness of the scallops and the richness of the almonds.

MARINADE
2   garlic cloves, minced
2   tablespoons fresh lime juice
1   teaspoon minced lime zest
2   tablespoons olive oil
1/4 teaspoon salt
1/8 teaspoon black pepper

2   pounds large sea scallops

RELISH
1/3 cup slivered blanched almonds
1/2 cup finely chopped parsley
1   medium shallot, finely chopped
1   garlic clove, minced
2   tablespoons finely chopped red bell pepper
1   tablespoon well-drained capers, finely chopped
1/4 cup fresh lime juice

1/4 teaspoon salt
1/8 teaspoon black pepper
1/4 cup olive oil

1. To prepare the marinade, place the garlic, lime juice, and zest in a small mixing bowl and mix to combine. Add the olive oil and blend completely. Add the salt and pepper and taste for seasoning.

2. Thread the scallops onto metal or bamboo skewers (soak bamboo in cold water for 1/2 hour before grilling) and lay them in a shallow large nonaluminum dish. Pour the marinade over the scallops and make sure they're all evenly coated. Cover and refrigerate for 1/2 hour; the citrus in the marinade will begin to "cook" the scallops if left longer.

3. To prepare the relish, preheat the oven to 350°F. Toast the almonds on a baking sheet for 5 to 7 minutes or until lightly browned. Cool and reserve.

4. Place all the relish ingredients except the oil and almonds in a medium mixing bowl and whisk until combined. Pour the oil in a steady stream into the mixture and whisk until well incorporated. Be careful not to puree the mixture. Spoon it into a serving dish and add the toasted almonds. Taste for seasoning.

5. Prepare a barbecue for medium-high-heat grilling. Remove the scallops from the marinade and grill about 3 inches from the heat for 3 to 4 minutes on each side, until done to taste.

6. Place the brochettes on a serving platter and spoon salsa on top or serve on the side. Serve immediately.

ADVANCE PREPARATION: The salsa can be prepared up to 4 hours ahead, covered, and left at room temperature. Add the almonds just before serving.

POULTRY

GRILLED ORANGE MUSTARD CHICKEN   195

GRILLED CHICKEN NIÇOISE   197

GRILLED CHICKEN WITH PESTO BEAN SAUCE   199

LEMON CHICKEN WITH ROASTED GARLIC SAUCE   201

CHICKEN WITH GARLIC AND LIME   204

ARROZ CON POLLO   206

CRISPY ROAST CHICKEN   208

GLAZED ORANGE-HOISIN CHICKEN   210

ROASTED CORNISH HENS WITH HONEY TANGERINE MARINADE   212

GRILLED TURKEY BREAST IN MUSTARD BOURBON SAUCE   214

MARINATED ROAST TURKEY   216

RICH TURKEY GRAVY   218

TURKEY VEGETABLE COBBLER   220

CHICKEN AND APPLE SAUSAGE   223

TURKEY SAUSAGES WITH SUN-DRIED TOMATOES   225

GRILLED ORANGE MUSTARD CHICKEN

S E R V E S 4 T O 6

GRAINY MUSTARD ADDS texture, and a mixture of fresh herbs brings out the flavor in this light and zesty marinade. Sweet orange juice is nicely balanced by the piquant mustard-herb combination. Adding a touch of balsamic vinegar brings the contrasting flavors together. Begin with Chilled Artichoke Halves with Red Pepper Aïoli (page 17) and serve the chicken with Ricotta Corn Cakes with Smoky Salsa Topping (page 33), or Sautéed Green and Yellow Beans with Garlic and Basil (page 271).

RECOMMENDED WINE: A ripe, oaky Chardonnay does well with this dish as does a crisp, young red such as a Zinfandel or a Rhône blend.

MARINADE

1/4	cup grainy mustard
1/4	cup Dijon mustard
1/4	cup fresh orange juice
1	teaspoon finely chopped orange zest
1	tablespoon balsamic vinegar
1	tablespoon olive oil
1/4 to 1/2	teaspoon hot pepper oil (page 412) or store-bought
2	tablespoons finely chopped fresh herb leaves: any combination of tarragon, mint, chives, thyme, basil, and flat-leaf parsley
1/4	teaspoon cracked black pepper
3	medium whole chicken breasts, halved, boned, and skinned if desired

GARNISH
fresh herb leaves
orange slices

1. Combine the marinade ingredients in a small bowl. Taste for seasoning. Arrange the chicken pieces in a shallow large nonaluminum dish and pour the marinade over the chicken to coat it well. Marinate, covered, for 30 minutes to 4 hours in the refrigerator.

2. Prepare a barbecue for medium-high-heat grilling. Remove the chicken from the marinade and grill 3 inches from the heat for 7 to 10 minutes on each side or until cooked through. Place the chicken on a platter or individual serving plates and garnish with fresh herb leaves and a slice of orange.

ADVANCE PREPARATION: Can be prepared up to 4 hours ahead through step 1, covered, and refrigerated.

GRILLED CHICKEN NIÇOISE
S E R V E S 4 T O 6

SUN-DRIED TOMATOES CONTRIBUTE a depth of flavor that fresh or canned tomatoes can't match. California dry-packed sun-dried tomatoes are about a quarter the price of the imported Italian variety and work well in this recipe. Be sure to soften the tomatoes in boiling water for at least 10 minutes before proceeding.

This thick Mediterranean-influenced marinade is low in acid, so you can marinate the chicken for up to 8 hours without changing the texture—in fact the flavor will improve. Begin with California Caponata (page 31) with Parmesan toasts (page 311) and serve the chicken with Garden Risotto (page 143) or Assorted Grilled Vegetables (page 13). For dessert try Tiramisu with Toasted Hazelnuts and Chocolate (page 369) or Orange, Almond, and Olive Oil Cake (page 353).

RECOMMENDED WINE: Try a fresh, youthful Pinot Noir with this full-flavored dish.

MARINADE AND SAUCE BASE

1/2	cup dry-packed sun-dried tomatoes
2 to 3	garlic cloves to taste
2	teaspoons olive oil
15	Niçoise or other black olives, pitted
1	teaspoon capers, well drained and rinsed
2	tablespoons finely chopped fresh basil
2	tablespoons finely chopped parsley
1	tablespoon Dijon mustard
1	tablespoon balsamic vinegar
1/4	teaspoon salt
1/8	teaspoon black pepper

3	large whole chicken breasts, boned, halved, and flattened

SAUCE

2	tablespoons reserved sun-dried tomato marinade
2	teaspoons fresh lemon juice
1/4	cup crème fraîche (page 425) or sour cream
1/4	teaspoon salt
1/8	teaspoon pepper

1. Pour boiling water over the sun-dried tomatoes in a small bowl. Let soften for 15 to 30 minutes. Drain the tomatoes well and pat them dry.

2. In a food processor fitted with the metal blade with the motor running, mince the garlic. Add the rest of the ingredients for the marinade and process until pureed and the consistency of a thick paste. Stop processing to scrape down the sides of the bowl. Reserve 2 tablespoons of the marinade for the sauce. Taste for seasoning.

3. Place the chicken breasts in a shallow large nonaluminum dish and coat them with the marinade until it is evenly distributed. Make sure you put some marinade *under* the skin. Cover and refrigerate the chicken for 2 to 8 hours, turning several times to make sure the marinade adheres.

4. To make the sauce, combine all the sauce ingredients, including the reserved marinade, in a small mixing bowl and whisk until smooth. Taste for seasoning.

5. Prepare a barbecue for medium-high-heat grilling. Grill the chicken 3 inches from the heat for 7 to 10 minutes on each side or until cooked through.

6. To serve, place the sauce in a small saucepan and gently heat it over medium-low heat until just simmering. (Watch carefully if you're using sour cream, because it tends to curdle if heated too long.) Place the chicken on serving plates and serve the sauce on the side. Serve immediately.

ADVANCE PREPARATION: Can be prepared up to 8 hours ahead through step 4 and refrigerated.

GRILLED CHICKEN WITH PESTO BEAN SAUCE

SERVES 4 TO 6

CHICKEN BREASTS ARE probably my favorite poultry because they're a perfect backdrop for sauces or marinades. Here beans are combined with pesto and made into a sauce to spoon over grilled chicken—a marvelous surprise. Serve this with steamed asparagus for a pretty presentation.

RECOMMENDED WINE: The herbal nature of this dish goes very nicely with an oak-aged Sauvignon Blanc. This dish is also complemented by soft-textured Merlots.

MARINADE
1/4 cup dry white wine
1/4 cup Mixed-Herb Pesto (page 402)
1/4 teaspoon salt
1/4 teaspoon black pepper

3   large whole chicken breasts, boned, halved, and flattened

SAUCE
2   cups cooked Italian red beans, cannellini, or black beans with 1/2 cup
      bean juice or chicken stock (page 397)
1/4 cup Mixed-Herb Pesto (page 402)
2   tablespoons sour cream

GARNISH
1/4 cup sour cream
2   tablespoons Mixed-Herb Pesto (page 402)
2   tablespoons freshly grated Parmesan
      fresh herb sprigs such as basil, thyme, or parsley

1. Combine the marinade ingredients in a small mixing bowl and mix until smooth. Taste for seasoning. Arrange the chicken breasts in a shallow large non-aluminum dish. Pour the marinade over it, making sure the chicken is coated evenly, and marinate covered for 30 minutes to 4 hours in the refrigerator.

2. Prepare a barbecue for medium-heat grilling. Remove the chicken from the marinade and grill about 3 inches from the heat for 7 to 10 minutes on each side or until no longer pink.

3. While the chicken is cooking, prepare the sauce. In a medium saucepan over medium heat, bring the beans, bean juice, and pesto to a simmer. Cook for about 5 minutes. Using a potato masher or hand blender, puree the beans in the pan, leaving some texture. Reduce the heat to low. Add the sour cream and cook only another minute, or the sauce may begin to curdle. If you want a thinner consistency, add a bit more sour cream, chicken stock, or bean liquid.

4. To serve, place the chicken on serving plates and spoon some bean sauce over it. Place a dollop each of sour cream and pesto on top. Sprinkle on some Parmesan and garnish with herbs. Serve immediately.

ADVANCE PREPARATION: Can be prepared up to 4 hours ahead through step 1 and refrigerated.

LEMON CHICKEN WITH ROASTED GARLIC SAUCE

S E R V E S 6

THIS IS A variation on my most requested party dish, which first appeared in *The Cuisine of California*. In this new version I've adjusted the flavor of the sauce with pureed roasted garlic and Dijon mustard and roasted the chicken instead of sautéing it. Easy to prepare and incredibly fragrant, these plump browned chicken breasts need only an accompaniment of Roasted Onions and Baby Potatoes (page 299) and Sautéed Green and Yellow Beans (page 271) to make a casually elegant statement. This is also wonderful served cold for lunch.

RECOMMENDED WINE: This is one of those dishes (most of them involve chicken) that will be great with almost any wine. Since it uses white wine, a barrel-fermented Sauvignon Blanc or a Chardonnay would be fine, but a medium-weight Cabernet Sauvignon would be good too.

MARINADE

1   tablespoon finely chopped lemon zest
1/3 cup fresh lemon juice
1   tablespoon olive oil
1/3 cup chicken stock
1/4 cup finely chopped fresh herbs: any combination of rosemary, thyme,
        parsley, basil, and oregano
1/3 cup dry white wine
1   teaspoon honey
1/2 teaspoon salt
1/4 teaspoon black pepper

4   large whole chicken breasts, boned and halved
1/4 cup whipping cream
2   teaspoons Dijon mustard

2   tablespoons roasted garlic puree (page 409)
     salt and pepper to taste
2   tablespoons finely chopped parsley

GARNISH
1   bunch of fresh watercress
1   lemon, sliced
2   tablespoons finely chopped parsley

1. Combine the marinade ingredients in a small bowl and whisk to blend. Arrange the chicken pieces in a large shallow nonaluminum dish and pour the marinade over them. Marinate the chicken for 1/2–2 hours in the refrigerator.

2. Preheat the oven to 425°F. Arrange the chicken pieces in a roasting pan, reserving the marinade, and roast for 20 to 25 minutes or until nicely browned, with no pink remaining. Remove chicken from oven, pour off the pan drippings and reserve.

3. While the chicken is roasting, add the reserved marinade to a medium saucepan and boil until reduced to about 1/2 cup, about 5 to 7 minutes. Add the cream, mustard, and garlic puree and boil for another few minutes or until the sauce is slightly thickened. When the chicken is cooked, add the reserved pan drippings and reduce for 3 more minutes or until slightly thickened. Add the salt, pepper, and parsley. Taste for seasoning.

4. To serve, arrange the chicken breasts on a platter, spoon some sauce over them, surround with the watercress and lemon slices, and sprinkle with parsley. Serve immediately. Serve the remaining sauce on the side.

ADVANCE PREPARATION: Can be prepared up to 2 hours ahead through step 1 and refrigerated.

GARLIC TIPS

I can't imagine what California cooking would be like without this scented pearl. It has a chameleonlike character when taken from its raw state to baked. Its basic integrity is still intact, but the subtle, nutty, magical flavor will surprise you.

• Roast a whole head of garlic and squeeze the mild, creamy cloves directly out of their skin onto a thick wedge of country bread. Place the heads, with most of the papery skin removed, in an earthenware casserole or on a square of heavy foil, drizzle with olive oil, add salt and pepper, and roast, covered, at 425°F for about 45 minutes to an hour. Plan on at least one whole head per person—these are addictive!

• Subtle garlic flavoring: Put a few garlic cloves in the water you are using to cook vegetables, potatoes, or rice and let the garlic flavor the food. Retrieve the garlic before serving.

• Sautéing garlic in oil can sometimes produce a burned flavor. To avoid that, use a good-quality olive oil or a combination of unsalted butter and oil and sauté over medium heat. Sauté the garlic after cooking the other ingredients, for no more than a minute. This will soften its sharp edge and bring out garlic's inherent qualities.

• To remove the garlic odor from your hands rinse them under *cold* water—hot will simply cook the smell onto your skin.

• Chop, press, or process? Hand-chopping garlic will yield the greatest quantity since you won't leave behind all that pulp in the press. (A garlic press may be quick and easy to use, but it often produces a strong, bitter flavor.) Adding any salt that is called for in the recipe to the cutting board while chopping makes it easier to scoop up the garlic afterward. Chopping garlic by hand will release its aromatic oils, giving it a more assertive bite. The more finely it is chopped, the more intensely flavored it will be. Mincing the garlic in a food processor fitted with the metal blade is a good technique since it brings out the garlic's aromatic oils without the bitterness.

CHICKEN WITH GARLIC AND LIME

S E R V E S   4   T O   6

CALIFORNIANS LOVE GARLIC. One method I use with the "stinking rose" is to sauté it lightly and then slowly simmer it in a stock until it's caramelized. In this dish a layered garlic flavor is achieved by simmering a garlic–lime juice sauce with the chicken and garnishing it with glazed baby pearl onions and whole garlic cloves. You'll need about 6 limes for this. Make sure your guests love garlic before you serve them this one! Begin with Farmer's Market Chopped Salad (page 78) and serve the chicken with simple roasted baby potatoes. For a refreshing finish, try Mixed Exotic Fruit Gazpacho (page 349).

RECOMMENDED WINE: This pungent dish needs a full-flavored wine as an accompaniment. A ripe Zinfandel, a Rhône varietal, or a big, complex Cabernet Sauvignon will work nicely.

2   tablespoons unsalted butter
2   tablespoons olive oil
4   medium whole chicken breasts, skinned, boned, and halved
2   heads of garlic, broken into cloves but unpeeled
1/3 cup fresh lime juice
2   cups veal or chicken stock (page 395 or 397)
2   tablespoons whipping cream
1/2 teaspoon salt
1/8 teaspoon white pepper

GLAZED ONIONS AND GARLIC
18 pearl onions or shallots

1   cup chicken or veal stock (page 397 or 395)
1/4 teaspoon salt
     pinch of pepper
1   head of garlic, cloves separated and peeled

GARNISH
2   tablespoons finely chopped parsley

1. In a medium skillet over medium-high heat, heat 1 tablespoon of the butter and 1 tablespoon of the oil. Add the chicken breast halves in batches and brown for about 5 minutes on each side. Transfer the chicken to a platter and cover it.

2. Place the unpeeled garlic cloves in the same skillet and brown them quickly. Don't worry—the papery peel will be removed during straining. Discard any excess oil and add the lime juice and stock and scrape up the brown bits from the pan. Bring the juice to a boil and reduce the heat to a simmer. Cover the skillet and cook the garlic for about 20 minutes or until the garlic is soft.

3. Place the mixture in a food processor fitted with the metal blade and puree. Put the mixture through a fine strainer and return it to the skillet. Add the cream, the juice from the chicken breasts that's collected on the platter, the salt, and the pepper and bring to a simmer. Keep warm.

4. Immerse the onions in boiling water in a medium saucepan for 10 seconds, then rinse them in cold water. Trim off the top and bottom, then remove the outer skin and first layer with your fingers. Pierce a cross at the root end so the onions will cook evenly and not burst. Dry the onions.

5. In a medium saucepan over medium heat, combine the remaining butter and oil, add the onions, and brown them for about 7 to 10 minutes, using a large spoon to roll them or shaking the pan occasionally. Add 1/2 cup of the stock, the salt, and pepper and bring to a simmer. Add the peeled garlic cloves and remaining stock, reduce the heat to medium-low, and continue cooking until tender. The onions and garlic should retain their shape but be tender when pierced with a fork. The liquid should be a glaze consistency. Watch carefully.

6. Return the chicken to the sauce and cook it for about 5 minutes or until tender but not overcooked. Taste for seasoning.

7. Place the chicken on a large serving platter and pour the sauce over it. Spoon the glazed garlic and onion on top of the chicken and garnish with chopped parsley. Serve immediately.

ADVANCE PREPARATION: Can be prepared up to 4 hours ahead through step 5 and refrigerated. Reheat gently.

ARROZ CON POLLO

SERVES 4

"THE POOR MAN'S paella" and "a Mexican party dish with Spanish ancestry" are just two descriptions given to this homey one-dish rice main course. According to Jacqueline Higuera McMahan, author of *California Rancho Cooking* (The Olive Press, 1988), Arroz con Pollo was served at large parties on the California ranches when it was not possible to barbecue outdoors.

I like to add fresh mint leaves to infuse the rice lightly and punch up the flavor. Traditionally *Arroz con Pollo* is served as is, but I prefer it with salsa and a dollop of sour cream. Make your own salsa or purchase a fresh store-bought variety that is as spicy as you like. Begin with Shrimp Salsa (page 11) and serve the Arroz con Pollo with a mixed green salad. Finish with Vanilla Caramel Cream (page 371) or Orange, Almond, and Olive Oil Cake (page 353).

RECOMMENDED WINE: A bright, well-oaked Chardonnay is the answer to this earthy dish, or you might try a brisk Gamay Beaujolais.

1	large whole chicken breast, skinned and boned
3	cups water
2	tablespoons olive oil
1	small onion, finely chopped
1-1/2	cups long-grain rice
1	medium carrot, peeled and diced into 1/2-inch pieces
2	tablespoons fresh lemon juice
3	large fresh mint sprigs
1/2	cup finely diced red bell pepper
1	cup frozen baby peas, thawed
1	teaspoon salt
1/4	teaspoon pepper

GARNISH
   fresh mint sprigs
1/4   **cup sour cream or plain nonfat yogurt**
1/4   **cup spicy green or tomato salsa (fresh or store-bought)**

1. Place the chicken breast in a 2-quart saucepan and add 3 cups of water. Bring to a simmer for 10 minutes. Cover the pan and remove it from the heat. Let sit for 10 minutes. Remove the chicken from the pan and shred it into bite-size pieces. Reserve the chicken and the stock.

2. In a medium saucepan over medium heat, heat the oil. Add the onion and sauté for 2 to 3 minutes or until slightly soft. Turn up the heat to high and add the rice and carrots. Brown them for about 3 minutes, stirring constantly.

3. Add the reserved stock and lemon juice to the rice, stir with a fork and bring to a boil. Reduce the heat to medium-low.

4. Add the reserved chicken, mint and red pepper, cover and cook for about 10 to 12 minutes or until the rice is almost cooked. Add the peas during the last 3 minutes of cooking and continue simmering until all the liquid has been absorbed and the rice is tender. Add the salt and pepper and taste for seasoning.

5. Remove the mint and spoon the rice into a serving dish. Garnish with fresh mint sprigs and serve the sour cream and salsa on the side.

ADVANCE PREPARATION: Can be prepared up to 2 hours ahead through step 4 and reheated gently.

CRISPY ROAST CHICKEN

SERVES 4

LIKE MOST COOKS, I've had many conversations on the proper way to roast a chicken. Some argue that roasting with the breast side down is the very best way to keep the bird moist enough, while others insist that method produces a zebra-striped bird stamped with its roasting lines. And what's the correct roasting temperature?

This controversy isn't new. In *The California Cookbook* (1946), Genevieve Callahan wrote, "I am inclined to feel that the temperature and the length of time of roasting have more bearing on juiciness than position during roasting." I agree with her, although her recipe suggests a 325°F oven. In an "unorthodox note," Ms. Callahan mentions high-heat roasting and cites "an old Italian short time–high temperature method." This roast chicken is modeled after that old Italian technique.

I find that cooking whole chickens at 425°F keeps them juicy inside and crispy-brown on the outside. The marinade adds color and depth of flavor to the chicken and its juices.

I like to carve the chicken and spoon the vegetables and juices on top. If you want to roast a larger bird, use a 5- to 6-pound roasting chicken and increase the cooking time by 20 to 25 minutes. Watch the chicken carefully and put a foil tent on top if it seems to be getting too brown.

This chicken is great with Soft Polenta with Sun-Dried Tomato Pesto (page 147). Begin with Peppery Greens with Gorgonzola and Pine Nuts (page 80). For dessert, try Banana Cake with Chocolate Fudge Frosting (page 377).

RECOMMENDED WINE: This dish calls for an assertive red wine, specifically a Merlot, a Cabernet Sauvignon, or a Rhône varietal such as a Syrah.

MARINADE

2   tablespoons grainy Dijon mustard

1/4 cup balsamic vinegar

2   tablespoons soy sauce

3   garlic cloves, minced

2   teaspoons minced fresh ginger

1/4 teaspoon black pepper

1   3-1/2- to 4-1/2-pound fryer chicken, cleaned and patted dry

1   onion, sliced

2   carrots, peeled and thinly sliced

2   cups chicken stock (page 397)

1. Combine the marinade ingredients in a small mixing bowl, mixing to blend. Taste for seasoning. Place the chicken in a large nonaluminum mixing bowl. Starting around the main body cavity, carefully slip your hand under the skin, being sure not to tear it. (You may need to use gloves if you have long fingernails.) Pat the marinade under the skin and all over the bird on both sides on top of the skin. Cover the chicken and marinate for at least a few minutes and up to 8 hours in the refrigerator.

2. Preheat the oven to 425°F. Place the chicken, breast side up, on a rack in a roasting pan or on a vertical roaster. Sprinkle the onion and carrots on the bottom of the pan and add 1 cup of the stock. Roast the chicken for about 45 minutes to 1 hour or until the juices run clear when the thigh is pierced with a knife. Halfway through the cooking, add the remaining cup of chicken stock to keep the bottom of the pan from scorching. Let the chicken rest for 10 minutes before carving. Carve the chicken and arrange on a serving platter. Scrape up the juices and vegetables and pour them over the chicken pieces to serve.

ADVANCE PREPARATION: Can be prepared up to 8 hours ahead through step 1 and refrigerated. This is also excellent served cold.

GLAZED ORANGE-HOISIN CHICKEN

SERVES 4

MY FRIEND BARBARA WINDOM is a great cook who typically produces delicious food that's short on preparation time and long on taste and presentation. Her Asian chicken can be served on a moment's notice as long as you have the ingredients in your pantry. Barbara prefers Dundee orange marmalade for this dish because it's not too sweet.

Glazed Orange-Hoisin chicken is superb right from the oven or chilled and served for lunch. If you're serving this warm, begin with Mixed Greens with Beets and Peppers and accompany the chicken with Rice Pilaf with Corn and Peanuts. If you're serving the chicken cold, a platter of Assorted Grilled Vegetables and a simple green salad would be fine accompaniments.

RECOMMENDED WINE: The strong, sweet flavors of this dish blend well with Zinfandel, Syrah, or Pinot Noir.

MARINADE

3   tablespoons hoisin sauce
1   teaspoon chile paste with garlic
1/3 cup soy sauce
1   tablespoon honey
1   tablespoon dark sesame oil
2   tablespoons finely chopped fresh ginger
1/4 cup Dundee orange marmalade

1   3-1/2- to 4-1/2-pound fryer chicken, cleaned, patted dry, and cut into quarters

GARNISH

2   tablespoons finely chopped scallions
    orange slices

1. Combine all the marinade ingredients except the marmalade in a large non-aluminum bowl. Add the marmalade and whisk the marinade well. Taste for seasoning.

2. Add the chicken quarters to the marinade and coat all the pieces evenly. Cover and marinate the chicken for 30 minutes to 2 hours in the refrigerator, turning it once or twice.

3. Preheat the oven to 425°F. Place the chicken quarters skin side up in a large shallow roasting pan and roast for 50 to 55 minutes or until the chicken is golden brown. Baste it with the juices once or twice while it is roasting.

4. To serve, remove the chicken from the pan and degrease the drippings. Arrange the chicken on a large serving platter, spoon some sauce over it, and garnish with scallions and orange slices. Serve immediately.

ADVANCE PREPARATION: Can be prepared 1 day ahead, refrigerated, and served chilled. Or prepare it up to 2 hours ahead through step 2 and refrigerate.

ROASTED CORNISH HENS WITH HONEY TANGERINE MARINADE

SERVES 6 TO 8

HONEY TANGERINES MAKE their market appearance in the winter months. If you've never treated yourself to a juicy exotic honey tangerine, you've missed a flavor sensation. This zesty marinade is a wonderful complement to the slightly gamy flavor of the Rock Cornish hen. You can use oranges if honey tangerines are unavailable. This goes well with Confetti Rice Pilaf (page 305).

RECOMMENDED WINE: The citrus flavors of this dish are matched nicely by a crisp Chardonnay. Pinot Noir is also quite compatible.

MARINADE

4   honey tangerines
1   tablespoon finely chopped fresh ginger
1   medium shallot, finely chopped
1   garlic clove, minced
2   tablespoons olive oil
2   tablespoons soy sauce
2   tablespoons finely chopped fresh mint
1/2 teaspoon black pepper
1/2 teaspoon salt

6   Rock Cornish hens, cleaned and split in half
1   cup water

SAUCE

1   cup reserved marinade
2   tablespoons heavy cream (optional)
3   tablespoons finely chopped fresh mint

GARNISH
tangerine or orange slices

1. Zest the tangerines and mince the zest. Juice 2 of the tangerines to make 1 cup juice.

2. In a large nonaluminum mixing bowl, combine the zest and juice with the remaining marinade ingredients and whisk until well incorporated. Taste for seasoning. Reserve 1 cup of the marinade for the sauce.

3. Carefully separate the skin from the hens by placing your fingers gently under the skin and loosening it. (You may need to wear gloves if you have long nails.) Place the hens in the bowl. Massage the marinade underneath the skin. Rotate the hens until they are completely covered with the marinade. Marinate for 2 to 4 hours in the refrigerator.

4. Preheat the oven to 425°F. Remove the hens from the marinade and reserve it for basting. Place the hens close enough together to fit on a large roasting rack set in a large roasting pan. Pour in the water to keep the drippings from burning. Roast the hens for 35 to 45 minutes, basting a few times. If some of the hens are not golden brown, put them under the broiler for a couple of minutes. Remove the hens from the oven and place them on a large serving platter. Garnish with the orange slices.

5. Pour the accumulated juices from the roasting pan into a fat separator, then transfer them to a medium saucepan. Add the 1 cup reserved marinade and heat the sauce over medium-high heat, reducing it by a quarter. Add the cream if desired and the mint and cook for another 3 to 4 minutes. Taste for seasoning and serve on the side.

ADVANCE PREPARATION: Can be prepared up to 2 days ahead and refrigerated—excellent served slightly chilled. Can be prepared up to 4 hours ahead through step 3, covered, and refrigerated.

GRILLED TURKEY BREAST IN MUSTARD BOURBON SAUCE

SERVES 4 TO 6

IT WASN'T SO long ago that veal scaloppine was the quick, last-minute dish that many home cooks relied on in a pinch. Now that veal is so expensive, turkey has become a healthful alternative. This southern-style marinade is zesty and simple to prepare. If you don't have a grill handy, you can broil or sauté the turkey. Serve this with Rice Pilaf with Corn and Peanuts (page 306) and Fava Beans with Red Onions and Bacon (page 281).

RECOMMENDED WINE: This dish goes equally well with a ripe, rich Chardonnay or a Pinot Noir.

MARINADE
2   tablespoons Dijon mustard
1/4   cup fresh orange juice
1   tablespoon bourbon
1   tablespoon molasses
1/4   teaspoon salt
1/4   teaspoon black pepper

1-1/2 pounds boneless turkey breast, cut into 1/2-inch slices

SAUCE
1/2   cup chicken stock (page 397)
1   tablespoon whipping cream
2   tablespoons finely chopped cilantro or parsley

1. Whisk all the marinade ingredients together in a small mixing bowl. Place the turkey slices in a shallow large nonaluminum dish. Pour half of the marinade over

the turkey, making sure it covers the turkey evenly, and marinate for 2 to 4 hours covered in the refrigerator. Reserve the remaining marinade for the sauce.

2. Prepare a barbecue for medium-high-heat grilling. Remove the turkey slices from the marinade and grill 3 inches from the heat about 2 to 3 minutes on each side. Remove from the heat and place on a platter.

3. Pour the reserved marinade into a small saucepan and add the stock and cream. Bring the stock/marinade mixture to a boil over high heat, reduce the heat to a simmer, and cook for about 5 minutes. Taste for seasoning. Pour the sauce over the turkey slices and sprinkle them with the cilantro or parsley. Serve immediately.

ADVANCE PREPARATION: The marinade can be prepared up to 1 day ahead and refrigerated.

"TRUSSING" POULTRY WITH SKEWERS

The easiest way to truss poultry is to use bamboo skewers. Insert one skewer in the thigh portion of the bird all the way through and out the other side. Do the same thing in the wing portion, being sure to go all the way through the bird and out the other side with each skewer. When you're ready to serve the bird, simply push the skewers all the way out in one swift motion. No fuss, no mess, and best of all, the bird looks great.

MARINATED ROAST TURKEY

SERVES 10 TO 14

THIS IS MY favorite recipe for roast turkey because the marinade infuses the skin and breast meat, producing a more tender, juicier bird. It is especially enjoyable for Thanksgiving. The soy and balsamic marinade forms the basis for a rich dark sauce or gravy. Use a fat separator when draining the drippings for the gravy. If you're roasting a larger bird, just increase the marinade ingredients accordingly. You can also stuff this turkey, but it takes a little longer to cook the turkey if it's stuffed, about an hour longer. This marinade is also excellent on a turkey breast when you don't feel like cooking the entire bird (see note). Remember to start this recipe a day ahead.

RECOMMENDED WINE: Pair this dish with Syrah, Pinot Noir, or Zinfandel.

MARINADE

2   medium shallots, finely chopped
3   tablespoons balsamic vinegar
2   tablespoons soy sauce
2   tablespoons olive oil
1/4 teaspoon salt
     pinch of pepper
2   tablespoons chopped fresh thyme leaves or 2 teaspoons dried

1   14- to 16-pound turkey, cleaned and patted dry
1   large orange, sliced with the skin on (if not stuffing)
1   onion, sliced (if not stuffing)
2   onions, coarsely chopped
2   carrots, peeled and sliced
2   cups chicken or turkey stock (page 397), or more as needed

1. The day before you want to cook the turkey, marinate it. Combine the marinade ingredients in a large nonaluminum mixing bowl. Taste for seasoning. Starting around the main body cavity, carefully slip your hand under the turkey skin, being sure not to break the skin. (You may need to wear gloves if you have long fingernails.) Place the turkey in the bowl. Pat the marinade under the skin and all over the bird on both sides on top of the skin. Marinate overnight in the refrigerator, covered with plastic wrap. Baste with the marinade a few times.

2. The next day, preheat the oven to 325°F. To stuff the turkey, place the stuffing loosely in the neck and main cavity and close the flaps with skewers. If you have not stuffed the turkey, place the sliced orange and sliced onion in the cavity and tie the legs together. Rub the marinade remaining in the bowl all over the turkey. Place the chopped onions and carrots on the bottom of a large roasting pan. Pour the stock over the vegetables. Set a nonstick roasting rack in the roasting pan and place the turkey on top, breast side up.

3. Place the turkey in the center of the oven and roast it, basting about every 45 minutes with the accumulated pan juices, until a thermometer inserted in the thickest part of the thigh registers 170°F and the juices run clear. You may need to add more stock if the pan becomes too dry. A 16-pound turkey should take about 4 hours; 5 hours if stuffed. Be sure to check the temperature at 30-minute intervals as the finish time approaches. A number of variables can affect the cooking time.

4. Remove the turkey from the oven and transfer it to a large platter or carving board. Let the turkey rest for at least 20 minutes before carving. Discard the vegetables and reserve the pan drippings for the gravy, using the fat separator to avoid excess fat.

ADVANCE PREPARATION: Can be prepared up to 1 day ahead through step 1, covered, and refrigerated.

NOTE: If you're roasting a turkey breast, use the same amount of marinade and roast at 325°F for 18 to 20 minutes per pound to an internal temperature of 170°F.

RICH TURKEY GRAVY

MAKES ABOUT 3-1/2 CUPS

PREPARING THE GRAVY at the last minute, after the turkey comes out of the oven, can create a lot of extra pressure when you still have to put everything on the table. Try this method and have the gravy ready and waiting for the defatted pan drippings from the turkey, cutting down the last-minute work to just a few moments.

To make this even easier, prepare your stock weeks ahead and freeze it. The intense flavor of rich brown turkey stock makes the difference between a good and a great gravy. You can add cooked giblets, mushrooms, diced chestnuts, or even roasted pureed garlic with equally good results.

1/2 cup unsalted butter
1/2 cup all-purpose flour
1   quart rich brown turkey stock (page 393), defatted and warmed
1/2 cup dry red wine
      salt and pepper to taste
      defatted drippings from a roast turkey

OPTIONAL ENRICHMENTS (CHOOSE ONE)
1/2 cup cooked chopped giblets
1/2 cup sautéed mushrooms
1/2 cup diced roasted chestnuts
1   tablespoon roasted garlic puree (page 409)

1. In a heavy large saucepan over medium heat, melt the butter, watching carefully so it does not burn. Add the flour slowly and whisk briskly until bubbles form. Continue whisking for a few minutes until the mixture thickens and turns a golden brown. The color of this roux is important, because it determines the final color of the sauce.

2. Add the stock and wine and whisk until the roux is completely blended into the liquid. Continue cooking the gravy over medium heat for 15 to 20 minutes, until it is thickened and no taste of flour remains. Add the salt and pepper and taste for seasoning.

3. After you remove the turkey from the oven, strain the pan drippings into a gravy separator and pour the defatted drippings into the gravy. Warm the gravy over medium heat and season to taste. If desired, add one of the enrichments to the gravy.

ADVANCE PREPARATION: Can be prepared 1 day ahead through step 2, covered, and refrigerated. Reheat gently.

GOOD GADGETS: THE FAT SEPARATOR

If you make soups, stock, or sauces, this gadget will be very useful. It looks like an old-fashioned garden watering can. The spout originates at the very bottom, and the grease rises to the top on its own when left to sit for a minute. The technique is to pour the stock or drippings off the bottom slowly until the grease line reaches the top of the spout hole. Then stop pouring and discard the grease.

TURKEY VEGETABLE COBBLER

SERVES 6

WHEN YOU CRAVE a comforting old-fashioned, home-cooked meal, look no further. This sophisticated version of pot pie includes a hefty sprinkling of mixed fresh California herbs and big chunks of turkey. A golden cobbler-style dough enriched with Parmesan crowns the top.

If you're in a hurry, use the defrosted small white frozen onions to save time. Fresh baby peas are at their peak in early spring; otherwise use frozen petit peas. Reddish orange chanterelles with their distinctive fruity, peppery, nutlike flavor add an elegant touch. Sometimes I add a few extra ounces of dried mushrooms to give the sauce an earthier flavor. Think of this cobbler when Thanksgiving is over and you can't face another plain turkey dinner.

RECOMMENDED WINE: A rich, well-oaked Chardonnay works very well with this dish, and so does a Pinot Noir or a Merlot.

10	ounces white pearl onions or a 10-ounce bag frozen, thawed
3	medium carrots, peeled and cubed, or 10 ounces baby carrots
1/2	cup unsalted butter
1	medium leek, white part only, cleaned and finely chopped
1/2	pound medium mushrooms, cut into large dice
1/4	pound fresh chanterelles, morels, cremini or shiitake, cut into large dice
1/4	cup dried shiitake or chanterelle mushrooms, softened in boiling water and drained (optional)
1	cup cooked fresh baby peas or frozen baby peas, thawed
1-1/2	pounds or 4 cups *large* chunks of cooked turkey breast
7	tablespoons all-purpose flour
2	cups extra-rich turkey or chicken stock (page 397)
1	cup half-and-half

1/4　　teaspoon salt
1/4　　teaspoon white pepper or to taste
2　　　tablespoons finely chopped parsley
2　　　tablespoons finely chopped fresh chives
1　　　teaspoon finely chopped fresh thyme
1　　　tablespoon finely chopped fresh winter savory (optional)

COBBLER DOUGH
1-3/4 cups all-purpose flour
1　　　tablespoon baking powder
1/2　　teaspoon salt
1/4　　cup freshly grated Parmesan
6　　　tablespoons unsalted butter, frozen and cut into small pieces
1/2　　cup whipping cream

1　　　large egg, beaten

1. If you're using fresh onions, immerse them in a pot of boiling water for 30 seconds, then rinse them in cold water. Trim off the fuzzy portion of the root, being sure not to cut it off completely. Remove the outer skin and the first layer of the onion with your fingers. Pierce a cross about 1/8 inch deep at the root end of each onion so they will cook evenly and not burst. Bring a medium saucepan of water to a boil and simmer the onions for 10 minutes or until slightly tender when pierced with a fork. Remove from the water and reserve in a large mixing bowl. If you're using frozen onions, just put the thawed onions in a large mixing bowl.

2. Immerse the carrots in a medium pan of boiling water and simmer for about 7 minutes or until crisp-tender. Remove, drain, and add the carrots to the onions.

3. In a medium skillet over medium heat, melt 2 tablespoons of the butter, add the leek, and sauté for about 3 minutes. Add all the mushrooms and continue to sauté for 3 minutes. Add the leeks and mushrooms along with the cooking juices to the other vegetables in the bowl. Add the peas and turkey chunks to the vegetables and reserve.

4. Melt the remaining 6 tablespoons of butter in a large saucepan over medium heat. Sprinkle in the flour and cook, stirring constantly, for 3 minutes. Slowly add the stock, half-and-half, salt, and pepper and whisk the sauce until thickened and smooth. Add the herbs and the turkey and vegetable mixture and mix well. Taste for seasoning.

5. Grease a deep 9- by 13-inch casserole dish with butter. Pour the cobbler mixture into the dish.

6. For the dough, combine the flour, baking powder, salt, and 3 tablespoons of the Parmesan in a food processor fitted with the metal blade. Add the frozen butter and process with the metal blade until all the flour is incorporated. Add the cream while the motor is running and process until the dough forms a ball.

7. Roll out the dough to fit the top of the casserole or drop spoonfuls of dough on top of the turkey mixture, distributing the dough evenly. Brush with the beaten egg and sprinkle the remaining Parmesan evenly over the top. Place the casserole on a baking sheet.

8. Preheat the oven to 400°F. Bake the cobbler for 30 to 35 minutes or until the crust is browned, checking during the last few minutes to make sure it does not burn. Serve immediately.

ADVANCE PREPARATION: Can be made 1 day ahead through step 7, covered well, and refrigerated. It also can be baked ahead, refrigerated, covered, brought to room temperature, and then reheated gently in a 325°F oven for 20 minutes or until bubbly hot.

CHICKEN AND APPLE SAUSAGE

Makes 3 pounds; serves 6 to 8

Bruce Aidells, sausage-maker extraordinaire, suggested that I use a combination of fresh and dried apples to give this chicken sausage a concentrated apple flavor. Fresh tarragon is a savory option. This sausage is delicious for breakfast or brunch. It's also an excellent foundation for Thanksgiving stuffing. Apples have residual sugar, so the sausages tend to burn when cooked over high heat. Be sure to slice them no more than 1/2 inch thick for even cooking.

RECOMMENDED WINE: On their own, these sausages combine well with Chardonnay. When among other dishes, other wines—Pinot Noir, Zinfandel, Merlot, or even Cabernet Sauvignon—might be appropriate.

3   **pounds chicken legs and thighs, boned**
2   **teaspoons salt**
1-1/2 **teaspoons black pepper**
1/2   **teaspoon ground coriander**
1/4   **teaspoon freshly grated nutmeg**
1/2   **cup cold water**
2   **cups peeled, cored, and diced Pippin apples in 1/4-inch pieces**
       (about 1 large apple)
1   **cup chopped dried apples, soaked in 1/2 cup hot water for 20**
       minutes, squeezed dry, and finely chopped
1 to 2 **teaspoons finely chopped fresh tarragon to taste (optional) or 1/2**
       teaspoon dried

1. Remove the chicken skin and finely mince it. Cut the chicken meat into 3/4-inch cubes. In a food processor fitted with the metal blade, process the meat and skin in small batches, about 1 pound at a time, by pulsing on and off until a fine texture is achieved. *Do not overprocess.* It should be slightly chunky, not a puree. Place the chicken mixture in a large mixing bowl.

2. Add the remaining ingredients to the chicken and mix together. Knead by hand until well blended.

3. Turn out the chicken mixture onto a 22-inch-long sheet of wax paper. Using 2 rubber spatulas, smooth the mixture into a long sausage shape extending to within 2 inches of each end of the paper. Fold the paper ends up and roll the paper around the sausage. Place the sausage on a cookie sheet with the paper seam down. Refrigerate overnight.

4. Divide up what you want to freeze in small batches. To cook, slice the sausages into 1/2-inch-thick slices and either sauté them in a combination of oil and unsalted butter or grill them on a barbecue over medium heat until browned on both sides, about 2 to 3 minutes each side. Serve immediately.

ADVANCE PREPARATION: Can be prepared up to 3 days ahead through step 3 and kept tightly wrapped in the refrigerator. It can be frozen for up to 2 months. If you're freezing the sausages, divide them into 4 portions so you can thaw a small amount for each occasion. Thaw before cooking.

TURKEY SAUSAGES WITH SUN-DRIED TOMATOES

MAKES 3 POUNDS OR ABOUT 14 4-OUNCE PATTIES; SERVES 6 TO 8

THESE ARE GREAT served like hamburgers on your favorite rolls, sautéed and sprinkled on pizza, or added to pasta sauce. The anchovies and capers lend a Mediterranean taste that works well with the simple but distinctive turkey flavor. Keep these in your freezer wrapped in single layers of foil for easy access.

RECOMMENDED WINE: Try a fruity young red such as a Zinfandel or Pinot Noir with this sausage.

3	pounds turkey thighs, boned
3/4	cup chopped oil-packed sun-dried tomatoes
1	tablespoon anchovy paste
1	tablespoon capers, well drained and rinsed
2	teaspoons salt
1-1/2	teaspoons black pepper
1/4	cup finely chopped fresh basil or 2 tablespoons dried
1	tablespoon finely chopped fresh thyme or 1-1/2 teaspoons dried
1/2	cup Zinfandel or Merlot

1. Remove the turkey skin and finely mince it. Cut the turkey meat into 3/4-inch cubes. In a food processor fitted with the metal blade, process the meat, the skin, and half the sun-dried tomatoes in small batches, about 1 pound at a time, by pulsing on and off until a fine texture is achieved. *Do not overprocess.* It should be slightly chunky, not a puree. Place the turkey in a large mixing bowl.

2. Add the remaining ingredients to the turkey and mix together. Knead by hand until well blended. Shape into desired-size patties separated by layers of wax paper and refrigerate.

3. Prepare a barbecue for medium-heat grilling. Grill the sausages 3 inches from the heat for about 4 to 6 minutes on a side, depending on their size. Or sauté the patties in a sauté pan with a bit of olive oil. Serve immediately.

ADVANCE PREPARATION: Can be prepared up to 3 days ahead through step 2, tightly wrapped, and refrigerated. The sausages can be frozen for up to 2 months.

MAKING POULTRY SAUSAGE

Sausages have become big business in California. They're not available only in supermarkets but also at baseball games, at specialty fast-food restaurants, and from carts on the street. You can find just about any variety imaginable. But sometimes I feel like making my own—they're really not difficult to make. You don't have to put sausages in a casing, just form them into logs or patties.

Bruce Aidells, Berkeley cookbook author and owner of the famous Aidells Sausage Company, suggests making a large quantity of poultry sausage at once since you can freeze it for future use at a moment's notice. Be sure, however, to freeze these sausages in small batches so they can be thawed for individual servings. Both of these sausage recipes can be halved if you prefer.

A meat grinder gives the best texture, but since most home cooks don't have one, a food processor does a good job. These recipes use chicken or turkey legs and thighs as the primary ingredients. Ask your butcher to leave the thighs and legs for you. The poultry skin is used instead of the customary pork fat to keep the sausage moist. Remove the skin and mince it before it goes into the food processor to avoid having large pieces of skin in the mixture, which the food processor cannot break down. When time is at a premium, you can simply sauté or grill either of these sausages as you would a hamburger.

MEAT

GRILLED SKIRT STEAK WITH AVOCADO-TOMATO SALSA   229

GRILLED ROAST BEEF WITH SHALLOT-CHIVE SAUCE   233

GRILLED FLANK STEAK WITH SMOKY SALSA   235

BRAISED BEEF WITH SUN-DRIED TOMATOES, ZINFANDEL,
    AND THYME   237

GRILLED STEAKS WITH OLIVADA AND PORT WINE SAUCE   240

GRILLED LAMB CHOPS WITH CRANBERRY-ROSEMARY MARINADE   242

RACK OF LAMB WITH MINT CRUST   244

LAMB BROCHETTES WITH CRUNCHY RAITA   247

INDONESIAN LEG OF LAMB   250

PANFRIED NOODLES WITH VEGETABLES   252

GRILLED VEAL CHOPS WITH ZUCCHINI-CORN RELISH   254

LIGHT MEATBALLS WITH DOUBLE-TOMATO HERB SAUCE   256

VEAL STEW WITH ORANGE SAUCE   258

BRAISED STUFFED SHOULDER OF VEAL   260

LOIN OF PORK WITH DRIED FRUITS AND GEWÜRZTRAMINER   264

ASIAN GLAZED PORK TENDERLOIN   266

GRILLED SKIRT STEAK WITH AVOCADO-TOMATO SALSA

SERVES 6

THIS MEXICAN-STYLE DISH is perfect for parties or for a last-minute dinner. Skirt steak should be purchased in long strips rather than rolled up for this recipe. This particularly tasty cut of beef is used frequently in Latin cooking.

If you have time, make your own tortillas or scout out good fresh ones at a Mexican delicatessen or restaurant. Begin with Griddled Quesadillas with Caramelized Onions, Chicken, and Jack Cheese (page 29) and serve Vanilla Caramel Cream (page 371) for dessert.

RECOMMENDED WINE: The lively, spicy flavors of the salsa are surprisingly compatible with a soft, well-rounded Cabernet Sauvignon or Merlot.

MARINADE
2   tablespoons olive oil
1/2 cup fresh lime juice (about 8 limes)
1   garlic clove, minced
1/2 small onion, thinly sliced
1/4 teaspoon salt
1/4 teaspoon black pepper

2   pounds skirt steak

SALSA
1   large tomato, peeled, seeded, and finely chopped
1   ripe medium avocado, peeled, pitted, and finely chopped
2   tablespoons finely chopped red onion
2   tablespoons finely chopped cilantro
1   jalapeño chile, seeded, finely chopped* or 1 tablespoon store-bought
      spicy green salsa or to taste

---

* When you're working with chiles, always wear rubber gloves. Wash the cutting surface and knife immediately.

1   tablespoon fresh lemon juice
1/2 teaspoon salt
1/4 teaspoon black pepper

12 medium corn tortillas (page 322), warmed

1. Place all the marinade ingredients in a large nonaluminum mixing bowl and whisk until combined. Taste for seasoning. Place the skirt steak in the mixing bowl, being sure to flatten it out and turn it well to coat all sides with marinade. Marinate for 2 to 4 hours covered in the refrigerator.

2. Meanwhile, mix all the salsa ingredients to combine in a medium mixing bowl. Taste for seasoning.

3. Prepare a barbecue for medium-heat grilling. Remove the steak and the onion slices from the marinade and grill it 3 inches from the heat for 4 to 6 minutes on each side for medium-rare. Grill the onion slices, making sure they don't fall through the grill, until they are lightly charred and soft.

4. Place the steak and onions on a carving platter and thinly slice the meat on a diagonal. Serve with a bowl of salsa and the warmed tortillas.

ADVANCE PREPARATION: Can be prepared up to 4 hours ahead through step 2 and refrigerated.

NOTE: The tortillas can be warmed right on the barbecue for 30 seconds on each side or on a gas burner, using tongs to turn them. Keep the tortillas warm by wrapping them in heavy napkins and placing them in a basket.

CHILE PEPPERS

Mexico's influence on California cooking is apparent from our extensive use of fresh and dried chiles that add depth and complexity to many dishes and marinades. There are those who like their food hot and spicy, but even people who don't enjoy hot food often appreciate a hint of chile flavoring.

Don't forget to wear rubber gloves when preparing chiles, and be sure to remove all interior ribs and seeds (where much of the heat resides). The volatility of chile oil should not be underestimated—some people are much more sensitive to it than others.

SOME COMMON CHILES

Anaheim: Six to eight inches long and tapering from a narrow base, the Anaheim is the mildest of the chiles (although occasionally it can be surprisingly hot) and turns from pale green to dark green to red as it ripens. Fresh Anaheim chiles are very popular for stuffing. They are also available canned.

Jalapeño (Chipotle When Dried and Smoked): This bright green, 1-1/2-inch-long pepper is hot to very hot and is one of the most commonly used and most versatile peppers. It is available canned or fresh and is sometimes seen in its bright red ripe state. Some jalapeños are smoked and dried to make chipotle pepper, usually available only canned in the United States. The chipotle's distinctive smoky flavor is well worth seeking out at a specialty market, where you will find it canned with garlic, tomatoes, and vinegar and labeled Chipotles en Adobo. Puree the chipotles in a food processor and store the paste in the refrigerator; it will keep for a few months. A little touch of chipotle puree enlivens many dishes.

Poblano (Ancho When Dried): From three to five inches long with a very wide base, the dark green poblano (sometimes called a *pasilla*) is also used for stuffing. Its hotness can range from mild to medium. The dried form, called the *ancho,* is the most commonly used in Mexican cooking. Ancho chiles should always be toasted briefly over high heat in a skillet and then covered with boiling water to soften them before being used.

Serrano: This little pepper packs an awful lot of punch for its size, which is just over one inch long and very slender. These bright green chiles turn red as they ripen and are usually very hot. This is the chile for true aficionados; serrano chiles should be used sparingly by those unfamiliar with their power.

PEELING CHILES

The poblano and Anaheim chiles need to be peeled. Select firm-fleshed, thick-skinned chile peppers so they will retain their texture when grilled or broiled. Place the chiles in a broiler pan or on a barbecue grill and broil approximately 4 inches from the heat until the skin is blistered and slightly charred on all sides. Always use long tongs to turn the peppers. Never pierce the pepper, or the juices will escape. Put the peppers in a brown paper bag and close it tightly. Let the peppers rest for 10 minutes. Remove the peppers from the bag and drain the peppers. Peel off the skin with your hands, being sure to use rubber gloves to protect yourself from the fiery resins. Make a slit in each chile and open it up. Core the chiles and cut off the stems. Scrape the seeds and ribs from the chiles and cut the chiles into the desired-size pieces. If you're in a pinch and don't have kitchen gloves, cover your hands in cooking oil to protect them.

GRILLED ROAST BEEF WITH SHALLOT-CHIVE SAUCE

SERVES 4 TO 6

FOR BARBECUED BEEF, my favorite cut is the triangle tip roast, sometimes called *bottom sirloin* or *tri-tip.* It is in fact triangular and is marbled with fat for flavorful results on the grill. The simple shallot-chive sauce is a refreshing accompaniment whether the meat is served hot or at room temperature. Serve with Pasta with Tomatoes, Basil, and Balsamic Vinaigrette (page 132). For dessert, consider Glazed Lemon Sour Cream Cake (page 355).

RECOMMENDED WINE: This beefy dish is compatible with virtually every full- to medium-bodied red wine: Cabernet Sauvignon, Merlot, Zinfandel, Syrah, and so on.

MARINADE
2   garlic cloves, minced
1   medium shallot, finely chopped
1   tablespoon fresh lemon juice
2   tablespoons olive oil
1/4 teaspoon pepper
1/2 teaspoon salt

1   2-pound triangle tip roast

SHALLOT-CHIVE SAUCE
1   medium shallot, finely chopped
1   tablespoon finely chopped fresh chives
2   tablespoons fresh lemon juice
1/4 cup olive oil
1/4 teaspoon hot pepper oil (page 412) or to taste
1/2 teaspoon salt
1/4 teaspoon white pepper

GARNISH
snipped fresh chives

1. Combine all the ingredients for the marinade in a small mixing bowl. Place the beef in a shallow nonaluminum dish and coat with the marinade until it is evenly distributed. Cover and refrigerate for 4 hours; turn several times to make sure the marinade covers all the meat.

2. Meanwhile, combine all the sauce ingredients in a small bowl and whisk together until well blended. Taste for seasoning. Cover and set aside until serving time.

3. Prepare a barbecue for medium-high-heat grilling. Remove the beef from the marinade and grill it about 3 inches from the heat for about 3 minutes on each side. Turn down the barbecue to medium heat. Cover the barbecue and grill each side for about 10 minutes longer. Check with an instant-read thermometer to get an exact reading (135°F for rare, 145°F for medium-rare).

4. If the meat is to be served hot, reheat the sauce over medium heat while you slice the beef about 1/4 inch thick on a diagonal. Overlap the slices on a platter, pour a little warmed sauce over the meat, and garnish the platter with fresh chives. To serve it chilled, let the beef come to room temperature, then refrigerate it, slice, and serve the sauce on the side.

ADVANCE PREPARATION: Can be prepared up to 1 day ahead and refrigerated, if it's to be served chilled. Remove the sauce from the refrigerator 1 hour before serving to bring it to room temperature. If you're serving the meat hot, the sauce can be prepared 1 day ahead and the meat can be marinated up to 1 day ahead and refrigerated.

GRILLED FLANK STEAK WITH SMOKY SALSA

SERVES 4 TO 6

SMOKY TOMATO SALSA and beer make up both the marinade and the sauce for this quick and tasty main course. It's best to marinate flank steak and then cook it quickly to achieve a robust flavor and tender texture. Cut the steak against the grain for best results. Serve these flank steak slices accompanied by warm corn tortillas (page 322), sour cream, Smoky Salsa (page 416), and Green Pea Guacamole (page 22).

RECOMMENDED WINE: The strong flavors in this dish need to be paired with a wine that has power and depth but not much subtlety. It goes well with Zinfandel, Petite Sirah, big and youthful Cabernet Sauvignon, and Rhône varieties.

1   cup Smoky Salsa (page 416)
1   cup full bodied beer
1 1/2 pounds flank steak

1. Combine 1/2 cup of the salsa and 3/4 cup of the beer in a medium mixing bowl and mix until well blended. Flatten out the flank steak in a shallow large non-aluminum dish. Pour the marinade over it and marinate for 2 to 24 hours covered in the refrigerator; the longer, the more tender.

2. In a small serving bowl, combine the remaining salsa and beer for the sauce and mix together. Taste for seasoning.

3. Prepare a barbecue for medium-heat grilling. Remove the steak from the marinade and grill it 3 inches from the heat for 5 to 7 minutes on each side for medium-rare. Place on a carving platter and thinly slice against the grain. Serve immediately with the sauce.

ADVANCE PREPARATION: Can be prepared up to 1 day ahead through step 2 and refrigerated.

FRESH TOMATOES VS. CANNED TOMATOES

For tomato sauce or recipes in which the tomatoes are cooked, you'll frequently get a better result using canned tomatoes if fresh tomatoes are not at their prime. Look for the organic canned variety that have extra flavor and a deep red color. These tomatoes have been packed at the peak of their ripeness and will give more flavor than a fresh unripened tomato. If you need fresh ripe uncooked tomatoes, skip the recipe until fresh tomatoes are in season.

BRAISED BEEF WITH SUN-DRIED TOMATOES, ZINFANDEL, AND THYME

S E R V E S 6 T O 8

THIS DISH MAKES a wonderful alternative to the usual family brisket served during the Jewish holidays. Based on a traditional pot roast recipe, the brisket brings together California ingredients in a sauce that tastes lighter than the family standby but is still flavorful and hearty. Don't forget to start this a day ahead.

Large plastic cooking bags work extremely well for long braises because they lock in moisture and slowly tenderize the meat. You can also cook the beef in a roasting pan with a cover. I prefer using the flat or first cut of brisket, which is a bit more expensive but has a much lower fat content. When braised it becomes very tender. Serve with Crispy Potato Pancakes with Vegetables (page 296) and a simple green vegetable.

RECOMMENDED WINE: Although most red wines will go nicely with this dish, I recommend sticking with the wine used in the recipe: full-bodied Zinfandel.

1   4- to 5-pound first-cut brisket

MARINADE
3   carrots, peeled and thinly sliced
1   large onion, thinly sliced
2   celery ribs, thinly sliced
3   garlic cloves, minced
1-1/2 ounces dry-packed sun-dried tomatoes, softened in boiling water for
        10 minutes and drained
1/2   teaspoon salt
1/4   teaspoon pepper
1   cup full-bodied Zinfandel

2   tablespoons all-purpose flour
2   large tomatoes, peeled, seeded, and diced
2   cups veal stock (page 395) or beef stock
1   teaspoon fresh thyme leaves or 1/2 teaspoon dried
1/2   cup full-bodied Zinfandel

SAUCE
2   tablespoons olive oil
1   pound mushrooms, sliced
1   teaspoon salt
1/4   teaspoon pepper
2   garlic cloves, minced
1/2   cup full-bodied Zinfandel
1   teaspoon finely chopped fresh thyme leaves or 1/2 teaspoon dried
1/2   cup finely chopped parsley

1. In a large plastic storage container or a large nonaluminum pan, place the brisket fat side down. Scatter the carrots, onion, celery, garlic, and dried tomatoes around the meat. Sprinkle the brisket with salt and pepper and pour 1 cup of Zinfandel over it. Cover the dish and marinate overnight in the refrigerator. Turn the meat over at least once to distribute the marinade ingredients evenly.

2. Preheat the oven to 325°F. Sprinkle the flour into a large plastic cooking bag. Place the meat, marinade ingredients, fresh tomatoes, stock, thyme, and 1/2 cup Zinfandel in the bag and close with the tie. Be sure to make slits in the top of the bag for even cooking. Place the bag in a large heavy-duty roasting pan. (You can also cook it directly in the roasting pan.) Roast for 3 to 4 hours, checking for tenderness after 3 hours. The meat should be very tender.

3. While the meat is cooking, heat the oil in a medium sauté pan over medium heat. Add and sauté the mushrooms for about 5 minutes, draining off and reserving the excess juice. When the mushrooms are cooked, add the salt, pepper, garlic, 1/2 cup Zinfandel, and thyme. Turn up the heat and boil for 2 to 3 minutes. Set aside.

4. When the meat is cooked, remove it from the oven and cool. Drain the braising liquid and vegetables into a large saucepan. Puree the sauce in the pan with a hand blender or in a food processor fitted with the metal blade, being sure to leave a slight texture. Add the mushrooms, their liquid, and 1/4 cup of the parsley and bring to a simmer over medium heat. If the sauce is too thick, add a bit of veal or beef stock. Taste for seasoning.

5. Place the brisket on a carving board. Slice the meat against the grain into 1/2-inch slices, place overlapping on a serving platter, and pour the sauce over the meat. Garnish with the remaining parsley and serve immediately.

ADVANCE PREPARATION: Can be prepared up to 1 day ahead. Reheat in a 350°F oven for 1/2 hour before serving.

GRILLED STEAKS WITH OLIVADA AND PORT WINE SAUCE

S E R V E S 4

EARTHY OLIVE PASTE offers a Mediterranean twist to grilled steaks that are also complemented by a slightly sweet port wine sauce. The first time I tasted this, at Campanile Restaurant in Los Angeles, a large entrecôte section of beef was served in a rustic presentation. At home, New York steaks work best on the grill, served attractively in overlapping slices.

Simple techniques for reducing the sauce and grilling the steak make this a dish that even the beginning cook can accomplish with finesse—a good thing, because this is a wonderful dinner party dish. You can easily double this recipe.

Olive paste is available at specialty food stores, or you can make your own: 25 pitted Niçoise olives pureed with 1 tablespoon olive oil in a food processor makes 3 tablespoons of olive paste.

Serve the steaks with White Bean Stew with Spinach and Tomatoes (page 283), Oven-Roasted Potatoes with Parmesan (page 298) or Roasted Winter Vegetables (page 274) for dinner on a cold night. Follow with Essencia Zabaglione with Fresh Fruit Compote (page 347) and biscotti.

RECOMMENDED WINE: This is another aggressively flavored dish that goes very nicely with Zinfandel, Syrah, Merlot, or a young Cabernet Sauvignon.

SAUCE
1 tablespoon unsalted butter
2 medium shallots, minced
1/2 cup dry red wine
1/2 cup port wine
1 cup veal stock (page 395) or beef stock
2 tablespoons whipping cream
1/4 teaspoon salt

1   teaspoon cracked black pepper

4   New York steaks, about 3/4 inch thick
     salt and pepper to taste

2   tablespoons black olivada

GARNISH
watercress or parsley sprigs

1. For the sauce, melt the butter in a heavy medium saucepan over medium heat, add the shallots, and sauté until soft, about 3 to 5 minutes. Add the red wine and port, turn up the heat to high, and reduce by half to make a syrupy glaze. Add the stock and reduce by a quarter or until the sauce barely coats the back of the spoon. Add the cream and reduce for another few minutes, until it coats a spoon. Add salt and cracked pepper and taste for seasoning. Reserve the sauce.

2. Prepare a grill for medium-high-heat grilling or preheat the broiler. Grill or broil the steak about 3 inches from the heat for about 4 to 5 minutes on each side or until browned but still rare. Place the steaks on a carving platter, season lightly with salt and pepper, and spread the top of each steak with a thin coat of the olive paste. Cut the steaks into 1/2-inch-thick slices. Spoon some sauce onto a serving plate and place the steak slices, slightly overlapping, on top. Garnish with watercress or parsley and serve immediately.

ADVANCE PREPARATION: The sauce can be prepared up to 4 hours ahead and refrigerated. Reheat gently over low heat.

OLIVADA

Use this luscious olive paste

- spread on Parmesan toasts;
- added to mashed potatoes;
- to flavor your favorite vinaigrette;
- spread on chicken breasts and roasted at high heat to create a crust;
- added to a tomato pasta sauce;
- added to sour cream, red onion, and capers to top corn cakes or pizza;
- added to steamed vegetables;
- added to garlic mayonnaise.

GRILLED LAMB CHOPS WITH CRANBERRY-ROSEMARY MARINADE

SERVES 4

THE RELATIVELY EXOTIC combination of lamb with pomegranate juice was a favorite in California rancho kitchens in the early 1900s. The pomegranate juice may have been intended to mask the strong-flavored lamb produced on the ranches in those days. On the other hand, the combination could have had appeal then, as now, simply because it tastes so good. Pomegranate juice is difficult to find in most markets, so I experimented with tangy cranberry juice and came up with this last-minute marinade with fragrant fresh rosemary and garlic. Pomegranate juice is sometimes available in health food stores and gourmet markets, and of course you can substitute it for the cranberry juice here.

It isn't necessary to marinate the lamb for a long time since today's lamb chops have a milder flavor. This quick entrée has been a lifesaver when I'm in a hurry and want something a bit out of the ordinary. Begin with La Scala Chopped Salad (page 92) and serve the lamb with Confetti Rice Pilaf (page 305) or Potatoes Vaugirard (page 294). For dessert, try Baked Pears in Burgundy and Port Glaze (page 345).

RECOMMENDED WINE: Ordinarily, Cabernet Sauvignon is the ideal wine for lamb, but the sweetness of the cranberry juice cocktail in the marinade suggests a fruitier wine such as Sangiovese, Pinot Noir, or Syrah.

MARINADE
1   garlic clove, peeled
1   shallot, peeled
1   tablespoon finely chopped fresh rosemary or 1-1/2 teaspoons dried

1/2 cup cranberry juice cocktail

1/4 cup full-bodied red wine such as Merlot or Cabernet Sauvignon

2 tablespoons olive oil

1/4 teaspoon salt

    pinch of black pepper

8 thick French rib lamb chops, up to 3/4 inch thick

GARNISH

fresh rosemary leaves

fresh cranberries (optional)

1. In a food processor fitted with the metal blade with the motor running, finely chop the garlic and shallot. Add the rosemary, cranberry juice, red wine, olive oil, salt, and pepper. Process until well blended. Taste for seasoning.

2. Arrange the lamb chops in a shallow large nonaluminum dish. Pour the marinade over the lamb chops, making sure the marinade is distributed evenly on both sides of the lamb chops. Marinate for 30 minutes to 4 hours covered in the refrigerator.

3. Prepare a barbecue for medium-high-heat grilling. Remove the lamb chops from the marinade and grill 3 inches from the heat for about 5 to 7 minutes on each side for medium-rare, depending on their thickness. Place the lamb chops on serving plates and garnish with the rosemary and the cranberries if desired. Serve immediately.

ADVANCE PREPARATION: Can be prepared up to 8 hours ahead through step 2.

RACK OF LAMB WITH MINT CRUST

S E R V E S   4   T O   6

AFTER I FINISHED training at the Cordon Bleu in London, I had a beginner's repertoire of classic dishes that I could prepare with panache. Rack of Lamb Persillade was a favorite among them. This adaptation adds the complementary flavor of fresh mint to the typical crispy bread topping. A standard brown sauce is enriched with mint-flavored nutty roasted garlic puree.

Rack of lamb is a wonderful company dish. For a pretty presentation, crisscross the ends of the lamb chops and surround them with some sauce. Begin with Smoked Salmon and Caviar Torta (page 5) and serve the lamb with Grilled Polenta with Confit of Red Onions and Prosciutto (page 149). For dessert, try Mango and Macadamia Nut Brown Butter Tart (page 364).

RECOMMENDED WINE: Here is a great opportunity to roll out your best well-aged Cabernet Sauvignon or Merlot. This lamb dish is an ideal foil for these complex wines, especially if they have some eucalyptus/mint character.

SAUCE

1	large head of garlic
1	teaspoon olive oil
5	fresh mint leaves
1	cup veal stock (page 395) or beef stock
1	teaspoon Dijon mustard
2	tablespoons dry red wine
1	tablespoon whipping cream
1	tablespoon unsalted butter, softened
1	tablespoon finely chopped fresh mint leaves
1/4	teaspoon salt
1/8	teaspoon black pepper

LAMB

2   racks of lamb (8 chops or about 3 pounds each), trimmed of excess fat
       and meat scraped 1-1/2 inches up on each bone (net weight 1-1/2–
       1-3/4 pounds each)
1   cup fresh French bread crumbs
2   medium shallots, finely chopped
2   tablespoons finely chopped fresh mint
2   tablespoons finely chopped parsley
1/4 teaspoon salt
1/8 teaspoon pepper
3   tablespoons olive oil
2   tablespoons chicken stock (page 397)

GARNISH
fresh mint leaves

1. For the sauce, preheat the oven to 425°F. Cut a piece of aluminum foil to fit a whole head of garlic. With a sharp knife, cut off the top of the head, then score it gently, cutting through just a few layers of the papery skin all around the diameter. Pull off all the loose skin from the top half, trying not to remove every shred. This will make it easier to squeeze out the cooked cloves later. Place the garlic head in the center of the foil, drizzle 1 teaspoon of olive oil over it, and surround the garlic with a few mint leaves that will infuse the garlic. Bake for 1 hour or until the cloves are very soft. When cooled, squeeze the garlic pulp with your fingers into a small ramekin.

2. In a medium saucepan over medium-high heat, combine the garlic pulp, veal stock, mustard, wine, and cream. Bring to a boil and reduce by a quarter. Swirl in the butter and add the mint, salt, and pepper. Taste for seasoning.

3. Preheat the oven to 450°F. Place the racks of lamb in a roasting pan, bone side down, and roast for 20 to 25 minutes, depending on their size, for medium-rare. Use an instant-read thermometer inserted into the thickest part of the lamb to check the inside temperature (135°F for medium-rare). Let the lamb rest for 5 minutes. Drain off all the fat in the roasting pan.

4. While the meat is roasting, combine the bread crumbs, shallots, herbs, salt, pepper, olive oil, and chicken stock in a small bowl and mix well.

5. Preheat the broiler. Spread the bread crumb mixture evenly on the meat side of the racks. Place the lamb under the broiler until it is lightly browned, about 2 to 3 minutes. Be careful not to burn it. Meanwhile, reheat the sauce.

6. To serve, place the racks on a serving or carving platter and slice by cutting between the bones. Serve 2 or 3 chops per person, garnished with fresh mint leaves, and pass the sauce on the side.

ADVANCE PREPARATION: Can be prepared up to 6 hours ahead through step 2, covered, and refrigerated. Gently reheat the sauce.

NOTE: If you use a larger rack of lamb, increase the cooking time. Test the temperature every few minutes.

LAMB BROCHETTES WITH CRUNCHY RAITA

SERVES 4 TO 6

COOLING MINTED YOGURT sauce, an Indian staple condiment, functions as both a marinade that tenderizes the meat and a crunchy, refreshing sauce to serve on the side. Serve the brochettes on a bed of Tomato-Mint Bulgur (page 302).

RECOMMENDED WINE: The creamy, tangy character of the yogurt suggests a young red such as a Zinfandel, Pinot Noir, or Syrah.

SAUCE AND MARINADE
2   cups plain nonfat yogurt
2   tablespoons finely chopped fresh mint
1   garlic clove, minced
1/4 cup fresh orange juice
1/8 teaspoon ground cumin
1/2 teaspoon salt
    pinch of white pepper

BROCHETTES
2   pounds boneless lamb loin, cut into 2-inch cubes

1/2 medium European cucumber, finely chopped

1. Prepare the sauce and marinade by combining all the ingredients. Taste for seasoning. Place the meat in a medium nonaluminum bowl and pour 3/4 cup of the marinade over it, mixing well so that all the meat is well coated. Reserve the remaining sauce. Marinate for 30 minutes to 4 hours covered in the refrigerator.

2. Place the lamb on metal skewers. Preheat the broiler or prepare a barbecue for medium-high-heat grilling. Cook the brochettes, about 3 inches from the fire, turning them a few times and basting with the marinade, until the meat is browned and done as desired, about 15 to 20 minutes.

3. Add the chopped cucumber to the reserved sauce and mix together.

4. Place the brochettes on serving plates and pass the remaining minted yogurt sauce.

ADVANCE PREPARATION: Can be prepared up to 8 hours ahead through step 1, covered, and refrigerated.

MARINADES

Marinades are an important technique in California cooking because they add flavor to whatever you're cooking, with minimum effort and without masking the natural flavor of the food.

Most marinades are a combination of an acid, such as citrus juice, vinegar, wine, or even yogurt, and vegetable or olive oil. Spices, herbs, and mustards are often added for distinctive flavor. Add a minimum of salt since it can toughen the meat. I like to use a ratio of two parts acid to one part oil. Let the marinade rest for a few minutes to allow the flavors to develop. Use glass, porcelain, or enamel for marinating since aluminum will give the food a metallic taste. Be sure all surfaces of the food are covered with the marinade.

Some general rules:

- Meats can be marinated for up to 24 hours without changing their texture.
- Generally, poultry needs a shorter time, up to 6 hours, and fish should never be marinated for more than 2 hours if there is a high acid content to the marinade.
- If you are marinating food in the refrigerator, remove it 1/2 hour before grilling so that it can come to room temperature before cooking.
- Use the marinade to baste during cooking to give it extra moisture and flavor.
- Don't forget about marinating vegetables, which are particularly good grilled. Marinate vegetables for 30 minutes to 4 hours.
- Pastes or herb coatings are another type of marinade. Plan on spreading the paste on the meat, poultry, or seafood up to 4 hours ahead of cooking. Pastes that contain little acid can marinate up to 8 hours.

Here are a few pastes that are delicious on meat, chicken, or fish:

- sun-dried tomato, garlic, basil, capers, and olive oil
- rosemary, thyme, garlic, shallots, olive oil, and fresh lemon juice
- dijon mustard, orange zest, balsamic vinegar, and chives
- hoisin, scallions, dark sesame oil, and ginger

INDONESIAN LEG OF LAMB

SERVES 8 TO 10

BASED ON A recipe from Mark Ellman's Avalon restaurant in Lahaina, Maui, this scrumptious dish is a good choice for a dinner party. Boned and butterflied leg of lamb works nicely for barbecuing. Ask your butcher to pound the lamb into a uniform thickness so it will cook evenly.

Star anise, the star-shaped spice from China, is included for its slight licorice flavor. If you have time, marinate the lamb overnight so it can soak up the exotic flavors. While I suggest reducing the marinade with a bit of stock as a sauce, you can also just serve the sliced lamb as is, with the lamb juices as the sauce.

Begin with Asian Gravlax with Ginger-Mustard Sauce (page 8) and accompany the lamb with Confetti Rice Pilaf (page 305) or Rice Pilaf with Corn and Peanuts (page 306). Try Tiramisu with Toasted Hazelnuts and Chocolate (page 369) for dessert. Since the leg is a large portion, I usually have some left over. Little cubes of this full-flavored lamb are a great addition to Panfried Noodles with Vegetables (page 252).

RECOMMENDED WINE: The forward, spicy flavors of this dish require a full-bodied red wine. I have found it does best with Zinfandel, Petite Sirah, Syrah, or other Rhône varieties.

MARINADE
1/4 cup soy sauce
1/4 cup sake
2   tablespoons honey
1   tablespoon crushed star anise
2   tablespoons minced fresh ginger
2   tablespoons minced garlic
1   tablespoon dark sesame oil
1/3 cup finely chopped fresh mint
1/4 cup grainy mustard

1   7-pound leg of lamb, boned and butterflied (about 4-1/2 to 5 pounds)
1   cup veal stock (page 395) or beef stock

1. In a large nonaluminum mixing bowl, combine all the ingredients for the marinade and mix well. Reserve 1/2 cup of the marinade. At least 12 hours and up to 24 hours ahead, place the lamb in the marinade and evenly distribute the marinade all over. Refrigerate the lamb, covering it with plastic wrap and occasionally turning it to marinate evenly.

2. Prepare a barbecue for high-heat grilling. Remove the lamb from the marinade and use the marinade for basting. Place the lamb on the grill 3 inches from the heat and sear the meat for 3 minutes on each side. Turn down the heat to medium, cover the barbecue, and grill each side for about 15 to 20 minutes, for a total cooking time of 35 to 40 minutes for medium-rare to medium. You may need to cut a piece off before the rest is finished if the lamb is much thicker in certain places. The meat should be pink on the inside for best flavor and texture. If you're using a charcoal grill without a lid, cook the meat over a medium fire and turn the meat every 5 to 7 minutes. Use an instant-read thermometer to get an exact reading (140°F for medium-rare, 150°F for medium). Transfer the lamb to a wooden platter and let it rest for about 10 minutes. Slice the meat against the grain on a diagonal into 1/4-inch slices.

3. Combine the reserved marinade with the stock in a medium saucepan over medium-high heat. Boil the sauce until it is reduced to about 3/4 cup. Taste for seasoning. Serve separately.

ADVANCE PREPARATION: The marinade can be prepared up to 2 days ahead and refrigerated. The meat can be marinated up to 24 hours ahead, covered, and refrigerated.

PANFRIED NOODLES WITH VEGETABLES

SERVES 4 TO 6

FOR THIS ONE-DISH main course I like to use the Japanese version of Chinese wheat noodles, chuka soba noodles, which are precooked and dried. By crisping the noodles first, you'll create varied textures. Use any leftover meat or chicken you have, but this is a last-minute meal that can't be made ahead, so plan accordingly.

RECOMMENDED WINE: Depending on which meat you use in this dish, there are lots of choices here. If you choose chicken and you serve the dish as part of a luncheon, you might think about accompanying it with a ripe, oaky Chardonnay. If you use the Indonesian lamb, a young Zinfandel or Cabernet Sauvignon would be a better choice.

1/2 cup dried shiitake mushrooms
1   8-ounce package chuka soba noodles
1/4 cup peanut oil
6   scallions, both white and green parts, finely sliced
1   tablespoon finely chopped fresh ginger
2   garlic cloves, minced
2   carrots, peeled and sliced
1/2 pound sugar snap peas, trimmed
6   mushrooms, sliced

SAUCE
2   tablespoons cornstarch
3   tablespoons soy sauce
2   tablespoons dry sherry
2   tablespoons dark brown sugar

1/2 cup chicken stock (page 397)
2   teaspoons dark sesame oil
     pinch of hot red pepper flakes

2   cups cubed cooked beef, chicken, or lamb

1. Pour boiling water over the shiitake mushrooms in a bowl and let them soften for at least 10 minutes.

2. In a large pot of boiling water, cook the noodles for about 3 to 4 minutes or until al dente. Do not overcook the noodles because they are going to be cooked again. Drain the noodles well and spread them out on a kitchen towel to dry slightly.

3. In a wok or large nonstick skillet over high heat, heat 2 tablespoons of the oil, add the noodles, and toss them with 2 large forks or spoons until they're crisp and golden brown, about 3 to 5 minutes. Transfer the noodles to a bowl.

4. Heat the remaining oil in the wok or skillet over medium-high heat and stir-fry the scallions, ginger, and garlic for about 1 to 2 minutes. Add the carrots, peas, and sliced mushrooms and continue to stir-fry, stirring continually, about 3 minutes until the vegetables are crisp-tender.

5. In a small mixing bowl, combine all the sauce ingredients and mix to blend, making sure the cornstarch is dissolved. Strain the shiitake mushrooms, reserving 1/2 cup of the soaking liquid, and add the liquid to the sauce mixture. Trim the stems and add the mushrooms to the vegetables. Add the sauce mixture to the vegetables and turn up the heat to high. Add the meat and stir until the sauce is slightly thickened. Taste for seasoning.

6. Just before serving, add the noodles to the stir-fry just to heat them through. Place the noodles in a serving bowl and serve immediately.

GRILLED VEAL CHOPS WITH ZUCCHINI-CORN RELISH

SERVES 4

VEAL CHOPS TASTE best grilled medium-rare. In the colder months, complex mushroom sauces are a wonderful counterpoint to the veal's delicate flavor. In the summer, when fresh corn is plentiful, this relish is a lighter, fresher approach, especially since the vegetables are grilled rather than sautéed.

Serve a bowl of Roasted Tomato Jam (page 418) alongside as well as Oven-Roasted Potatoes with Parmesan (page 298) for a satisfying meal. For dessert, try Peach Melba Buckle (page 359).

RECOMMENDED WINE: Sangiovese, Rhône varieties, and Pinot Noir are the best choices for this dish.

RELISH

2　medium zucchini, cut lengthwise into 1/4-inch slices
1/2 small red onion, cut into 1/4-inch slices (about 3 slices)
1/2 medium roasted red pepper, peeled (page 287) and finely chopped
1　ear of fresh corn, husked
3　tablespoons olive oil
2　tablespoons balsamic vinegar
2　tablespoons fresh lemon juice
2　tablespoons finely chopped fresh basil
2　tablespoons finely chopped parsley
1/2 teaspoon salt
1/4 teaspoon black pepper

VEAL

3   tablespoons olive oil

1   tablespoon balsamic vinegar

6   veal loin chops, 8 to 10 ounces each

SAUCE

1/2 cup veal stock (page 395) or beef stock

GARNISH

large fresh basil leaves

1. Prepare a barbecue for medium-heat grilling. Place the zucchini and red onion slices on the grill 3 inches from the heat and grill them for about 4 minutes on each side or until slightly charred. Remove the zucchini and onions from the grill, chop them into 1/4-inch pieces, and place them in a medium mixing bowl along with the red pepper.

2. Place the corn on the barbecue and grill it, turning the corn as it just begins to darken, about 3 to 4 minutes. Remove the corn from the grill, and when it is cool enough, shuck the corn kernels off with a sharp knife into the mixing bowl. Add the remaining ingredients for the relish and mix to combine. Taste for seasoning.

3. Combine the oil and vinegar in a small mixing bowl and brush each side of the veal chops with this mixture. Turn up the grill to medium-high-heat. Place the veal on the grill about 3 inches from the heat and grill for 5 to 7 minutes on each side. The veal should be very pink inside. Meanwhile, combine the stock with 1/4 cup of the relish in a small saucepan and bring it to a simmer. Keep the stock hot. In another small saucepan, heat the remaining relish. Keep it warm.

4. To serve, take the veal off the grill, place it on serving plates, and spoon a tablespoon of the sauce on top. Place the basil leaves on the plate and spoon a large dollop of the warm relish on top of the basil. Serve immediately.

ADVANCE PREPARATION: Can be prepared 8 hours ahead through step 2 and refrigerated. Reheat the relish over low heat.

LIGHT MEATBALLS WITH DOUBLE-TOMATO HERB SAUCE

MAKES ABOUT 30 MEATBALLS; SERVES 8 TO 10

A MIXTURE OF veal and turkey instead of beef lightens these unusual baked meatballs. Airy and fluffy, these meatballs owe much of their flavor and moistness to the shredded carrot and zucchini that replace the usual fat or cream. Shred or grate the carrot and zucchini very finely, and taste the zucchini to make sure it isn't bitter. Serve these alone, with your favorite pasta, or on a baguette with the tomato sauce spooned over them.

This recipe can also be adapted as a meat loaf. Form the mixture into a large loaf shape, place it in a baking pan, and bake it for 1 hour at 400°F. For extra flavor, spoon over some of the sauce while the meat loaf is cooking.

RECOMMENDED WINE: Here a ripe, full-bodied Chardonnay does very nicely. If you want to pour a red wine, try Pinot Noir.

2	tablespoons olive oil
1	medium onion, finely chopped
2	garlic cloves, minced
2	medium carrots, peeled and finely shredded
1	medium zucchini, finely shredded
1	pound lean ground turkey
1	pound lean ground veal
1/3	cup fine dried bread crumbs
2	large eggs
1	large egg white
1/4	cup finely chopped parsley
1/4	cup freshly grated Parmesan

2   tablespoons Dijon mustard
1   teaspoon finely chopped fresh rosemary or 1/2 teaspoon dried
1/2 teaspoon finely chopped fresh thyme or 1/4 teaspoon dried
1   teaspoon salt
1/4 teaspoon pepper
3   cups Double-Tomato Herb Sauce (page 400)

1. In a medium skillet over medium heat, heat the oil, add the onions, and sauté them for about 7 to 10 minutes, stirring frequently, until they're soft and translucent. Add the garlic and sauté for another minute. Add the carrots and zucchini, blend with the onion mixture, and cook for about 2 minutes.

2. Transfer the cooked vegetables to a large mixing bowl and add the remaining ingredients except the sauce. Blend well, using a large spoon or your hands to mix all the ingredients together.

3. Preheat the oven to 375°F. With your hands, gently roll the mixture into meatballs about 1-1/2 inches in diameter. Place them in a large roasting pan that has been lined with aluminum foil. Bake for 35 minutes. Meanwhile, heat the tomato sauce.

4. To serve, arrange the meatballs in a serving dish and spoon the hot sauce over them.

ADVANCE PREPARATION: Can be prepared 1 day ahead through step 3 and refrigerated. Reheat in a 350°F oven for 20 minutes, occasionally basting with tomato sauce. The cooked meatballs can also be frozen.

VEAL STEW WITH ORANGE SAUCE

SERVES 4 TO 6

IN THIS SPLENDID flavor combination, cubes of veal are braised in a light orange sauce subtly flavored with bacon. Ask your butcher for veal shoulder meat, which retains its tenderness when stewed slowly. Begin with Mixed Greens with Beets and Peppers (page 85). Simple buttered egg noodles are all that you need to accompany the stew.

RECOMMENDED WINE: The hearty flavors of this dish require a hearty wine to balance. Best would be Zinfandel, but a big Merlot, Syrah, or even Cabernet Sauvignon does almost as well.

3　pounds veal stew, cut into 2-inch cubes and patted dry
2　medium onions, finely chopped
1/4 pound bacon, finely chopped
3　tablespoons all-purpose flour
　　juice of 1 medium orange (about 1/2 cup)
1　cup dry white wine
1　tablespoon finely chopped orange zest
2　tablespoons balsamic vinegar
2　garlic cloves, minced
10 ounces baby carrots, peeled, or regular carrots, peeled and sliced into
　　　1-inch pieces
1　tablespoon olive oil
1　pound medium mushrooms, quartered
1　cup chicken or veal stock (page 397 or 395), optional
1/2 teaspoon salt
1/4 teaspoon white pepper

GARNISH

1/4 cup finely chopped parsley
   thin orange slices
1   tablespoon finely chopped orange zest

1. Preheat the oven to 450°F. In a large ovenproof roasting pan, combine the veal, onions, bacon, and flour, making sure the flour covers everything evenly. Place the pan in the oven and, with long oven mitts and a long-handled spoon, toss the meat mixture every 10 minutes so that the meat is lightly browned, for a total roasting time of about 30 minutes.

2. Remove the pan from the oven and transfer all the ingredients to a large ovenproof, flameproof casserole. Place the roasting pan over medium heat on top of the stove and add the orange juice and wine, deglazing the pan by scraping up the brown bits. Add the deglazed juices to the casserole and place over medium heat. Add the orange zest, vinegar, and garlic and bring the mixture to a simmer. Cover the casserole and simmer over low heat for 1-1/4 hours or until the meat is tender, stirring once or twice to cook the meat evenly.

3. Immerse the carrots in a medium saucepan of boiling water over high heat and simmer for 10 minutes or until the carrots are cooked but slightly firm. Drain and set aside.

4. While the meat is cooking, heat the oil in a large skillet over medium heat, add the mushrooms, and sauté until softened about 3 to 4 minutes.

5. Add the mushrooms to the stew and continue cooking, covered, for 15 minutes over low heat. If the sauce is too thick, add the stock to reach the desired consistency. Add the carrots, salt, and pepper and cook for about 5 minutes or until the carrots are heated through. Taste for seasoning.

6. Spoon the stew into a large serving bowl, garnish with the parsley, orange slices, and orange zest, and serve immediately.

ADVANCE PREPARATION: Can be prepared 5 days ahead, covered, and refrigerated. The stew also freezes well. Thaw before reheating. Adjust seasonings before serving.

BRAISED STUFFED SHOULDER OF VEAL

SERVES 8 TO 10

WHILE A STUDENT at Cal Berkeley in the late 1960s, I visited many ethnic restaurants in nearby San Francisco. One of my fondest memories finds me sitting at Vanessi's counter watching one of the first California-style open kitchens operate in high gear. Aromatic sizzling pans, the clicking of wire whisks against copper bowls preparing zabaglione, and the smell of just-baked bread—it was easy to imagine I was in Italy.

When I decided to re-create this memory at home, I chose Vanessi's braised veal, a favorite of mine. I didn't realize how long the recipe would take to prepare. But don't be put off by the long preparation time; just plan a day when you can enjoy leisurely cooking. I usually make this one day ahead because the flavors improve with time. You'll need a trussing needle for this.

If your time is at a premium, prepare the veal without the stuffing. It will still be delicious, but *much* less work will be required. The veal will still need to be tied, a task your butcher can perform, and will take about 2 hours to cook without the stuffing.

The clod portion of the veal shoulder is country-elegant, filled with Italian-style stuffing, rolled into a tight package, browned, and braised in a fragrant tomato-Madeira sauce until tender. When sliced, the green mushroom-flecked filling is a perfect contrast to the milky white veal interior. Enjoy this with steamed green beans or sweet spring peas.

RECOMMENDED WINE: There is a definite affinity between wines and dishes of similar geographic provenance, so an Italian variety such as Sangiovese, Barbera, or Dolcetto goes nicely with this Italian dish. Zinfandel, which is thought to be an Italian variety, is also an excellent match.

STUFFING

1/3 cup pine nuts

2 medium bunches of spinach, leaves only, cleaned and left wet

1 tablespoon olive oil

4 medium shallots, finely chopped

1/2 pound mushrooms, coarsely chopped

2 garlic cloves, minced

1/3 cup dry white wine

2 cups fresh French bread crumbs

1/4 pound thinly sliced prosciutto, coarsely chopped

1/4 pound thinly sliced mortadella, coarsely chopped

2 tablespoons finely chopped parsley

1 tablespoon chopped fresh thyme or 1 teaspoon dried

1 tablespoon chopped fresh rosemary or 1 teaspoon dried

1/2 teaspoon salt

1/4 teaspoon pepper

2 large eggs

5 pounds boned veal shoulder, clod portion, with a pocket made in the thick part of the shoulder

FOR COOKING THE VEAL AND THE SAUCE

3 tablespoons olive oil

1 large onion, finely chopped

2 medium carrots, peeled and finely chopped

2 celery ribs, finely chopped

1/2 cup dry white wine

1/2 cup Madeira

2 cups veal stock (page 395)

3 large fresh tomatoes, peeled, seeded, and finely chopped, or 1-1/2 cups chopped drained canned tomatoes

2 garlic cloves, minced

1 tablespoon chopped fresh rosemary or 1 teaspoon dried

1 teaspoon salt

1/4 teaspoon pepper

3 tablespoons finely chopped parsley

1. For the stuffing, preheat the oven to 350°F and toast the pine nuts on a baking sheet for 5 minutes or until light brown. Remove from the oven and reserve.

2. Place the moist spinach in a large skillet over medium-high heat, partially cover it, and steam for about 2 minutes. Remove the spinach from the heat and place it in a strainer. Pour cold water over it to stop the cooking. Drain carefully and place it in a dry kitchen towel. Wring the spinach out until all excess liquid is removed. Finely chop the spinach and reserve.

3. In a large skillet over medium heat, heat the oil, add the shallots, and sauté for about 3 minutes or until soft. Add the mushrooms and continue cooking, stirring often, for about 2 minutes or until just tender. Add the garlic and sauté for 30 seconds. Pour in the wine, cook for another minute, and remove from the heat.

4. In a medium mixing bowl, combine the spinach, mushroom mixture, bread crumbs, prosciutto, mortadella, herbs, salt, and pepper. Add the eggs and pine nuts and mix again. Taste for seasoning.

5. To stuff the veal, slide the stuffing, a small handful at a time, into the pocket, making sure the filling is distributed evenly. Pat the veal down to help distribute it.

6. With a trussing needle threaded with string, sew up the end of the veal that has the pocket opening. Make sure it is sewn securely so the stuffing won't escape during cooking.

7. Press the veal into a compact package with your hands. Using kitchen string, wrap the veal in a tight package. Tie it lengthwise and crosswise to hold it together.

8. To cook the veal, preheat the oven to 350°F. In a 6- to 8-quart ovenproof, flameproof casserole that will hold the veal, heat 2 tablespoons of the oil over medium-high heat. Add the veal and brown it evenly on all sides, using 2 spoons to turn it. Transfer it to a platter.

9. Turn down the heat to medium. Add the remaining tablespoon of oil to the casserole and the onion, carrots, and celery. Sauté over heat until slightly softened, about 5 minutes. Pour in the wine and Madeira and boil for 3 minutes, scraping the bits from the bottom of the pan to enrich the sauce. Add the stock, tomatoes, garlic, and rosemary.

10. Return the veal to the casserole, cover, and bake for 2-1/2 hours or until a meat thermometer inserted in the meat and not touching the stuffing reaches 160°F. Remove the veal from the oven and remove all the string from around the meat. Place the veal on a carving board and let it rest.

11. Boil the sauce down for about 5 minutes, until slightly thickened. Skim off the fat from the surface. Add salt, pepper, and 1 tablespoon of the parsley. Taste for seasoning.

12. Slice the veal into 1-1/2-inch slices so that the stuffing remains intact. Overlap the slices on a large white serving dish and pour the sauce around the veal. Ladle the sauce down the center of the slices and garnish with the remaining parsley. Serve immediately.

ADVANCE PREPARATION: Can be prepared up to 1 day ahead, covered, and refrigerated. Reheat in the sauce before slicing.

LOIN OF PORK WITH DRIED FRUITS AND GEWÜRZTRAMINER

SERVES 6

CALIFORNIA WINERIES HAVE taken an active role in educating food and wine lovers on the successful pairing of wines with California-style foods. Fetzer winery led the way with its Valley Oaks Garden Center in Mendocino County. This facility includes a 4-1/2-acre organic garden with more varieties of herbs, fruits, and vegetables than you can possibly imagine and a stunning demonstration kitchen and conference center. Throughout the year food events are held there to celebrate contemporary California cooking.

Fetzer's chef, John Ash, has a job most of us in the food field would envy. Each day he picks his produce sparkling fresh from the garden and puts his unique signature on each recipe by reinterpreting classic dishes. Here I've adapted one of John's recipes that shows off the natural attraction between pork and spicy fruit flavors like ginger, Gewürztraminer, and dried fruit. Serve this pork on a chilly winter evening accompanied by Crispy Potato Pancakes with Vegetables (page 296).

RECOMMENDED WINE: It would seem appropriate to stick with the Gewürztraminer used in the recipe. Try to find one that is not too high in residual sugar (more than 3 percent is excessive). If you want to branch out, try a Syrah or a fresh, young Pinot Noir.

2 tablespoons olive oil
1 2-1/2- to 3-pound boneless loin of pork, tied

SAUCE
1 medium red onion, finely chopped
2 garlic cloves, minced
2 tablespoons finely chopped fresh ginger

2 teaspoons finely chopped orange zest
2 cups fresh orange juice
1 serrano chile, seeded and finely chopped*
1 cup Gewürztraminer
1 cup chicken stock (page 397)
1 cup dried apple slices, coarsely chopped
1 cup dried apricot halves, coarsely chopped
1 teaspoon ground allspice
1 2-inch cinnamon stick
2 teaspoons dark brown sugar
2 tablespoons whipping cream
  salt and pepper to taste

GARNISH
2 tablespoons finely chopped parsley

1. In a heavy large flameproof casserole that will hold the pork, heat 1 tablespoon of the oil over medium-high heat. Add the pork and brown evenly on all sides, turning the meat with 2 large spoons or tongs, about 15 minutes. Transfer the pork to a dish.

2. Turn down the heat to medium and add the remaining tablespoon of oil to the casserole, add the onion, and sauté over medium heat for 3 minutes or until softened. Add the garlic and sauté for another minute. Add the remaining sauce ingredients except the brown sugar, cream, and salt and pepper and return the pork to the casserole. Cover the casserole and simmer over low heat, turning the meat occasionally for even cooking, for 45 to 60 minutes or until a meat thermometer inserted into the middle of the loin reads 160°F.

3. Remove the loin from the sauce and keep it warm. Remove the cinnamon stick. Add the brown sugar and cream and reduce the sauce until it is slightly thickened, about 3 to 5 minutes. Add salt and pepper to taste and taste for seasoning.

4. To serve, remove the strings from around the pork, cut it into 1/2-inch slices, and overlap the slices on a platter with a rim. Spoon the sauce over the meat, garnish with chopped parsley, and serve immediately.

ADVANCE PREPARATION: Can be prepared up to 8 hours ahead through step 3 and refrigerated. Reheat the sauce and the meat gently over low heat.

---

* When you're working with chiles, always wear rubber gloves. Wash the cutting surface and knife immediately.

ASIAN GLAZED PORK TENDERLOIN

SERVES 4

THESE TENDER PORK tenderloins are bathed in a fragrant Asian-Californian mix of ingredients. You can either roast the pork in the oven or grill it on the barbecue. Hoisin sauce and sesame oil are available in the Asian section of your supermarket.

Begin with Asian Guacamole (page 24) and serve the pork with Rice Pilaf with Corn and Peanuts (page 306). For dessert, try Nectarine Cobbler with Dried Cherries (page 357).

RECOMMENDED WINE: To balance the sweetness in the glaze, the best wine choices are Zinfandel, Pinot Noir, and Syrah.

MARINADE
1   garlic clove, minced
1   teaspoon finely chopped fresh ginger
1   tablespoon hoisin sauce
2   scallions, white and light green parts only, finely sliced
1   tablespoon sherry vinegar
1   teaspoon finely chopped orange zest
1/3 cup fresh orange juice
1/2 teaspoon dark sesame oil
1   tablespoon vegetable oil
1/4 teaspoon salt
    pinch of black pepper

2   pork tenderloins, about 3/4 pound each

SAUCE
1/2 cup chicken stock (page 397)

GARNISH
orange slices

1. In a medium mixing bowl, combine all the marinade ingredients and whisk them until well blended. Taste for seasoning. Reserve 1/4 cup of marinade for the sauce. Place the tenderloins in a shallow medium nonaluminum dish. Pour the remaining marinade over the tenderloins, rolling them around until they are well coated. Marinate, covered, in the refrigerator for 2 to 4 hours.

2. Preheat the oven to 400°F. Place the pork tenderloins in a roasting pan and roast for 15 to 20 minutes or until an instant-read thermometer registers 160°F. Remove the pork from the oven and let it stand for 10 minutes. Or grill the pork on a medium-high-heat barbecue 3 inches from the heat for about 15 to 20 minutes, turning it as it browns.

3. While the pork is roasting, combine the reserved marinade with the stock and bring it to a boil.

4. To serve, slice the pork into 1/4-inch pieces and arrange the slices overlapping on a platter. Garnish with orange slices and spoon the sauce over the meat. Serve immediately.

ADVANCE PREPARATION: Can be prepared 4 hours ahead through step 1 and refrigerated.

SIDE DISHES

SAUTÉED GREEN AND YELLOW BEANS WITH GARLIC AND BASIL   271

TRICOLOR VEGETABLE SAUTÉ   272

CAULIFLOWER PUREE WITH TWO CHEESES   273

ROASTED WINTER VEGETABLES   274

ORANGE-GLAZED BEETS   276

BUTTERNUT SQUASH GRATIN WITH TOMATO FONDUE   277

HOME RANCH BUTTERNUT SQUASH   279

FAVA BEANS WITH RED ONIONS AND BACON   281

WHITE BEAN STEW WITH SPINACH AND TOMATOES   283

CORN BREAD, LEEK, AND RED PEPPER STUFFING TERRINE   285

ONION, PRUNE, AND CHESTNUT COMPOTE   288

ROASTED GARLIC MASHED POTATOES WITH LEEKS   290

LIGHT AND FLUFFY MASHED POTATOES   292

POTATOES VAUGIRARD   294

CRISPY POTATO PANCAKES WITH VEGETABLES   296

OVEN-ROASTED POTATOES WITH PARMESAN   298

ROASTED ONIONS AND BABY POTATOES   299

SPICED SWEET POTATO PUDDING   300

TOMATO-MINT BULGUR   302

SPICY ALMOND COUSCOUS   303

CONFETTI RICE PILAF   305

RICE PILAF WITH CORN AND PEANUTS   306

SPINACH RICE TIMBALES   307

SAUTÉED GREEN AND YELLOW BEANS WITH GARLIC AND BASIL

SERVES 4 TO 6

SAUTÉING YELLOW WAX beans and green beans over high heat in olive oil gives them a rich golden brown color. Mixing the beans with the Italian favorite combination of garlic and fresh basil brings out their inherent sweetness. Be sure to buy tender medium-size beans for best results. When I'm in the mood for just vegetables, a plate of these beans with a baked potato makes a satisfying supper. Or serve these with any simple grilled, roasted, or braised main course.

3/4 pound tender yellow wax beans, ends removed
3/4 pound tender green beans, ends removed
2 tablespoons olive oil
1 garlic clove, minced
2 tablespoons finely chopped fresh basil
   salt and pepper to taste

1. In a large saucepan, bring enough water to cover the beans to a boil. Immerse the beans and cook until tender but slightly resistant, about 5 to 7 minutes. Rinse the beans in cold water and drain them well.

2. Heat the olive oil in a medium skillet over medium heat. When the oil begins to sizzle, add the beans and stir, turning up the heat. Continue stirring the beans until they just begin to brown. Add the garlic and basil and cook for another 30 seconds. Remove the beans from the heat, add salt and pepper, and toss to combine. Taste for seasoning. Place the beans in a serving dish and serve immediately.

ADVANCE PREPARATION: Can be prepared up to 4 hours ahead through step 1 and kept at room temperature.

TRICOLOR VEGETABLE SAUTÉ

S E R V E S 4 T O 6

THIS SIMPLE, COLORFUL vegetable accompaniment goes with many entrées. Be sure to cut the vegetables the same size for even cooking.

1   tablespoon olive oil
2   medium zucchini, cut into 2- by 1/2-inch pieces
2   medium Japanese eggplant, cut into julienned or 2- by 1/2-inch pieces
1   red bell pepper, cut into julienne or 2- by 1/2-inch pieces
1   garlic clove, minced
2   tablespoons finely chopped scallions, light green and white parts only
1/4 cup chicken stock (page 397)
     salt and pepper to taste

1. In a medium skillet over medium-high heat, heat the oil, add the vegetables, and sauté, turning frequently, until slightly browned, about 3 to 5 minutes. Lower the heat, add the garlic and 1 tablespoon of the scallions, and continue sautéing for another minute. Turn up the heat, add the chicken stock, and continue cooking until the liquid is just about evaporated, about 1 to 2 minutes. Add salt and pepper and taste for seasoning. Place the vegetables in a serving dish and garnish with the remaining scallions. Serve immediately.

CAULIFLOWER PUREE WITH TWO CHEESES

SERVES 4

CAULIFLOWER AND CHEESE have a natural affinity. Here a puree of steamed cauliflower is enhanced by piquant yogurt and a combination of cheddar and Parmesan. Sometimes I'll serve this puree instead of mashed potatoes. Sweet petit peas make a nice accompaniment.

1   large head of cauliflower, cut into florets, tough stems removed
3   tablespoons plain nonfat yogurt or sour cream
1/2 cup shredded sharp cheddar cheese
1/4 cup freshly grated Parmesan
1/2 teaspoon salt
    pinch of white pepper

GARNISH
2   tablespoons finely chopped parsley

1. Place the cauliflower florets in a large saucepan with a steamer insert and cover a quarter of the way up with water. Cover, bring to a boil, reduce the heat to simmer, and cook for about 12 to 15 minutes or until tender. Drain well.

2. Place the cauliflower in a food processor fitted with the metal blade and puree. Add the remaining ingredients and process until well blended. Taste for seasoning. Spoon the cauliflower into a serving bowl and garnish with parsley.

ADVANCE PREPARATION: Can be prepared up to 1 day ahead and refrigerated. Reheat gently.

ROASTED WINTER VEGETABLES

S E R V E S   4

SWEET POTATOES, SWEET peppers, zucchini, and mushrooms are just a few other vegetables that can be added to this cozy vegetable mélange. It's difficult to make enough of this dish because even people who are not ordinarily vegetable lovers will ask for seconds. If you're feeding a crowd, it's easy to double or even triple this recipe.

Chicken stock adds moisture while reducing the need for excess oil. Adding the corn kernels at the end provides a delightful fresh corn flavor. Serve these colorful vegetables with Grilled Veal Chops with Zucchini-Corn Relish (page 254), Chicken with Garlic and Lime (page 204), or Rack of Lamb with Mint Crust (page 244).

3	carrots, peeled and cut into 1-inch chunks
2	medium leeks, white part only, cleaned and finely chopped
1	quart medium Brussels sprouts, cut in half if large
3	tablespoons olive oil
1-1/2	cups chicken stock (page 397)
1	teaspoon finely chopped fresh thyme leaves or 1/2 teaspoon dried
1/4	teaspoon salt
1/4	teaspoon black pepper
1	cup fresh corn kernels (about 2 medium ears) or thawed frozen

GARNISH
2　tablespoons finely chopped parsley

1. Preheat the oven to 400°F. In a large metal roasting pan, combine the carrots, leeks, and Brussels sprouts with 2 tablespoons of the oil and 1 cup of the stock. Add the thyme, salt, and pepper and mix well, being sure to coat all the vegetables evenly.

2. Place the roasting pan in the oven and roast for 30 minutes, turning the vegetables occasionally. Add the remaining oil and stock to the pan and continue roasting for 30 more minutes. The mixture should be brown and caramelized. You may need to turn up the oven to 425°F to help the vegetables caramelize a few minutes before adding the corn.

3. Five minutes before removing the vegetables from the oven, add the corn and cook until heated through and browned. Taste for seasoning. Spoon the vegetables into a large serving bowl and garnish with parsley. Serve immediately.

ADVANCE PREPARATION: Can be prepared 4 hours ahead through step 1, covered and kept at room temperature. Make sure the oven is preheated to 425°F before continuing.

HIGH-HEAT ROASTING

Whether you're roasting meat, poultry, or fish, high-heat roasting (425°F to 450°F) produces a crisp outer skin and a moist inner flesh. Certain vegetables with natural sugar, like corn, onions, and carrots, become particularly delicious and slightly caramelized when cooked in this manner with a little olive oil and simple seasoning. Tomatoes come alive when the high heat concentrates and enhances their natural sweetness. Make sure to use a low-sided roasting pan that is large enough to avoid overcrowding the vegetables. It's difficult to give an exact cooking time for each of the vegetables because of all of the variables—freshness, thickness and variety. Occasional stirring is necessary to brown the vegetables uniformly and keep them from sticking. The key is they should be nicely browned and slightly caramelized. This efficient method is a good alternative to traditional cooking methods.

ORANGE-GLAZED BEETS

SERVES 4 TO 6

I THINK OF beets as one of nature's culinary wonders because of their unique natural sweetness and deep rich red color. These simmered beets are finished with a light orange glaze that reinforces the sweet beet flavor. A helpful tip to deal with the red-dye effect beets leave on your skin is to wear rubber gloves and place a sheet of wax paper on your cutting board. Serve these with Grilled Lamb Chops with Cranberry-Rosemary Marinade (page 242) or Crispy Roast Chicken (page 208).

6   medium beets, peeled, cleaned, and quartered (2-inch wedges)
1   cup chicken stock (page 397)
2   tablespoons balsamic vinegar
1/4 cup fresh orange juice
1   teaspoon olive oil
1/2 tablespoon unsalted butter
1   tablespoon finely chopped parsley
1/2 teaspoon salt
1/8 teaspoon pepper

1. Combine the beets, stock, vinegar, orange juice, and oil in a medium non-aluminum Dutch oven over medium heat. Bring to a simmer, then reduce the heat and braise for about 30 to 45 minutes or until fork-tender when pierced with a fork.

2. Over high heat, reduce the remaining stock until it glazes the beets, stirring occasionally to coat the beets evenly. Add the butter, parsley, salt, and pepper and toss to coat the beets. Taste for seasoning and serve immediately.

ADVANCE PREPARATION: Can be prepared up to 1 day ahead through step 1 and refrigerated. Bring to room temperature to finish cooking.

BUTTERNUT SQUASH GRATIN WITH TOMATO FONDUE

SERVES 6 TO 8

I USED TO make this dish by first sautéing the squash in olive oil. Now I steam the squash to eliminate extra oil, and it actually tastes better. You can use any cheese you like. My favorites here are nutty Swiss, mild Monterey Jack, and extra-sharp cheddar. Serve this with a simple grilled entrée or as a substantial main dish. Begin with Mixed Greens with Beets and Peppers (page 85).

3   pounds butternut or other winter squash
2   tablespoons olive oil
3   medium leeks, white and light green parts only, cleaned and finely
        chopped
2   pounds fresh tomatoes, peeled, seeded, and chopped, or 4 cups diced
        drained canned tomatoes
1   tablespoon finely chopped fresh basil or 1/2 tablespoon dried
1   teaspoon finely chopped fresh thyme or 1/2 teaspoon dried
1   teaspoon salt
1/2 teaspoon black pepper
1/3 pound sharp cheddar, Monterey Jack, or Swiss cheese, shredded (1-1/2
        cups)

1. Carefully cut the peel from the squash, cut the squash in half, scoop out the seeds, and cut the flesh into 1-inch slices. Put 2 inches of water in the bottom of a large steamer and bring to a boil. Using tongs, carefully place the squash slices in the steamer, cover, and steam over medium heat for 15 to 20 minutes or until fork-tender. Transfer the squash to an oiled 9- by 12-inch oval gratin dish.

2. In a medium skillet over medium heat, heat the oil, add the leeks, and sauté for about 5 minutes or until softened. Add the tomatoes and cook over medium-high

heat, stirring frequently, for 10 minutes. Add the basil and thyme and cook until the sauce is quite thick, about 5 minutes. Add the salt and pepper and taste for seasoning.

3. Spoon the tomato mixture over the squash and then sprinkle the cheese evenly over the top.

4. Preheat the oven to 425°F. Bake for about 15 to 20 minutes or until the cheese is lightly browned and bubbly. Serve immediately.

ADVANCE PREPARATION: Can be prepared up to 8 hours ahead through step 3, covered, and refrigerated. Bring to room temperature before baking.

HOME RANCH BUTTERNUT SQUASH

SERVES 4

ON A TRIP to the Home Ranch in Steamboat Springs, Colorado, I tasted a dish of quickly sautéed butternut squash that was memorable for its simple, clear flavor. Inspired by that taste memory, I experimented with adding garlic and cumin to bright orange butternut squash with a surprisingly savory and slightly sweet result. This is a wonderful accompaniment to Glazed Halibut with Orange-Chive Sauce (page 176) or any simple grilled chicken, beef, or fish dish.

1   2-pound butternut squash
2   tablespoons olive oil
1   garlic clove, minced
1/4 teaspoon ground cumin
3/4 cup chicken stock (page 397)
1/2 teaspoon salt
1/4 teaspoon white pepper
2   tablespoons finely chopped parsley

1. Carefully cut the peel from the squash, cut the squash in half, scoop out the seeds, and cut the flesh into 1/4-inch dice.

2. In a large sauté pan over medium heat, heat the oil, add the squash, and sauté for about 3 to 5 minutes, until lightly browned, stirring frequently. Add the garlic and cumin and toss to coat, sautéing for a minute. Add the stock, turn up the heat to

medium high, cover, and cook for 5 to 7 minutes or until the squash is fork-tender. Remove the squash from the heat and add salt, pepper, and parsley, mixing to combine.

3. Taste for seasoning. Heat further if any excess moisture remains. Spoon into a serving bowl and serve immediately.

ADVANCE PREPARATION: Can be prepared up to 4 hours ahead through step 1, covered, and kept at room temperature.

FAVA BEANS WITH RED ONIONS AND BACON

SERVES 4 TO 6

FAVA BEANS, SOMETIMES called *broad beans* or *horse beans,* have a distinctive creamy, nutty flavor. In the past the best place to find fava beans was the local Italian market. Today, in the spring and summer months fava beans make their appearance in farmer's markets across the state as well as in many supermarkets.

While it takes a bit of time to shell and peel fresh fava beans, it's fun to enlist a friend or your kids to do the work together, discovering the different textures inside. Look for the smaller, younger beans, which have better flavor and are more tender. These beans go well with a simple grilled fish or chicken dish. This dish also makes a good first course, served slightly chilled with a touch of basic vinaigrette (page 410).

3   pounds fresh young fava beans
3   strips of bacon
1   tablespoon olive oil
1   medium red onion, finely chopped
2   teaspoons balsamic vinegar
2   tablespoons finely chopped parsley
1/4 teaspoon salt
    pinch of pepper

1. Shell the fava beans by removing them from the pod. If the beans are very young, they may not need to be skinned after shelling (the skin feels spongy), but if they are older and larger, the outer skin should be removed because it makes the beans tougher. Place these beans in a medium saucepan.

2. In a medium skillet over medium heat, cook the bacon until crisp. Drain on paper towels and cool. Crumble into tiny pieces and reserve.

3. In a medium skillet over medium heat, heat the oil, add the onion, and sauté slowly for about 10 minutes. Add 1 teaspoon of the vinegar and continue cooking until the onions are light brown and just beginning to caramelize. Reserve in the pan.

4. Cover the beans with water by 1/2 inch and bring them to a simmer. Simmer over medium heat for a few minutes or until tender, 2 to 5 minutes.

5. When the beans are cooked, add them to the pan with the onions. Add the bacon, remaining vinegar, parsley, salt, and pepper and cook over medium heat until heated through, about a minute, mixing to combine. Taste for seasoning. Serve immediately.

ADVANCE PREPARATION: The fava beans can be shelled 8 hours ahead and the dish prepared up to 4 hours ahead through step 3 and kept at room temperature.

WHITE BEAN STEW WITH SPINACH AND TOMATOES

SERVES 6

WHITE BEANS BECOME creamy as they cook, allowing the juices to thicken slightly. Fresh seasonings of tomato and spinach heighten the simple white bean's taste. Serve this as an accompaniment to Grilled Steaks with Olivada and Port Wine Sauce (page 240). I also like to serve this stew as a main-course dish for a luncheon that begins with Peppery Greens with Gorgonzola and Pine Nuts (page 80). If you're serving this as a main course or first course, present it in shallow soup bowls and pass the Parmesan separately.

2   cups (1 pound) dried large white beans
2   tablespoons olive oil
1   medium onion, finely chopped
2   garlic cloves, minced
2   medium tomatoes, peeled, seeded, and finely chopped
4   cups chicken stock (page 397)
1   large bunch of spinach, leaves only, cleaned and torn into bite-size
     pieces
1   teaspoon salt
1/4 teaspoon pepper
1   teaspoon balsamic vinegar
1/4 cup freshly grated Parmesan

1. Cover the beans with cold water and soak overnight or do a quick soak by bringing the beans and just enough water to cover them to a boil, cooking for 2 minutes, covering, and letting them stand for 1 hour. Drain the soaked beans and set aside.

2. In a medium Dutch oven over medium heat, heat the oil, add the onion, and sauté for about 3 minutes or until softened. Add the garlic and sauté for another minute. Add the tomatoes, stock, and beans. Simmer, covered, for 1-1/2 to 2-1/4 hours or until the beans are tender.

3. Add the spinach and braise, covered, for 3 minutes or until slightly wilted. Add the salt, pepper, and vinegar and mix to combine. Taste for seasoning.

4. To serve, spoon the beans into a serving bowl or individual bowls and sprinkle with Parmesan. Serve immediately.

ADVANCE PREPARATION: Can be prepared up to 8 hours ahead and refrigerated. Bring to room temperature and reheat gently over low heat.

CORN BREAD, LEEK, AND RED PEPPER STUFFING TERRINE

SERVES 8 TO 10

THIS SAVORY DISH is a holiday showstopper. Crusty corn bread stuffing is molded in a terrine shape, then baked, unmolded, and surrounded by a parsley garnish or, my favorite, Roasted Winter Vegetables (page 274). Be sure to have both a flat serving spatula and a large serving spoon on hand for serving. Canned water chestnuts impart a crunchy contrast to the smooth stuffing texture. You can substitute toasted pecans for the water chestnuts if you prefer. Serve this with turkey, chicken, or duck.

In my home, stuffing is a highly prized part of the holiday dinner, so I make at least two. If you like a more complex stuffing, omit the red pepper and water chestnuts and add to this one 1/2 pound cooked Chicken and Apple Sausage (page 223), 1/2 cup finely chopped dried apricots, 1/2 cup dried cranberries, and some cooked chestnuts. Add up to 1/2 cup extra melted butter and 1/2 cup chicken stock. This will stuff a 16-pound bird with enough left over to fill a medium casserole.

3 tablespoons unsalted butter
2 tablespoons olive oil
3 medium leeks, white part only, cleaned and finely chopped
4 celery ribs, sliced
1 pound mushrooms, sliced
1 medium red bell pepper, chopped into 1/2-inch pieces
2 garlic cloves, minced
6 cups corn bread for stuffing (page 399), crumbled and toasted
1 8-ounce can sliced water chestnuts, rinsed well and drained
1/2 cup finely chopped parsley
1/4 teaspoon black pepper

1/2 teaspoon salt
1   teaspoon finely chopped fresh sage or 1/2 teaspoon dried
1   teaspoon finely chopped fresh thyme or 1/2 teaspoon dried
1/2 cup chicken or turkey stock (page 397)
4   tablespoons unsalted butter, melted
2   tablespoons crumbled corn bread

1. In a large skillet over medium heat, melt 2 tablespoons of the butter and 1 tablespoon of the olive oil, add the leeks, and sauté stirring frequently, until softened about 3 minutes. Transfer the leeks to a large mixing bowl. Melt the remaining butter and olive oil in the skillet, add the celery and mushrooms, and sauté until slightly softened about 3 to 5 minutes. Add the red pepper and garlic and sauté for a few more minutes, making sure the red pepper is still firm. Transfer to the large bowl.

2. Add the toasted corn bread, water chestnuts, parsley, pepper, salt, sage, and thyme to the stuffing and mix well. Slowly add the stock and 3 tablespoons of the melted butter. Mix carefully, making sure the stuffing is moist but not too compact, especially if you're planning to stuff a turkey. Taste for seasoning.

3. Grease a 9-1/2- by 5-1/2-inch loaf pan and transfer the stuffing to it. The stuffing can be compacted because it will not expand in the pan. Sprinkle the crumbled corn bread on top and drizzle with the remaining tablespoon of melted butter. Cover the stuffing well with foil. You can also place this stuffing in a medium baking dish and serve it right from the dish.

4. Preheat the oven to 375°F. Bake the stuffing for 1 hour. Remove the foil for the last 15 minutes of baking to create a crunchy topping. Unmold the stuffing onto a platter and then reverse it onto a rectangular platter so that the brown side is right side up. Garnish with watercress, parsley, or colorful cooked vegetables and serve immediately. A cake slicer works best for serving.

ADVANCE PREPARATION: Can be prepared up to 1 day ahead through step 3, covered, and refrigerated. Remove from the refrigerator 1 hour before baking.

HOW TO PEEL A BELL PEPPER

Select firm-fleshed, thick-skinned peppers so they'll retain their texture when grilled or broiled. Place the whole peppers on a broiler pan or a barbecue grill and broil approximately 4 inches from the heat until the skin is blistered and slightly charred on all sides. Always use long tongs to turn the peppers. Never pierce the pepper, or the juices will escape. Put the peppers in a brown paper bag and close it tightly. Let the peppers rest for 10 minutes. Remove the peppers from the bag and drain them. Peel off the charred skin with your fingers. Make a slit in each pepper and open it up. Core and cut off the stem. Scrape the seeds and ribs from the peppers. Cut the peppers with a sharp knife or a pizza cutter into slices.

ONION, PRUNE, AND CHESTNUT COMPOTE

SERVES 8 TO 10

MY FRIEND LAURIE Burrows Grad suggested I prepare a version of this compote on Thanksgiving a few years back. This particular combination of tastes and textures—California prunes, cooked chestnuts, and braised baby onions—turned out to be inspired. Now I include this compote on my holiday table each year, served warm or at room temperature. Buy vacuum-packed cooked chestnuts to save a lot of time shelling them. Although similar to a relish, this compote seems more like a vegetable when served warm.

1	pint pearl onions
3	tablespoons unsalted butter
1-1/2	cups veal stock (page 395) or beef stock
1	cup good-quality sweet or semi-sweet port wine, divided
2	cups pitted, dried medium prunes
2	cups whole chestnuts, roasted and peeled
1/2	teaspoon salt
1/2	teaspoon pepper
2	teaspoons finely chopped fresh thyme (lemon thyme if possible) or 1 teaspoon dried

GARNISH
fresh thyme leaves

1. Immerse the onions in a large pan of boiling water for 15 seconds. Rinse them with cold water and drain. Trim off the top and bottom of the onion, being sure to keep the root on. Remove the outer skin and first layer with your fingers. Pierce a cross about 1/8 inch deep at the root of each onion so that they will cook evenly and not burst.

2. Melt 2 tablespoons of the butter in a medium skillet over medium heat. Add the peeled onions and sauté, rolling them on all sides to coat them evenly, until all sides are nicely browned, about 7 to 10 minutes. Add 1 cup of the stock and bring it to a boil. Reduce the heat and simmer, covered, until the onions are translucent and soft, about 20 to 25 minutes. (If the heat is too high, the onions will burst before they finish cooking.) Reserve.

3. Combine 3/4 cup of the port, the prunes, and the remaining 1/2 cup of stock in a medium saucepan over medium-high heat. Bring the prunes to a boil, then reduce the heat and simmer for about 10 minutes or until the prunes are soft but not mushy. Transfer the prunes and juice to the onion mixture and reduce the liquid to a thin glaze over medium heat, about 3 more minutes.

4. Melt the remaining tablespoon of butter in a medium skillet over medium heat. Add the chestnuts and heat them through. Add the remaining 1/4 cup port and reduce the mixture until the chestnuts are lightly glazed, about 3 minutes. Transfer the chestnuts to the onion-prune mixture and add the salt, pepper, and thyme. Taste for seasoning. Spoon into a serving bowl and garnish with the fresh thyme. Serve warm or at room temperature.

ADVANCE PREPARATION: Can be prepared 3 days ahead, covered, and refrigerated. Bring the compote to room temperature before gently reheating it over low heat. The mixture may become very thick. To thin it out, add a small amount of additional stock and port and heat gently until the sauce is slightly thickened. Taste for seasoning.

ROASTED GARLIC MASHED POTATOES WITH LEEKS

SERVES 6 TO 8

WHEN YOU'RE IN the mood to indulge, try these creamy mashed potatoes. Nutty-rich roasted garlic, sweet sautéed leeks, and fruity olive oil add a California-Mediterranean touch to simple mashed potatoes. These are a must on my holiday dinner table. Try them as a bed for simple grilled salmon or as an accompaniment to Marinated Roast Turkey (page 216), or Roasted Cornish Hens with Honey Tangerine Marinade (page 212).

2 tablespoons unsalted butter
1 medium leek, white and light green parts only, cleaned and finely chopped
3 pounds Yellow Finn, Yukon Gold, or White or Red Rose potatoes, peeled and cut into 3-inch chunks
  pulp of 1 head of roasted garlic (about 1 tablespoon) (page 203)
2 tablespoons unsalted butter, cut into pieces
1 tablespoon olive oil
1 cup half-and-half, heated
  salt and white pepper to taste

GARNISH
2 tablespoons finely chopped parsley

1. In a medium sauté pan over medium heat, melt the butter, add the leeks, and sauté for 5 to 7 minutes or until softened, stirring occasionally. Reserve.

2. Immerse the potatoes in cold water for 5 minutes to remove excess starch. In a large pot of boiling salted water, cook the potatoes for about 15 minutes or until

fork-tender. Drain and return them to the pot. Over high heat, dry them, tossing occasionally, for about 1 or 2 minutes or until all the moisture is evaporated.

3. Put the potato cubes and garlic pulp through a ricer or mash them with a masher in a large mixing bowl. Add the butter and oil and slowly pour in the half-and-half, stirring until the potatoes are very creamy but not soupy. Add the reserved leeks, salt, and pepper. To serve, transfer the potatoes to a serving bowl and garnish with parsley. Serve immediately.

ADVANCE PREPARATION: Can be prepared up to 2 hours ahead, covered, and kept at room temperature. Reheat gently in the top of a double boiler over medium heat. Add extra half-and-half as needed. Taste for seasoning.

LIGHT AND FLUFFY MASHED POTATOES

SERVES 6 TO 8

THIS LIGHTER VERSION of mashed potatoes is slightly tangy because it contains yogurt. Yukon Gold or Yellow Finn potatoes have a pleasing consistency for mashed potatoes. I have also used the exotic Peruvian purple potato for this recipe, much to the amusement of my guests, who are invariably fascinated by the color. The choice of potato is yours: starchy potatoes like russets will turn out fluffier; yellow, red, or white potatoes will have a creamier texture. Serve this with Crispy Roast Chicken (page 208), Baked Salmon with Red Onion Sauce (page 169), or Veal Stew with Orange Sauce (page 258).

3   pounds Yellow Finn, Yukon Gold, or Idaho baking potatoes, peeled
        and cut into 3-inch chunks
2   tablespoons unsalted butter
3/4 cup low-fat milk
1   cup plain nonfat yogurt
1/2 teaspoon salt
     pinch of white pepper
1   tablespoon finely chopped fresh chives

1. Immerse the potatoes in cold water for 5 minutes to remove excess starch. In a large pot of boiling salted water, cook the potatoes for about 15 to 20 minutes or until fork-tender. Drain and return them to the pot. Over high heat, dry the potatoes tossing them occasionally, for about 1 or 2 minutes or until all the moisture is evaporated.

2. Put the potatoes through a potato ricer or mash them with a potato masher in a large mixing bowl. In a medium saucepan over medium heat, combine the butter and milk and bring to a simmer. Pour over the potato mixture and blend well. Add the yogurt, salt, pepper, and chives and blend well into the potatoes. Taste for seasoning. Transfer to a serving bowl and serve immediately.

ADVANCE PREPARATION: Can be prepared up to 2 hours ahead, covered, and kept at room temperature. Reheat gently in the top of a double boiler over medium heat. Add extra milk as needed. Taste for seasoning.

POTATOES VAUGIRARD

SERVES 6

WHEN I LIVED in Paris, I often made this simple dish using potatoes from the open-air market and cheese from the local *fromagerie.* Named after the Vaugirard market where I shopped each Sunday, these potatoes are easy to make and a real favorite among my family and friends.

I tried many different cheeses and potatoes for those leisurely Sunday lunches and thought I had found the best varieties. When I returned to Los Angeles, however, I discovered that the creamy Yellow Finn or Yukon Gold potatoes work best for this potato dish. They also give off their own buttery qualities, making the addition of butter to flavor and moisten the potatoes unnecessary. Don't worry if you can't find these golden gems, however. The recipe works well with plain old Idahos. I serve this dish frequently with roasted meats, grilled meats, and poultry.

2-1/2 pounds Yellow Finn, Yukon Gold, or Idaho baking potatoes
3   garlic cloves, minced
2   tablespoons finely chopped parsley
1-1/2 cups shredded Swiss Gruyère cheese
1/4   teaspoon black pepper
1-1/2 cups chicken stock (page 397)

1. Preheat the oven to 375°F. Slice (do not peel) the potatoes using the medium slicing disk on a food processor or a sharp knife into 1/4-inch slices. Combine the garlic, parsley, cheese, and pepper in a small mixing bowl.

2. Grease a 2-quart baking dish such as a soufflé dish. Layer the potatoes in thirds, sprinkling the garlic-cheese mixture over each layer, reserving the last third of the

garlic-cheese mixture. Pour the chicken stock over the potatoes and then sprinkle the rest of the garlic-cheese mixture evenly over the top.

3. Bake, uncovered, for 50 to 60 minutes, or until the top is brown and crusty and the potatoes are fork-tender. Serve immediately.

ADVANCE PREPARATION: Can be prepared up to 2 hours ahead through step 2, covered, and kept at room temperature.

CRISPY POTATO PANCAKES WITH VEGETABLES

MAKES 12 TO 14 PANCAKES; SERVES 6 TO 8

FRESH POTATO PANCAKES or latkes taste best when they're still warm, but it's a trick to cook large quantities and keep them crisp and warm at the same time. From years of experience I have found a number of shortcuts to make the chore more manageable.

If you follow my method for freezing the pancakes, you'll get excellent results. Also, with thanks to my colleague and good friend Ellen Brown, the one-step food processor method makes the usually tedious work of making the pancakes a snap. You can make up the batter without shredding the potatoes and vegetables, yielding near-perfect results.

Remember, you can make as many batches of potato pancakes as you want, pour them into a large mixing bowl, and fry the pancakes as needed. In this version, carrot and zucchini are added for color and texture. If you prefer all potatoes, simply omit the carrot and zucchini and add an additional potato. Serve these with Asian Pear-Quince-Apple Sauce.

1   medium onion, quartered
2   large eggs
1   medium baking potato, peeled and cut into 1-inch cubes
1   small zucchini, cut into 1-inch cubes
1   small carrot, cut into 1-inch cubes
1/2 teaspoon salt
     pinch of black pepper
2   tablespoons all-purpose flour
     vegetable oil for frying

1   cup Asian Pear-Quince-Apple Sauce (page 423) or your
        favorite apple sauce

1. Puree the onion and eggs together in a food processor fitted with the metal blade until they're smooth and fluffy. Add the potatoes, zucchini, and carrot cubes and pulse until the mixture is finely chopped but retains some texture. Add the salt, pepper, and flour and quickly process to combine. *Do not overprocess.* Pour the batter into a medium mixing bowl.

2. Let the batter sit for 15 minutes, covered with plastic wrap to prevent discoloration.

3. Heat 3/4 inch of oil in a large nonstick skillet over medium-high heat. Pour a tablespoon of batter into the skillet to test the oil. If it is hot enough, the pancake will begin to sizzle and brown. Spoon tablespoons of the batter into the skillet, making sure there's a little room between pancakes. Flatten them with the back of a spoon and use the spatula to round out the sides if necessary. Fry the pancakes until golden brown on one side, then turn them and brown the other side.

4. Transfer the pancakes to a cookie sheet lined with 2 layers of paper towels. Allow the excess oil to drain. If you're serving these immediately, place the pancakes on a platter and serve with the Asian Pear-Quince-Apple Sauce.

ADVANCE PREPARATION: To freeze the latkes, lay them on a double sheet of aluminum foil and enclose the pancakes tightly in the foil. Make sure the pancakes are cool and then place on a flat surface in the freezer. When you're ready to serve, preheat the oven to 425°F and place the foil packets on a baking sheet. Remove the top sheet of foil so that the pancakes will bake and become crispy. Bake the frozen pancakes for 5 to 7 minutes until brown and crisp.

OVEN-ROASTED POTATOES WITH PARMESAN

SERVES 6

THESE TASTE LIKE french-fried potato wedges, though very little oil is used. Serve these crispy potatoes as an accompaniment to Broiled Orange Roughy with Salsa Glaze (page 181) or Grilled Roast Beef with Shallot-Chive Sauce (page 233).

3   pounds medium Idaho, Yellow Finn, or Yukon Gold potatoes,
      unpeeled
3   tablespoons olive oil
1   teaspoon salt
1/4 teaspoon black pepper
1/2 cup freshly grated Parmesan
2   tablespoons finely chopped parsley

1. Preheat the oven to 425°F. Rinse the potatoes and pat them dry. Cut each potato into 2-inch wedges.

2. Combine the oil, salt, and pepper in a large mixing bowl and mix well. Toss the potato wedges in the oil mixture until they're evenly coated.

3. Arrange the potato wedges on an oiled baking sheet and bake them for 25 to 30 minutes, turning every 10 minutes since they tend to stick to the pan. The potatoes are done when they're tender and golden brown.

4. Turn the potatoes into a large serving dish and toss them with the Parmesan and parsley, evenly coating all the wedges. Serve immediately.

ADVANCE PREPARATION: Can be prepared up to 2 hours ahead through step 3 and kept at room temperature. Reheat in a 350°F oven for 10 to 15 minutes and then toss with the Parmesan and parsley just before serving.

ROASTED ONIONS AND BABY POTATOES

Serves 4 to 6

THIS IS ONE of those versatile potato dishes that go with almost any main course. The potatoes turn incredibly smooth on the inside and crusty and brown outside, while the onion slices and leeks add a rich caramel crispness. I like to use golfball-size or even smaller creamer potatoes for this dish. If you can't find small ones, just cut the larger ones into 1 1/2-inch pieces. This dish is equally appropriate as an accompaniment to a frittata at brunch or with Grilled Veal Chops with Zucchini-Corn Relish (page 254), or Rack of Lamb with Mint Crust (page 244) at dinner.

2   pounds red or purple new potatoes
2   tablespoons olive oil
3/4 teaspoon salt
1/4 teaspoon pepper
2   medium onions, cut into eighths and sectioned
1   medium leek, white part and light green part only, thinly sliced
1/2 cup chicken stock (page 397)
1   tablespoon finely chopped chives

1. Preheat the oven to 425°F. Combine the potatoes, olive oil, salt, and pepper in a roasting pan. Coat the potatoes evenly with a large spoon or shake the pan from side to side until all the potatoes are coated.

2. Roast the potatoes for 20 minutes. Add the onion sections, leeks, and chicken stock and stir to combine evenly. Continue shaking every 10 to 15 minutes, until the potatoes are brown and crusty and the onions are lightly caramelized, about 3/4 to 1 hour more. Taste for seasoning. Spoon into a serving bowl and garnish with chives. Serve immediately.

SPICED SWEET POTATO PUDDING

SERVES 8 TO 12

DURING THE HOLIDAYS people seem to gravitate toward the familiar no matter how adventurous they are in their eating habits during the rest of the year. I find myself at odds with my family each year as I try to suggest a different version of sweet potatoes with marshmallows. Spiced Sweet Potato Pudding has been my only success.

With its a creamy interior and sweet, crunchy topping, this soufflé pudding begs the question—is it a side dish or dessert? However you serve this comforting dish, it's always a hit. I prefer the deep reddish mahogany–skinned sweet potato (often called a *yam*) for its sweeter flesh and creamier texture over the lighter-colored sweet potato.

You can usually find Amaretti cookies by Lazzaroni, wrapped two to a package, at Italian delicatessens. If they aren't available, substitute gingersnaps. A 2-quart soufflé dish makes a pretty presentation. Serve this with Marinated Roast Turkey (page 216).

TOPPING

1/2 cup coarsely chopped blanched slivered almonds
10 Amaretti cookies, crumbled (5 packages of 2)
1/4 cup packed dark brown sugar

PUDDING

4   medium sweet potatoes (about 2 pounds) to make 4 cups puree
1/2 cup half-and-half
2   tablespoons unsalted butter, melted
1/3 cup fresh orange juice
3   tablespoons packed dark brown sugar

2   tablespoons orange marmalade
1   teaspoon ground cinnamon
1/4 teaspoon ground ginger
1/4 teaspoon ground allspice
1/8 teaspoon white pepper
1/8 teaspoon freshly grated nutmeg
2   teaspoons finely chopped orange zest
4   large egg yolks
5   large egg whites
1/4 teaspoon salt
1/4 teaspoon cream of tartar

2   tablespoons unsalted butter, cut into small pieces

1. For the topping, preheat the oven to 350°F and toast the almonds on a baking sheet for 7 to 10 minutes or until brown. Combine the toasted almonds with the cookie crumbs and brown sugar. Set aside.

2. Preheat the oven to 400°F. Wrap each sweet potato in foil, place on a cookie sheet, and bake for 45 to 60 minutes or until very soft. Turn the oven temperature down to 350°F (or turn the oven off if you're preparing this ahead). Cool and spoon the pulp into a medium mixing bowl, measuring out 4 cups. Add the half-and-half, melted butter, orange juice, brown sugar, marmalade, all of the spices, and the orange zest and mix with an electric mixer on low speed. Slowly add the egg yolks, incorporating one at a time.

3. In a large mixing bowl, beat the egg whites until foamy and then add the salt and cream of tartar. Continue beating until stiff peaks form. Fold them into the potato mixture carefully, making sure no streaks remain. Spoon the mixture into a greased deep 2-quart casserole dish. Sprinkle the topping mixture over the potato mixture evenly. Dot with the cut-up butter.

4. Bake the pudding in a 350°F oven for 1-1/4 hours. When puffed and browned, remove it from the oven and serve immediately.

ADVANCE PREPARATION: Can be prepared up to 1 day ahead through step 2 and refrigerated. The topping can be covered and kept at room temperature. Bring the potatoes to room temperature before continuing.

TOMATO-MINT BULGUR

SERVES 6

BULGUR IS WHEAT that has been steamed and then dried before being ground or crushed, which is why it cooks so quickly. Don't mistake bulgur for cracked wheat, which takes much longer to cook and has an entirely different texture. This Mediterranean-inspired dish gives the heavy-textured bulgur grain a fresh, light style. Serve this with Lamb Brochettes with Crunchy Raita (page 247).

2	tablespoons olive oil
1	medium onion, finely chopped
1-1/2 cups	coarsely ground bulgur
3	cups chicken stock (page 397)
2	tablespoons finely chopped fresh mint
8	red or yellow cherry tomatoes or a combination, quartered
1/2	teaspoon salt
1/4	teaspoon black pepper

GARNISH
fresh mint sprigs

1. In a deep large skillet over medium heat, heat the oil, add the onion, and sauté for 5 minutes or until softened. Add the bulgur to the skillet and toast it for 2 or 3 minutes, stirring frequently.

2. Add the stock and bring the mixture to a boil. Reduce the heat, cover, and cook over low heat for 12 to 15 minutes or until all the liquid is absorbed. Remove the bulgur from the heat and add the mint and tomatoes, blending carefully so that the tomato pieces stay whole. Add the salt and pepper and taste for seasoning. Garnish with mint sprigs and serve immediately.

SPICY ALMOND COUSCOUS

SERVES 4

BE SURE TO buy the five-minute couscous for this recipe. This is a wonderful last-minute side dish with assertive flavors, so match it up with harmonious-flavored dishes. You can double this recipe if you're serving a large group. Try serving this with Grilled Lamb Chops with Cranberry-Rosemary Marinade (page 242) or Glazed Orange-Hoisin Chicken (page 210).

2	tablespoons slivered blanched almonds
1-1/2	cups water
1	small zucchini, diced into 1/4-inch pieces
1-1/2	cups chicken stock (page 397)
1	tablespoon unsalted butter
1	cup quick-cooking couscous
1/4	teaspoon ground cumin
1	tablespoon finely chopped cilantro
1	tablespoon finely chopped fresh mint
3	tablespoons golden raisins
1/2	teaspoon salt
1/4	teaspoon black pepper

1. Preheat the oven to 350°F. Place the almonds on a baking sheet and toast them in the oven for 5 to 7 minutes or until lightly browned. Or place them in a nonstick skillet over medium heat and toast for 3 or 4 minutes or until lightly browned. Set aside.

2. Heat the water in a medium saucepan over medium-high heat until it is simmering. Add the zucchini, cover, and cook for 4 minutes. Drain the zucchini in a colander and set aside.

3. Heat the stock and butter in a medium saucepan over medium heat and bring it to a boil. Add the couscous and cover. Remove the couscous from the heat and let it stand for 5 minutes.

4. Add the remaining ingredients, toss to combine, and taste for seasoning. Serve immediately.

ADVANCE PREPARATION: Can be prepared up to 2 hours ahead and kept at room temperature. Reheat carefully in the top of a double boiler over medium heat for 10 minutes.

CONFETTI RICE PILAF

Serves 4 to 6

WHEN YOU'RE LOOKING for a rice side dish that is flavorful but not overpowering, this is it, the dish I fall back on time and time again. Sautéing the rice first results in a more intense flavor. Leeks, carrots, zucchini, and parsley add lots of color. Serve this dish with Asian Glazed Pork Tenderloin (page 266), Glazed Halibut with Orange-Chive Sauce (page 176), or Roasted Cornish Hens with Honey Tangerine Marinade (page 212).

2	tablespoons olive oil
1	small leek, white part only, cleaned and finely chopped
1-1/2	cups long-grain rice
1	small carrot, peeled and shredded
1	small zucchini, shredded
3	cups hot water or chicken stock (page 397)
1	teaspoon salt
1/4	teaspoon pepper
2	tablespoons finely chopped fresh parsley
2	tablespoons freshly grated Parmesan

1. In a medium saucepan over medium heat, heat the oil, add the leek, and sauté for 3 minutes or until it is slightly soft. Turn up the heat to high and add the rice. Brown the rice for about 3 minutes, stirring constantly. Reduce the heat to medium, add the carrot and zucchini, and continue to stir for another minute.

2. Add the hot water to the rice, stir with a fork, and bring to a boil. Cover and reduce the heat to medium-low. Let the rice simmer for about 20 minutes, cooking until all liquid has been absorbed and the rice is tender.

3. Add the salt, pepper, parsley and Parmesan and blend them in with a large fork. Taste for seasoning and serve immediately.

ADVANCE PREPARATION: Can be prepared up to 2 hours ahead and kept at room temperature. Reheat carefully in the top part of a double boiler over medium heat for 10 minutes.

RICE PILAF WITH CORN AND PEANUTS

SERVES 4

HERE'S A RICE dish that easily multiplies and goes well with Asian entrées like Indonesian Leg of Lamb (page 250) or Glazed Orange-Hoisin Chicken (page 210). Dry roasted peanuts and corn create unusual textural interest.

1   tablespoon olive oil
4   scallions, white and light green parts only, finely chopped
1   cup long-grain rice
2   cups chicken stock (page 397)
1/2 cup corn kernels (about 1 medium ear)
1/2 teaspoon salt
1/4 teaspoon pepper
1/4 cup roasted peanuts
2   tablespoons finely chopped parsley

1. In a medium saucepan over medium heat, heat the oil, add the scallions, and sauté for 3 minutes or until slightly soft. Turn up the heat to high and add the rice. Brown the rice for about 3 minutes, stirring constantly.

2. Add the stock, stir with a fork, and bring to a boil. Reduce the heat to medium-low, cover, and simmer for 12 to 15 minutes, cooking until almost all the liquid has been absorbed. Add the corn and cook for about 3 to 5 minutes, until the rice is tender.

3. Add the salt, pepper, peanuts, and parsley and blend them in with a large fork. Taste for seasoning and serve immediately.

ADVANCE PREPARATION: Can be prepared up to 2 hours ahead and kept at room temperature. Reheat carefully in the top part of a double boiler over medium heat for 10 minutes.

SPINACH RICE TIMBALES
SERVES 6 TO 8

THESE LITTLE TOWERS of green rice make a particularly pretty presentation. You can also serve this as a side dish without molding the rice. Just spoon it into a bowl and serve it as is.

2   tablespoons olive oil
2   medium shallots, minced
4   medium mushrooms, finely chopped
1   10-ounce bunch of spinach, cleaned and torn into 1-inch pieces
1   quart water or chicken stock (page 397)
2   cups long-grain rice
1/4 teaspoon salt
     pinch of black pepper
1   cup freshly grated Parmesan
2   tablespoons finely chopped fresh basil or parsley

1. In a large skillet over medium heat, heat 1 tablespoon of the oil, add the shallots, and sauté for 3 minutes. Add the mushrooms and continue sautéing until the mushrooms are soft and there is no liquid in the pan, about 3 to 4 minutes. Add the spinach, turn up the heat to medium high, cover, and cook for 2 or 3 minutes or until the spinach is wilted, stirring once. Reserve.

2. Combine the water and remaining olive oil in a medium saucepan and bring it to a boil over medium-high heat. Stir in the rice, cover, and reduce the heat to medium-low. Cook the rice for 15 to 20 minutes or until all the liquid is absorbed. Stir in the vegetable mixture, salt, pepper, Parmesan, and herbs with a large fork. Taste for seasoning.

3. Lightly oil six 8-ounce or eight 6-ounce timbale molds or custard cups. Spoon the rice mixture evenly into the molds, making sure the mixture is compact. To serve, invert the molds onto serving plates by tapping the molds to release them. Serve immediately.

ADVANCE PREPARATION: Can be prepared up to 4 hours ahead through step 1 and kept at room temperature.

BREADS

PARMESAN TOASTS   311

SUN-DRIED TOMATO TOASTS   312

SPICED PUMPKIN-HAZELNUT BREAD   313

CIJI'S SCONES WITH CURRANTS   315

ORANGE–POPPY SEED BREAD   317

FRESH PEAR BREAD   318

MAPLE CORN MUFFINS   320

CORN TORTILLAS   322

CRISP TORTILLA CHIPS   324

COUNTRY SOURDOUGH BREAD   327

SOURDOUGH RYE ROLLS   330

WALNUT BREAD   332

JALAPEÑO CHEESE BREAD AND RUSTIC BREAD STICKS   334

FOCACCIA   337

PIZZA DOUGH   340

PARMESAN TOASTS

MAKES 24 TOASTS

IN THE 1950s Perino's Restaurant in Los Angeles was famous for what we used to call continental cuisine and for its warm pumpernickel toasts. These delectable little toasts of French bread with a melted layer of freshly grated Parmesan are more traditional, though they're also good made with pumpernickel. I like to serve the crispy toasts with a variety of tapenades. Or sprinkle slivers of marinated sun-dried tomatoes over them. You can easily double or triple this recipe for a large party.

24 thin slices of French or sourdough baguette
2   tablespoons unsalted butter, melted
2   tablespoons olive oil
1/3 cup freshly grated Parmesan

1. Preheat the oven to 375°F. Place the bread slices on a cookie sheet and toast them for 5 minutes.

2. Meanwhile, combine the melted butter with the olive oil in a small bowl. Brush each toast with the mixture. Place the Parmesan on a flat plate and press each slice into the cheese to coat it evenly. Return the toasts to the baking sheet and bake them for about 5 to 7 minutes or until the cheese is melted but not browned. Watch carefully. Cool.

ADVANCE PREPARATION: Can be prepared up to 1 week ahead and stored in an airtight container.

SUN-DRIED TOMATO TOASTS

MAKES 24 TOASTS

YOU CAN MAKE your own sun-dried tomato paste by combining softened sun-dried tomatoes with a bit of olive oil in a food processor fitted with the metal blade and pureeing until the mixture becomes a paste. But of course store-bought paste works perfectly here. These crispy toasts are delicious with cheese and on top of soups or salads for extra flavor.

24   thin slices of French or sourdough baguette
1/3   cup olive oil
2 to 3 tablespoons sun-dried tomato paste or pesto (page 404)

1. Preheat the oven to 375°F. Place the bread slices on a cookie sheet and toast them for 5 minutes.

2. In a small mixing bowl, combine the oil and tomato paste and mix until well blended. Brush the tomato mixture evenly on each toast. Return the toasts to the baking sheet and bake for 5 minutes or until baked through. Cool and store in an airtight container.

ADVANCE PREPARATION: Can be prepared up to 1 week ahead and stored in an airtight container.

SPICED PUMPKIN-HAZELNUT BREAD

MAKES TWO 4- BY 8-INCH LOAVES

I LOVE THE smell of bread baking in my kitchen, and this recipe has a particularly wonderful fragrance. Toasted hazelnuts add just the right flavor to the orange-scented bread. If you can't find hazelnuts, sliced almonds are a good alternative.

Offer small slices of this quick bread accompanied by orange-honey butter and a hot cup of tea on a cool afternoon. If you're wondering why this recipe makes two loaves, look in the dessert chapter. There you'll find Pumpkin Bread Pudding with Eggnog Brandy Sauce (page 373), a sublime ending to any cold-weather meal, which uses the second loaf.

1/2 cup chopped hazelnuts
4   tablespoons unsalted butter, softened
1/2 cup plus 2 tablespoons firmly packed dark brown sugar
1/2 cup granulated sugar
2   large eggs
1   teaspoon finely chopped orange zest
1/2 cup fresh orange juice
1   cup canned pumpkin puree
2   cups all-purpose flour
1/4 teaspoon salt
2   teaspoons baking powder
1/2 teaspoon baking soda
2   teaspoons pumpkin pie spice or 1/2 teaspoon each of ground
       cinnamon, nutmeg, ginger, and allspice
1/2 cup golden raisins

1. Preheat the oven to 350°F. Grease and flour two 4- by 8-inch loaf pans. Place the hazelnuts on a baking sheet and bake for 5 to 7 minutes or until lightly browned. Reserve.

2. In a large bowl, cream the butter with the sugars using an electric mixer on medium speed until well blended. Add the eggs, orange zest, juice, and pumpkin and blend well on low speed.

3. Combine the dry ingredients and add them to the mixture on low speed, mixing until well blended. *Do not overmix.* Add the raisins and hazelnuts and mix just enough to combine.

4. Transfer the mixture to the loaf pans and bake for 45 to 50 minutes or until a toothpick inserted in the center comes out clean. Cool in the pan at for least 15 minutes and then turn the bread out onto a cooling rack.

ADVANCE PREPARATION: This bread tastes best on the day it's baked. It freezes well wrapped in foil for up to 2 months.

CIJI'S SCONES WITH CURRANTS

MAKES 16 TO 18 SCONES

MY FRIEND CIJI Ware, the historical novelist, is also a serious scone maker. Teatime, California style, means enjoying a basketful of these warm crumbly treats with your favorite fruit spread instead of the traditional thick clotted cream. Ciji's recipe calls for low-fat milk for glazing the scones instead of the usual cream, yet the scones still become golden brown. This currant-studded quick bread is perfect for a late-afternoon break.

2   cups all-purpose flour
1   tablespoon baking powder
1   teaspoon baking soda
     pinch of salt
1/4 cup sugar
6   tablespoons cold unsalted butter
1/3 cup dried currants
1   large egg plus enough low-fat milk to make 3/4 cup

1. Preheat the oven to 350°F. Sift the flour, baking powder, soda, and salt into a bowl. Stir in the sugar.

2. Cut the butter into small pieces and blend it with the dry ingredients with a wooden spoon to create a crumbly mixture. Add the currants.

3. In a glass measuring cup, mix the egg and milk and reserve 2 tablespoons to glaze the scones. Add the rest to the flour mixture, mixing just enough to create a dough mixture that can be pressed into a ball. Pat the dough into a circle.

4. On a floured board, roll or pat out the scone dough about 1 inch thick. Dust a round 1-1/2- to 2-inch cookie cutter with flour and cut the dough into rounds. Pat

the trimmings into a ball, roll out the dough again, and cut more scones. Place the scones on a large greased baking sheet. Brush the remaining glaze on the scones.

5. Place the scones in the middle of the oven and bake them for about 18 minutes or until they are golden brown and firm to the touch. Serve them hot, with small bowls of assorted fruit spreads.

ORANGE–POPPY SEED BREAD

MAKES ONE 9- BY 5-INCH LOAF

SLIGHTLY SWEET AND moist, this bread works equally well for breakfast, tea or dessert. It will keep for a few days and is also delicious toasted.

2	large eggs
1/2	cup sugar
1/2	cup milk
1/2	cup unsalted butter, melted
	zest of 2 oranges, finely chopped
1/2	cup plus 1 tablespoon fresh orange juice
1-1/2	cups all-purpose flour
1	teaspoon baking powder
1	teaspoon baking soda
1/2	teaspoon salt
2	tablespoons poppy seeds

1. Preheat the oven to 325°F. Butter and flour a 9- by 5-inch loaf pan. In a medium bowl, beat the eggs until frothy. Slowly add the sugar and beat the mixture until light and fluffy. Slowly beat in the milk, melted butter, orange zest, and juice.

2. Sift together the flour, baking powder, baking soda, and salt and add along with the poppy seeds to the batter. Blend well by stirring with a wooden spoon or in a mixer on low speed.

3. Transfer the batter to the prepared pan and bake for 50 to 60 minutes, until the top is golden and a cake tester inserted in the center comes out clean. Cool the bread in the pan for 10 to 15 minutes and then turn it out on a rack. Let it cool completely. Serve at room temperature.

ADVANCE PREPARATION: This bread tastes best the day it's baked, but it can be prepared up to 2 days ahead and kept at room temperature, wrapped in aluminum foil to retain its moisture. Serve lukewarm or at room temperature.

FRESH PEAR BREAD

MAKES ONE 9- BY 5-INCH LOAF

SELECT PEARS THAT are slightly underripe, since the cooking process tends to soften them. Fresh winter pears, unlike most other fruits, develop their sweet flavor and superb juiciness when ripened off the tree. Use the juicy, fine-textured Comice or Bosc pear. The pleasing contrast of the sweet fruit and the nutty pecans, nutmeg, and ginger makes this a satisfying fresh quick bread that can be served at breakfast or with eggs for brunch.

2/3 cup coarsely chopped pecans
2   cups all-purpose flour
1   teaspoon baking soda
1/2 teaspoon salt
1/4 teaspoon ground ginger
1/4 teaspoon freshly grated nutmeg
1/2 cup unsalted butter at room temperature
3/4 cup sugar
2   large eggs
1/4 cup sour cream
1   teaspoon vanilla extract
1   large Comice or Bosc pear, peeled, cored, and coarsely chopped
     zest of 1 lemon, finely chopped

1. Preheat the oven to 350°F. Butter and flour a 9- by 5-inch loaf pan. Toast the pecans on a baking sheet for 5 to 7 minutes or until lightly browned. Sift together the flour, baking soda, salt, ginger, and nutmeg.

2. In the large bowl of an electric mixer, beat the butter and sugar on medium speed until light and fluffy. Add the eggs one at a time. Beat in the sour cream and vanilla. Add the sifted flour mixture and blend well on low speed. Stir in the pear, pecans, and lemon zest and combine well on low speed.

3. Spoon the mixture into the prepared pan and bake for about 1 hour, until a cake tester inserted in the center comes out clean.

4. Cool the bread for 10 to 15 minutes in the pan, then turn it out on a rack. Let it cool completely before slicing.

ADVANCE PREPARATION: This bread tastes best on the day it's baked, but it can be prepared up to 1 day ahead and kept at room temperature, wrapped in aluminum foil to retain its moisture. Serve lukewarm or at room temperature.

MAPLE CORN MUFFINS
MAKES 12 REGULAR OR 48 MINI-MUFFINS

THESE SWEET LITTLE corn nuggets are a big hit on my holiday table served with orange-honey butter. To make orange-honey butter, combine some orange zest with softened unsalted butter and orange blossom honey and mix them together until they are well blended. Combining flour with cornmeal lightens the batter, and the sweet maple and brown sugar flavors bring out the inherent creamy sweetness of the corn. You can also make these in the mini-muffin size to serve with tea in a pretty napkin-lined basket with your favorite butter and preserves.

2   cups all-purpose flour
1   cup yellow cornmeal
1   tablespoon baking powder
1/2 teaspoon salt
1/4 cup packed light brown sugar
2   large eggs
6   tablespoons melted unsalted butter
1   cup milk
1/3 cup maple syrup
1/2 cup corn kernels (about 1 medium ear)

1. Preheat the oven to 350°F. Grease the muffin tins. Combine the flour, cornmeal, baking powder, and salt in a large bowl.

2. In a medium mixing bowl, whisk the brown sugar into the eggs until well blended. Add the melted butter, milk, and syrup and mix until combined.

3. Pour the liquid mixture over the dry ingredients and fold them together with a rubber spatula until the dry ingredients are completely blended. Add the corn kernels and mix to combine.

4. Spoon the batter into the muffin cups two thirds of the way up. Bake for 20 minutes for mini-muffins or 25 to 30 minutes for regular muffins or until the tops are golden brown and a toothpick inserted in the center comes out clean. Cool the muffins in the pan for 15 minutes. Serve them immediately with orange-honey butter if desired.

ADVANCE PREPARATION: The muffins can be prepared up to 8 hours ahead and reheated in a 350°F oven just before serving.

CORN TORTILLAS

MAKES 12 TORTILLAS

THERE IS NOTHING better than a properly cooked fresh tortilla. If you make fresh tortillas frequently, you might want to invest in an electric tortilla maker, a clever gadget that really works. Just shape the masa into small balls of dough, then place one in the middle of the tortilla maker and press down to flatten and cook the dough at the same time. The process is even easier if you buy good-quality fresh masa dough at a *tortilleria.*

It's very entertaining to make these up as your guests watch. This method is the traditional one, which requires a conventional tortilla press, available in most Mexican markets or a gourmet cookware store. Tortillas are particularly good with Sweet Potato–Jalapeño Soup with Tomatillo Cream (page 45), Grilled Chicken, Black Bean, and Corn Salad with Salsa Dressing (page 103), and Grilled Skirt Steak with Avocado-Tomato Salsa (page 229).

2   cups masa harina
1-1/2 cups warm water
or
1   pound prepared masa from a tortilla factory

1. Have ready 24 seven-inch squares of wax paper. If you're not using prepared masa, combine the masa harina and warm water in a medium bowl. Blend the mixture with a fork until it forms a smooth ball. Then divide the dough into 12 pieces. Form each piece into a ball and cover the balls of dough with an inverted bowl.

2. Put a piece of wax paper on the bottom half of a tortilla press and arrange a dough ball on it, opposite the handle and slightly off center toward the edge of the press. Flatten the ball slightly and cover it with another wax paper square. Lower the top of the press onto the wax paper and press down firmly on the lever until the

tortilla measures about 6 to 6-1/2 inches in diameter. Make all the tortillas in the same way with the remaining dough.

3. Heat a griddle over high heat until hot. Carefully peel off the top paper square from a tortilla and invert the tortilla onto the griddle. After 5 seconds, peel off the remaining wax paper. Cook the tortilla for 1 minute; turn it over and cook until it looks dry and flecked with golden spots, about another 30 seconds to 1 minute. Transfer the tortilla to a plate or a napkin-lined basket. Cook the remaining tortillas in the same manner. If they're not used immediately, wrap them in a plastic wrap.

ADVANCE PREPARATION: Tortillas can be prepared up to 1 day ahead and refrigerated. Reheat in foil in a 350°F oven for 10 minutes for best taste or place them on a gas burner for 20 seconds on each side, using tongs to turn them.

CRISP TORTILLA CHIPS

SERVES 6

THESE TASTY, CRUNCHY chips are not deep-fried or greasy. Serve them with Shrimp Salsa (page 11), Asian Guacamole (page 24), or Green Pea Guacamole (page 22).

6 corn tortillas (page 322), cut into triangles
   salt and pepper to taste

1. Preheat the oven to 400°F. Place the triangles on a baking sheet. Heat the tortilla chips in the oven for 10 minutes or until crisp. Remove the tortilla chips from the oven and put them in a bowl. Season with salt and pepper and serve immediately.

ADVANCE PREPARATION: These can be made up to 8 hours ahead and stored in an airtight container.

BREAD DOUGH

Here are three basic methods for preparation of yeast bread. The difference between homemade and store-bought bread is enormous. Ingredient amounts are not specified since they will vary with each recipe.

active dry or fresh yeast
sweetener
lukewarm water
all-purpose flour
salt

To make dough by hand:

1. Sprinkle dry yeast or crumble fresh yeast into a bowl with the sweetener. Pour a little of the warm water over the yeast and let it stand until it becomes foamy, about 10 minutes. Stir to dissolve the yeast.

2. Reserve 1/2 cup of flour. Mix the flour and salt and any other dry ingredients together in a bowl and make a well in the center. Mix the yeast mixture with the remaining liquid ingredients and stir them into the flour. Mix well to obtain a soft dough, adding reserved flour as needed.

3. Knead the dough on a lightly floured work surface until it is smooth and elastic, about 8 to 10 minutes, flouring the surface occasionally if the dough sticks to it. Achieving elasticity will vary with room temperature and air humidity.

4. Transfer the dough to an oiled bowl and turn it over to oil its entire surface. Cover the dough with a damp cloth and let it rise in a warm place for about 1-1/2 hours or until it is doubled in volume.

5. Punch the dough down and knead it again briefly on a floured surface until smooth. Shape the dough into the desired loaf form and place it in an oiled pan. Cover the dough lightly with a cloth and let it rise until doubled in volume, about 1 hour.

6. Bake as directed in the recipe.

To make dough in a food processor:

1. Sprinkle dry yeast or crumble fresh yeast into a bowl with the sweetener. Pour a little of the warm water over the yeast and let it stand until it becomes foamy, about 10 minutes. Stir to dissolve the yeast.

2. Reserve 1/2 cup of flour. In a food processor, process the flour, salt, and any other dry ingredients briefly to mix them. Add the remaining liquid ingredients to the yeast mixture. Process the dough until it gathers into a ball, adding a little of the reserved flour at a time.

3. Process for 1 minute to knead the dough until the dough is smooth. Continue with steps 4, 5, and 6 from the first method.

To make dough in a mixer with a dough hook:

1. Sprinkle dry yeast or crumble fresh yeast into a bowl with the sweetener. Pour a little of the warm water over the yeast and let it stand until it becomes foamy, about 10 minutes. Stir to dissolve the yeast.

2. Reserve 1/2 cup of flour. Put the flour, salt, and any other dry ingredients into the large bowl of a mixer. With a dough hook turning at low speed, gradually pour in the yeast mixture.

3. Let the machine run until the dough is very smooth, adding reserved flour as needed. Continue with steps 4, 5, and 6 from the first method.

To freeze dough:

1. After the first rising, punch the dough down and shape it as directed. Wrap the dough tightly in plastic wrap and then in foil and freeze it for up to 1 month. When you're ready to use it, remove the dough from the freezer and place it in a pan as directed, allowing it to complete its second rising. Proceed with individual recipe directions.

COUNTRY SOURDOUGH BREAD
MAKES TWO 11- BY 3-1/2-INCH LOAVES

SAN FRANCISCO IS famous the world over for its sourdough bread. The bakers there rightly claim that the special wild yeasts and moist sea air of the Bay Area give their dough its unique taste. But sourdough, which had its origins in the mining camps of the California gold rush, can be baked anywhere.

What exactly is sourdough? It's simply bread that uses natural, airborne yeast cultures for its leavening rather than commercially cultured yeast. In this recipe, sourdough starter—which takes about three days to develop—is used for its flavor, and a little yeast is added to ensure that the dough rises properly. Your own sourdough will be different from everyone else's because the wild yeasts vary from place to place. Some starters are handed down from generation to generation, getting more and more sour and delicious as they are repeatedly used and replenished.

After you've tried this basic bread, experiment with the Sourdough Rye Rolls (page 330). Sourdough bread is extremely versatile and is excellent with pâtés, spreads, cheeses, and soups.

SOURDOUGH STARTER

1	1/4-ounce envelope active dry yeast or 1 3/5-ounce cake fresh
1	teaspoon sugar
2	cups lukewarm water
2	cups unbleached all-purpose flour

BREAD

1	cup sourdough starter
1-1/2 cups lukewarm water
5	cups unbleached all-purpose flour

1	1/4-ounce envelope active dry yeast or 1 3/5-ounce cake fresh
1	tablespoon sugar
2	teaspoons salt

1. For the starter, sprinkle the dry yeast or crumble the fresh yeast and sugar over 1/2 cup of the lukewarm water in a large glass bowl and leave it for 10 minutes or until small bubbles form.

2. Set aside 1/4 cup of the remaining water. Stir the remaining starter ingredients into the yeast mixture and beat with a wooden spoon until fairly smooth. If a few small lumps remain, they will dissolve during fermentation. Stir in the reserved water and beat briefly. The consistency of the mixture will be like that of thin crepe batter.

3. Cover the starter with a cloth and leave it in a warm place free from drafts for 2 or 3 days or until the mixture smells sour. If you like a strong sourdough flavor, leave the mixture for up to 5 days. Stir it once every day. If you forget to stir it, a skin may form on top. The skin should be removed.

4. For the bread, mix 1 cup of the starter with 1 cup of the water and 1 cup of the flour. Cover the dough and let it stand in a warm place for at least 3 hours or overnight.

5. Sprinkle the yeast and sugar over 1/4 cup of the remaining water in a cup or small bowl and leave for 10 minutes. Stir to dissolve the yeast.

6. Sift the remaining flour into a large bowl and make a well in the center. Add the starter mixture, dissolved yeast, remaining water, and salt. Gradually stir the flour into the mixture in the center of the well. When it becomes difficult to stir, knead in the remaining flour. If the dough is dry, knead in an extra tablespoon of water. If the dough is very sticky, knead in 1 or 2 tablespoons of flour.

7. Knead the dough thoroughly on a floured surface until it is smooth and elastic, flouring the surface occasionally if the dough sticks to it. Transfer the dough to an oiled bowl and turn the dough over to oil its entire surface. Cover the dough with a damp cloth and let it rise in a warm place for about 1 to 1-1/2 hours or until it doubles in volume.

8. To shape the dough, divide it in half and on a lightly floured surface roll out each half to 2 oval loaves of about 11 by 3-1/2 inches, with the ends slightly tapered. Grease 2 baking sheets and set a loaf on each. Cover the dough and let it rise in a warm place for about 1 hour or until it nearly doubles in volume.

9. Preheat the oven to 400°F. Put a pan of water on the bottom of the oven while preheating to provide steam.

10. Brush the loaves lightly with water. Using a very sharp knife, cut a few parallel diagonal slashes across the tops of the loaves. Cut the loaves carefully and without pressing too hard to avoid deflating the dough.

11. Bake for 40 to 45 minutes or until the loaves are golden brown. When you tap the bottom of each loaf with your fist, it should sound hollow. Let the bread cool on a rack.

ADVANCE PREPARATION: This bread is best on the day it is baked.

NOTE: Never prepare starter in a metal container. Reserve any unused starter, covered with plastic wrap with a few holes poked in it, in the refrigerator. About once a week, stir in 1/2 cup water and 1/2 cup flour. Leave the mixture out overnight, then refrigerate.

SOURDOUGH RYE ROLLS

MAKES 20 ROLLS

THESE EARTHY BROWN rolls feature a balance of three distinct flavors to achieve one original taste. The aromatic sourdough blends well with the heavier rye; both flours are strengthened by the addition of flavor-packed caraway. Serve this as an accompaniment to a first course, soup, or salad.

1/2 cup starter (page 327), stirred before measuring
1   1/4-ounce envelope active dry yeast or 1 3/5-ounce cake fresh
1   teaspoon sugar
2/3 cup lukewarm water
1   cup rye flour
2   cups all-purpose flour
2   tablespoons vegetable or olive oil
4   teaspoons caraway seeds
2   teaspoons salt

1. Prepare the starter at least 3 days before making the rolls.

2. Sprinkle the dry yeast or crumble the fresh yeast and the sugar over 1/3 cup of the lukewarm water in a cup or small bowl. Leave for 10 minutes and stir to dissolve the yeast.

3. Mix both flours together in a large bowl, reserving 1/2 cup, and make a well in the center. Add the starter, dissolved yeast mixture, and remaining ingredients and mix briefly with the ingredients in the middle of the well.

4. Gradually stir in the flour. When it becomes difficult to stir, knead in the remaining flour. If the dough is dry, knead in an extra tablespoon of water. If the dough is very sticky, knead in 1 or 2 tablespoons of flour.

5. Knead the dough thoroughly on a floured surface until it is smooth and elastic, flouring the surface occasionally if the dough sticks to it. Transfer the dough to an oiled bowl and turn it over to oil its entire surface. Cover with a damp cloth and let it rise in a warm place for 1 to 1-1/2 hours or until doubled in volume.

6. Grease a baking sheet. Knead the dough briefly on a lightly floured surface. Roll it out to a rope about 18 inches long. Cut the rope into 4 equal lengths, then cut each length into 5 equal pieces. Roll each piece into a ball between cupped palms. Roll each ball on the working surface into an oval roll about 1-1/4 by 3 inches. Arrange the rolls on a baking sheet, leaving room between them so they can rise. Cover them with a damp cloth and let them rise in a warm place for about 1 hour or until doubled in volume. Preheat the oven to 425°F.

7. Bake the rolls for 10 minutes. Reduce the oven temperature to 400°F. Bake for 10 minutes more or until the rolls are firm and brown on top and bottom. Let them cool on a rack. Serve them lukewarm or at room temperature.

ADVANCE PREPARATION: This bread is best on the day it is baked.

WALNUT BREAD

MAKES ONE 10-INCH-LONG LOAF

THOUGH THE NUT itself is originally from Persia, the term *English walnut* is attributable to English merchant marines trading in this delicious commodity around the world. Walnuts were first introduced to California by the Franciscan fathers in the 1700s. The nuts have been grown commercially in California since 1867. Today California produces 99 percent of our domestic supply, all of them English walnuts.

Walnuts take on different flavors depending on what they are paired with. Chocolate makes them seem bitter, while cream and cheddar cheese bring out their underlying sweetness. This bread has a double-walnut flavor because it's made with walnut oil. California walnut oil lacks the depth of flavor unique to its imported counterpart, so I recommend that you invest in a small bottle of French walnut oil and keep it refrigerated after opening.

For an interesting variation, add 1/2 cup of brandy-soaked currants to the dough after adding the walnuts. This bread is an excellent ending to a light meal when paired with semisoft cheese such as Monterey Jack or goat cheese and fresh fruit. It is also good as a breakfast bread served with butter or cream cheese.

1	1/4-ounce envelope active dry yeast or 1 3/5-ounce cake fresh
1	teaspoon sugar
1-1/4	cups lukewarm water
1/2	cup whole wheat flour
2-1/2	cups unbleached all-purpose flour
3	tablespoons imported walnut oil
1	teaspoon salt
1	cup chopped walnuts

1. Sprinkle the dry yeast or crumble the fresh yeast and sugar over 1/4 cup of the lukewarm water in a cup or small bowl. Leave for 10 minutes and then stir to dissolve the yeast.

2. Mix the flours together in a large bowl, reserving 1 cup, and make a well in the center. Pour the yeast mixture into the well. Add the remaining water, walnut oil, and salt and mix briefly with the ingredients in the middle of the well. Stir until the ingredients are thoroughly blended and begin to form a ball.

3. Knead the dough on a lightly floured work surface until it is very smooth and elastic, adding some of the remaining flour if the dough sticks. Knead in the walnuts by sprinkling about one fourth of them over the dough and the remainder over the work surface. Roll the dough in the nuts while kneading it gently. Transfer the dough to an oiled bowl and turn it over to oil its entire surface. Cover with a damp cloth and let it rise in a warm place for 1-1/2 hours or until doubled in volume.

4. Punch dough down and knead briefly, about 1 minute on a lightly floured surface. On a floured surface, roll it out to a smooth cylindrical loaf about 10 inches long. Grease a baking sheet and set the loaf on it. Cover the loaf with a damp cloth and let it rise in a warm place for about 1 hour or until nearly doubled in volume. Preheat the oven to 400°F.

5. Bake the bread for about 15 minutes or until it begins to brown. Reduce the oven temperature to 375°F and continue baking for 25 minutes. When you tap the bottom of the loaf with your fist, it should sound hollow.

ADVANCE PREPARATION: This bread is best on the day it is baked.

JALAPEÑO CHEESE BREAD AND RUSTIC BREAD STICKS

MAKES TWO 9- BY 5-INCH LOAVES OR 24 BREAD STICKS

WHETHER YOU BAKE this in a loaf or make the rustic bread sticks, you'll enjoy this spicy but not overpowering California-style bread. The spiciness of the bread can be altered by increasing or reducing the number of jalapeño chiles. This bread goes nicely with Golden Frittata with Tomatillo Salsa (page 117) or Herbed Scrambled Eggs with Goat Cheese (page 122), especially when toasted. I also recommend this with Chicken Minestrone with Mixed-Herb Pesto (page 63).

2	1/4-ounce envelope active dry yeast or 2 3/5-ounce cakes fresh
1	tablespoon sugar
2-1/4	cups lukewarm water
1/4	cup oil or unsalted butter, melted
1	cup whole wheat flour
5	cups unbleached all-purpose flour
1	tablespoon salt
4 to 6	jalapeño chiles or to taste, seeded and finely chopped*
2	cups shredded sharp cheddar cheese (1/2 pound)

EGG GLAZE

1	egg
1	tablespoon water
	cornmeal for sprinkling

---

* When you're working with chiles, always wear rubber gloves. Wash the cutting surface and knife immediately.

1. Sprinkle the dry yeast or crumble the fresh yeast and sugar over 1/2 cup of the lukewarm water in a cup or small bowl. Leave it for 10 minutes, then stir to dissolve the yeast. Add the remaining water and oil.

2. Sift the flours together into a large mixing bowl. Set aside 2 cups of the mixture. Add the salt to the remaining mixture and make a well in center. Pour the yeast mixture into the well, add the chopped chiles, and mix briefly.

3. Gradually stir in the reserved flour, 1/2 cup at a time, until the dough loses its stickiness and can be kneaded easily. Knead the dough thoroughly on a floured surface until it is smooth and elastic, flouring the surface occasionally if the dough sticks to it. Transfer the dough to an oiled bowl and turn it over to oil its entire surface. Cover with a damp cloth and let it rise in a warm place for about 1-1/2 hours or until doubled in volume. Punch down the dough and let it rest, about 5 minutes, covered with a cloth. (This allows the dough to regain its elasticity.)

4. Knead the dough again on a lightly floured surface. Knead in the cheese by sprinkling it on the bread all at once and kneading until distributed.

5. Grease two 9- by 5-inch loaf pans. Divide the dough into 2 equal parts and on the floured surface roll out each part to a smooth, cylindrical loaf about 9 inches long. Put the loaves in the pans seam side down, slash the top lightly 3 times with a serrated knife, cover with a damp cloth, and let rise in a warm place for about 1 hour or until nearly doubled in volume.

6. For the egg glaze, whisk the egg and water together until slightly foamy. Brush the loaves with the egg glaze. Sprinkle lightly with cornmeal. Preheat the oven to 375°F.

7. Bake the loaves for about 15 minutes or until they begin to brown. Reduce the temperature to 350°F and continue baking for another 45 minutes or until the bread sounds hollow when tapped. Let the loaves cool on a rack. Serve lukewarm or at room temperature.

ADVANCE PREPARATION: This bread is best on the day it is baked.

NOTE: If you're using a food processor to knead the dough, add the chiles and cheese by hand so that the pieces stay intact.

For Rustic Bread Sticks

1 / 2   R E C I P E   O F   B R E A D   D O U G H   W I L L   M A K E   10   T O   12   B R E A D   S T I C K S

After the dough has been punched down and allowed to rest (step 3):

4. On a floured board, shape the dough into a roll about 20 inches long. With a sharp knife, cut the dough into 10 to 12 equal pieces. Let it rest again, covered with a cloth or plastic wrap.

5. Using the palms of your hands, roll each piece of dough into a roll 3/4 to 1 inch in diameter and about 9 to 10 inches long (or whatever size will fit on your baking sheet). Twist each piece, if desired, to make twisted bread sticks. Place each piece on a lightly oiled baking sheet sprinkled with cornmeal. (Make sure the pieces are about 2 inches apart; use 2 baking sheets, but be sure to put them on the same rack.)

6. Cover the dough loosely with a cloth or plastic wrap and let it rise in a warm place until doubled in size. Lightly brush each bread stick with egg glaze and sprinkle with cornmeal.

7. Preheat the oven to 350°F. For soft bread sticks, bake for 12 to 15 minutes, until lightly browned. Watch carefully, or they will become too dry if overcooked. Cool on a wire rack and store in an airtight container. Serve warm with cilantro, garlic, and cumin-spiced soft butter. If you like harder bread sticks, bake them in a 300°F oven for about 30 minutes or until very crispy and nicely browned.

VARIATIONS: For a spicy finish, try any of these toppings, which go on after you brush on the egg glaze: hot red pepper flakes, coarse salt, chile powder, or garlic salt.

ADVANCE PREPARATION: This bread tastes best on the day it is baked.

GOOD GADGETS: THE OIL MISTER

Fill a plastic-triggered spray bottle with your favorite oil for the times when you want just a spritz for sautéing, dressing your salad, basting your vegetables, or finishing your baked bread. You'll be able to control exactly how much oil you're using, and the ingredients will have a perfectly light, even coating. Spray the oil about 6 inches from the food. Store the mister in a cool, dark place.

FOCACCIA

MAKES TWO 9-INCH ROUND LOAVES OR ONE 10- BY 15-INCH LOAF

BACK IN 1946 Genevieve Callahan (*The California Cook Book*) described a bread called *fugaccio* that was available in onion or raisin flavor at her local San Francisco Italian bake shop. Today we call it *focaccia*. However you spell it, this is a satisfying bread that Ms. Callahan properly explained "should look rather rough and bubbly, not smooth and flat."

I like a bready focaccia, so I bake it in a pan with a rim to encourage that quality. A pan with higher sides also helps to keep olive oil from dripping onto the bottom of the oven. Choose either the traditional onion or the spicier olive topping, depending on what you are serving with the focaccia. Serve this bread hot from the oven before dinner with little bowls of extra virgin oil for dipping. It's a comforting companion to a big bowl of soup or Warm Grilled Vegetable and Shrimp Salad (page 111).

2   1/4-ounce envelopes active dry yeast or 2 3/5-ounce cakes fresh
1   teaspoon sugar
1   cup lukewarm water
2-3/4 cups all-purpose flour
2   tablespoons rye flour
2   tablespoons coarse yellow cornmeal (semolina)
1-1/2 teaspoons salt
1   teaspoon chopped fresh thyme or 1/2 teaspoon dried
1/4   cup olive oil
1   teaspoon coarse salt

OLIVE TOPPING
1/4   cup Mediterranean green olives, rinsed, drained, pitted, and coarsely
          chopped

1/2   fresh jalapeño chile, seeded and minced*
1/4   teaspoon coarsely ground black pepper

ONION TOPPING
3   tablespoons coarsely chopped red onion
3   tablespoons coarsely chopped fresh rosemary
1/4   teaspoon coarsely ground black pepper

1. In a 2-cup measuring cup, sprinkle the yeast and sugar over 1/2 cup of the lukewarm water. Leave for 10 minutes and stir to dissolve the yeast. Add the remaining water.

2. In the bowl of a food processor fitted with the metal blade, combine the flours, cornmeal, salt, thyme, and 2 tablespoons of the olive oil and process briefly to mix. Stir the yeast and water mixture just to blend, and with the motor running, add the yeast mixture to the flour in a slow but steady stream. It should take about 10 seconds to add the liquid, and the dough should form a loose ball within 20 to 30 seconds. If the dough does not form a ball, sprinkle over more water, 1 teaspoon at a time. If the dough is too wet and quickly begins to climb up the center column, you will need to sprinkle over more flour, 1 tablespoon at a time. Process the dough for a total time of 60 seconds, in three bursts.

3. Turn out the dough onto a lightly floured board and knead very briefly, just to bring it together into a ball. The dough should be loose and soft, just on the verge of being sticky. Don't be tempted to add too much flour at this stage, because it will inhibit the rising of the dough. Place the dough in an oiled bowl and cover it with a damp cloth or plastic wrap. Let it rise at warm room temperature for 2 to 3 hours or until doubled in bulk, puffy, and wobbly in appearance.

4. Punch down the dough, divide it into 2 pieces, and press the pieces firmly into 2 oiled 8- or 9-inch cake pans, pressing them well into the corners (or press the full quantity into 1 oiled 10- by 15-inch rectangular pan). Note: if you like your focaccia thin and crispy, proceed directly to step 6. If you like a deep and bready loaf, proceed with step 5.

5. Cover the dough again with a damp cloth or plastic wrap and leave it at warm room temperature for about 30 minutes, until it is slightly puffed and wobbly.

---

* When you're working with chiles, always wear rubber gloves. Wash the cutting surface and knife immediately.

6. Preheat the oven to 475°F. Poke the dough with your finger in 5 or 6 places to give it a dimpled effect. Brush the dough with 1 tablespoon of the remaining olive oil for each round loaf or 2 tablespoons for the large rectangular loaf and sprinkle the coarse salt over the dough. Sprinkle with the topping of your choice and bake for 20 to 25 minutes, turning the pan around halfway through if it seems to be browning unevenly, until the focaccia is golden and nicely risen. Remove the bread from the oven and let it cool in the pan for a softer crust or on a rack for a crisp crust, then serve it slightly warm or at room temperature. Brush or spray the focaccia with a little more olive oil before serving.

ADVANCE PREPARATION: Can be prepared through step 3 and the dough wrapped and frozen, in which case it will take at least 3 hours to thaw and begin to rise again. *This cannot be hurried in the microwave.* Alternatively, it can be prepared through step 3, refrigerated overnight, and then brought to room temperature before proceeding.

PIZZA DOUGH

MAKES TWO 9-INCH PIZZAS

THIS FOOD PROCESSOR method for pizza dough is very easy. Rye and cornmeal are combined with all-purpose flour for a more interesting flavor.

PIZZA DOUGH

2   1/4-ounce envelopes active dry yeast or 2 3/5-ounce cakes fresh
1   teaspoon sugar
1   cup lukewarm water
2-1/2 cups all-purpose flour
1/2   cup rye flour
2   tablespoons yellow cornmeal
1-1/2 teaspoons salt
2   tablespoons olive oil

1. Sprinkle the dry yeast or crumble the fresh yeast and sugar over 1/4 cup of the lukewarm water in a glass measuring cup and leave it for 10 minutes. Stir to dissolve the yeast.

2. In a food processor fitted with the metal blade, process the flours, cornmeal, and salt briefly to mix them. Add the remaining lukewarm water and the oil to the yeast mixture. With the blades turning, gradually pour in the yeast-liquid mixture. If the dough is too dry to come together, add an extra tablespoon of water and process it again. Process for 1 minute to knead the dough.

3. Transfer the dough to a lightly oiled bowl. Cover the dough with a damp cloth and let it rise in a warm place for about 1 hour or until doubled in volume.

4. Punch the dough down and knead it again briefly on a floured surface until smooth. Form the dough into 2 balls and press each out with your fingertips to a

9-inch round on an oiled baking sheet. Cover the dough with a damp towel or plastic wrap and let it rise for 30 minutes.

5. Shape as directed in the recipe.

ADVANCE PREPARATION: Can be prepared up to 1 day ahead through step 4, wrapped in plastic wrap, and refrigerated. To continue, remove it from the refrigerator, allow at least 1 hour for the dough to come to room temperature, and then let it rise for 20 to 30 minutes. Shape as directed in the recipe. Or the dough can be frozen indefinitely, but it takes at least 3 hours to thaw (*this cannot be hurried in the microwave*). Let the dough rise for 20 to 30 minutes and shape as directed in the recipe.

DESSERTS

BAKED PEARS IN BURGUNDY AND PORT GLAZE 345

ESSENCIA ZABAGLIONE WITH FRESH FRUIT COMPOTE 347

MIXED EXOTIC FRUIT GAZPACHO 349

FRESH APRICOTS AND STRAWBERRIES WITH SOUR CREAM
    AND BROWN SUGAR 351

QUICK FRUIT DESSERTS 352

ORANGE, ALMOND, AND OLIVE OIL CAKE 353

GLAZED LEMON SOUR CREAM CAKE 355

NECTARINE COBBLER WITH DRIED CHERRIES 357

PEACH MELBA BUCKLE 359

PEAR-RASPBERRY ALMOND TART 361

MANGO AND MACADAMIA NUT BROWN BUTTER TART 364

APRICOT GLAZE 366

BLUEBERRY LEMON TART 367

TIRAMISU WITH TOASTED HAZELNUTS AND CHOCOLATE 369

VANILLA CARAMEL CREAM 371

PUMPKIN BREAD PUDDING WITH EGGNOG BRANDY SAUCE 373

CHOCOLATE CHIP COFFEE CAKE 375

BANANA CAKE WITH CHOCOLATE FUDGE FROSTING 377

CHOCOLATE FREAK-OUT 379

BITTERSWEET CHOCOLATE HAZELNUT TORTE WITH
    BANANA CUSTARD SAUCE 381

BANANA SPLIT ICE CREAM TORTE 384

CHOCOLATE TRUFFLE BROWNIES 386

WHITE CHOCOLATE AND PISTACHIO COOKIES 387

SPICY CRINKLE COOKIES 388

BAKED PEARS IN BURGUNDY AND PORT GLAZE

SERVES 8

I ALWAYS USED to peel pears before cooking them. What a wonderful discovery it was when I decided to cook the pears whole and unpeeled. As the pears bake, the skin becomes wrinkled with a shiny caramelized exterior, reminiscent of a French country dessert. These make a marvelous simple dessert for a dinner party. Serve with a plate of biscotti or White Chocolate and Pistachio Cookies (page 387).

2 cups burgundy wine
1 cup tawny port wine
1 cup sugar
1 cinnamon stick
   a 2-inch piece of lemon and orange zest
8 Bosc pears, ripe but firm with stems attached

GARNISH
fresh mint leaves

1. Preheat the oven to 350°F. In a medium nonaluminum saucepan over medium heat, bring the red wine, port, sugar, cinnamon, lemon, and orange zest to a simmer and dissolve the sugar. Remove the cinnamon stick.

2. Core the pears from the bottom and then cut the bottom flat so that they can stand upright. Place the pears stem side up in a large baking pan and then pour the wine mixture over them. Bake the pears for about 1 hour or until tender when pierced with a knife, basting every few minutes with the wine mixture.

3. Remove the pears from the oven and pour off the remaining wine mixture into a medium saucepan. Reduce the wine until it becomes a glaze. Spoon the glaze over the pears on a large serving platter or on individual dessert plates, garnish with fresh mint leaves, and serve warm, with vanilla ice cream if desired. These pears are also excellent served at room temperature.

ADVANCE PREPARATION: Can be prepared up to 8 hours ahead through step 3 and kept at room temperature.

ESSENCIA ZABAGLIONE WITH FRESH FRUIT COMPOTE

SERVES 6 TO 8

ZABAGLIONE IS A quick last-minute dessert that is always well received. California's Essencia wine is substituted for Marsala in this variation on the classic zabaglione with outstanding results. Andy Quady, the owner of Quady Winery, also makes an orange muscat low-alcohol 4 percent dessert wine called Electra that has hints of melons and berries. If you prefer less alcohol, substitute Electra for the Essencia. Pass a plate of Spicy Crinkle Cookies (page 388).

6   medium egg yolks
3   tablespoons sugar
1/2 cup Essencia wine
3   tablespoons whipping cream

FRUIT
4   medium oranges, peeled and sectioned
2   pints strawberries, hulled and thinly sliced

GARNISH
fresh mint sprigs

1. In the top of a medium-size double boiler, place the egg yolks, sugar, and Essencia and beat until well blended.

2. Place the double boiler over medium heat and whisk the mixture vigorously until it becomes foamy and begins to thicken. Remove the mixture from the heat, add the cream, and whisk until incorporated. (The mixture should be thick and custardlike and should coat a spoon.) Place the oranges and strawberries in a mixing bowl and toss.

3. To serve, spoon the compote into individual small serving bowls (wine goblets look pretty). Pour on the zabaglione, garnish with mint, and serve immediately. You can also serve the zabaglione chilled. Be sure to whisk it right before serving.

ADVANCE PREPARATION: If you're serving the zabaglione chilled, it can be prepared up to 6 hours ahead through step 2, covered, and refrigerated.

MIXED EXOTIC FRUIT GAZPACHO

SERVES 6

SITTING ON THE terrace of the Ritz-Carlton, Laguna Niguel, I was served a version of this elegant, refreshing dessert gazpacho. The chef prepares a fresh basil sorbet to accompany this dessert soup, but any quality fruit sorbet works here. Decorate the soup with the fruit, sorbet, and mint leaves. If you prefer a pure red soup, cook the mint leaves in the sugar syrup and strain them out before continuing.

1-1/2   cups water
3/4   cup sugar
2   pints fresh strawberries, cleaned and hulled
1   pint fresh raspberries
      juice of 1 lemon
2   tablespoons finely chopped fresh mint
1   mango, peeled and cut into small balls with a small melon baller
1   papaya, finely diced
1   kiwifruit, peeled and cut into julienne

GARNISH
1   pint fruit sorbet (raspberry or strawberry works well)
      fresh mint leaves

1. In a medium saucepan over medium heat, combine the water and sugar and simmer until the sugar is completely dissolved. Reserve.

2. Set aside 1/2 pint of the smaller strawberries for garnish and combine the rest with the raspberries and lemon juice in a blender or food processor fitted with the metal blade. Puree them until they liquefy. Using a fine strainer, strain the berries

into a large nonaluminum bowl and add the reserved sugar syrup and chopped mint. Mix well to combine, cover and chill in the refrigerator for at least 2 hours.

3. To serve, cut the reserved strawberries into julienne. Ladle some berry puree into 6 shallow soup bowls, then arrange the fruits on top in a whimsical pattern. Place a small scoop of sorbet in the center of each bowl and garnish with fresh mint leaves. Serve immediately.

ADVANCE PREPARATION: Can be prepared up to 1 day ahead through step 2 and refrigerated.

FRESH APRICOTS AND STRAWBERRIES WITH SOUR CREAM AND BROWN SUGAR

SERVES 6

HERE'S A QUICK dessert idea that lets summer produce shine. Picture big, juicy red strawberries and velvety apricot quarters on a platter surrounded by small pots of brown sugar and sour cream for dipping. A plate of biscotti or White Chocolate and Pistachio Cookies (page 387) are perfect with the fruit. Serve with a cooling glass of late harvest Riesling.

12 ripe but firm medium apricots
1   pint large strawberries, cleaned but not hulled
1   cup dark brown sugar
1   cup sour cream or crème fraîche (page 425)

GARNISH
fresh mint sprigs

1. Cut the apricots into quarters, removing the pits. On the outer edge of a serving platter, arrange the apricot quarters alternating with whole strawberries. In the center, place bowls of brown sugar and sour cream. Garnish with mint sprigs and serve immediately.

QUICK FRUIT DESSERTS

WHEN YOU FIND you're in a last-minute pinch for dessert, think of simple fruit desserts. Fruit looks particularly appealing when served in a large balloon wineglass. Here are some suggestions:

- strawberries with a splash of balsamic vinegar and freshly ground black pepper
- cut-up nectarines or peaches with Muscat Canelli
- blueberries with a vanilla crème anglaise
- sliced ripe pears with chunks of Roquefort
- dried cherries marinated in a brandied sugar syrup and served in compote dishes with crumbled Stilton cheese
- sliced and peeled apples or pears sautéed in butter and then caramelized with sugar, spooned over French vanilla ice cream
- fresh figs, quartered and served with honey ricotta cheese
- sliced oranges with candied orange zest

ORANGE, ALMOND, AND OLIVE OIL CAKE

SERVES 8

IN *FEAST OF the Olive*, Maggie Blyth Klein demonstrates how to cook with olives and olive oil in ways you wouldn't have imagined. This variation on Ms. Klein's citrus and almond cake is pure California, brimming with oranges, almonds, and, surprisingly, olive oil.

I love the complex flavors in this cake and the curious taste that the olive oil brings to it. Baking with olive oil provides a fruitier flavor and a bit heavier texture. Use an extra virgin olive oil with a strong fruity character to bring the almond and orange flavors together in a unique way. Select blood oranges if in season. Blood oranges will provide a more pronounced citrus flavor and also make a beautiful garnish. If you want, accompany this with a big bowl of mixed berries. Try a California orange afterdinner wine like Quady Winery's Essencia or Electra with this and you'll wish dessert would go on forever.

6   ounces blanched almonds
1   cup all-purpose flour
1   tablespoon baking powder
4   large eggs at room temperature
1-1/2 cups sugar
      zest of 1 medium orange, finely chopped
      juice of 1 medium orange (about 1/2 cup)
1/2   cup fruity extra virgin olive oil

GARNISH
powdered sugar
thinly sliced oranges
fresh mint leaves
whipped cream or crème fraîche (page 425)

1. Preheat the oven to 350°F. Oil a 9-inch springform pan with olive oil. In a food processor fitted with the metal blade, process the almonds until finely ground, almost like bread crumbs. In a medium mixing bowl, combine the ground almonds, flour, and baking powder and set aside.

2. With an electric mixer on medium speed, in a large mixing bowl beat the eggs until frothy. Slowly add the sugar and beat the mixture until it is light, thick, and lemon colored. Slowly add the flour mixture and then add the orange zest, juice, and olive oil, mixing just to combine.

3. Pour the mixture into the prepared pan and bake for 50 to 60 minutes or until a skewer inserted in the center comes out clean. Cool and remove the sides of the pan. Place the cake on a serving platter and sprinkle powdered sugar in a decorative pattern on top. To serve, place a piece of cake on a dessert plate and arrange orange slices, mint leaves, and a dollop of cream on the side.

ADVANCE PREPARATION: Can be prepared one day ahead and kept at room temperature, tightly covered.

GLAZED LEMON SOUR CREAM CAKE

SERVES 8 TO 10

I HAVE TRIED at least 10 different lemon cakes in search of one that would satisfy my personal preference for a clean lemon flavor, a fine crumb, moist texture, and ease of preparation. Most recipes called for lemon juice in the cake, which seems to cause textural problems. I finally experimented with lemon extract in the cake and fresh lemon juice for the glaze with an outstanding result, bursting with flavor.

Lightweight bundt pans bake at a more even temperature, so invest in one if you're doing a lot of baking. I like the way this cake freezes and usually keep one on hand for last-minute emergencies. Serve with seasonal berries and a dollop of whipped cream, Essencia Zabaglione with Fresh Fruit Compote (page 347) or a scoop of French vanilla ice cream. You might also try serving this for afternoon tea or even for breakfast.

1-3/4 cups all-purpose flour
1 teaspoon baking soda
1 teaspoon baking powder
1 cup unsalted butter at room temperature
1 cup sugar
3 large eggs at room temperature
1 tablespoon minced lemon zest
2 teaspoons lemon extract
1 cup sour cream

GLAZE
1-1/2 cups powdered sugar
1/2 cup strained fresh lemon juice
2 teaspoons finely chopped lemon zest

1. Preheat the oven to 350°F. Grease and flour a 9-inch lightweight bundt pan. Sift the flour, baking soda, and baking powder together in a medium mixing bowl. Set aside.

2. In a medium bowl with an electric mixer on medium speed or in a food processor fitted with the metal blade, beat the butter and sugar together until light and fluffy, about 4 minutes. Beat in the eggs, zest, and lemon extract and mix for 2 minutes.

3. Reduce the mixer to the lowest speed, add half the flour mixture, and mix until well combined. Add half the sour cream, mixing constantly, and then add the rest of the flour and sour cream, ending with the sour cream.

4. Pour the mixture into the prepared bundt pan and bake for about 35 to 40 minutes or until a cake tester inserted in the center comes out clean. Cool in the pan for 10 minutes, then invert onto a cake rack. Make the glaze.

5. Using a wire strainer, sift the powdered sugar into a small nonaluminum bowl. Add the juice and lemon zest and whisk to break up any lumps.

6. Place the cake on a wax paper–lined rimmed baking sheet. Using a long skewer, poke holes in the cake *almost* going through the bottom at 1-inch intervals. Slowly pour the glaze over the cake, making sure it's absorbed as you pour. Let the cake come to room temperature.

ADVANCE PREPARATION: Can be prepared up to 3 days ahead and kept at room temperature, tightly covered. The cake can also be tightly wrapped and frozen in aluminum foil for up to 2 months.

NECTARINE COBBLER WITH DRIED CHERRIES

SERVES 6 TO 8

QUICK TO ASSEMBLE and great for parties, this simple dessert is loaded with fresh fruit flavor. The flavor is enhanced by leaving the peel on the nectarines and adding intensely rich dried cherries. The crust is drizzled with melted butter for a cakey-crunchy baked topping. You can find dried cherries in the dried fruit section of your supermarket or at a gourmet specialty store.

3/4	cup coarsely chopped pecans
3/4	cup all-purpose flour
1-1/8	teaspoons baking powder
3/4	cup sugar
1/2	teaspoon ground cinnamon
	pinch of freshly grated nutmeg
	pinch of ground ginger
1	large egg
10	medium nectarines, pitted and sliced into 1-inch pieces
1	3-ounce package dried cherries, cut in half
6	tablespoons unsalted butter, melted

1. For the topping, preheat the oven to 350°F and toast the pecans on a baking sheet for about 7 to 10 minutes or until lightly browned. Cool. Don't turn the oven off. Butter and flour a square or oval 9- by 12-inch baking dish.

2. In a medium mixing bowl, combine the pecans, flour, baking powder, sugar, and spices. Add the egg and mix together with your hands until the mixture is crumbly. Set aside.

3. Place half the nectarine slices in the prepared pan and then sprinkle on the dried cherries. Cover with the remaining nectarine slices, making an even layer.

4. Sprinkle the nut mixture over the fruit and then drizzle on the butter evenly. Bake for about 35 to 45 minutes or until the top is golden brown and bubbling. Serve with French vanilla ice cream or Eggnog Brandy Sauce (page 424) if desired.

ADVANCE PREPARATION: Can be prepared up to 8 hours ahead and kept at room temperature.

PEACH MELBA BUCKLE

SERVES 6 TO 8

A BUCKLE IS one of those early American country desserts like a pandowdy, grunt, or cobbler that combines fruit with biscuits or cake. The source for this recipe idea is Florida Chef Clair Epting, who prepared a blood peach raspberry crisp with a peach honey sauce for dessert one evening at the Cakebread winery in Napa Valley. The late summer peaches grown by the Cakebread's neighbors were unbelievably fragrant and juicy with bright red centers. This buckle takes a similar approach to California's wonderful peaches, combining them with raspberries, a spiced cake, and a toasted almond streusellike topping.

TOPPING
1/2 cup coarsely chopped almonds
1/2 cup all-purpose flour
1/2 cup packed dark brown sugar
1/4 cup granulated sugar
1/2 teaspoon ground cinnamon
    pinch of freshly grated nutmeg
    pinch of ground ginger
1/2 cup unsalted butter, cut into small pieces

CAKE
1/2 cup unsalted butter
3/4 cup sugar
1   large egg at room temperature
2   cups all-purpose flour
2   teaspoons baking powder
1/2 teaspoon ground ginger
1/2 cup milk

1   pint fresh raspberries, cleaned and picked over
3   medium peaches, peeled, pitted, and cut into 1/4-inch pieces

1. For the topping, preheat the oven to 350°F and toast the almonds on a baking sheet for about 7 to 10 minutes or until lightly browned. Cool. Don't turn the oven off. Butter and flour a 9- by 12-inch baking dish.

2. In a medium mixing bowl, combine the almonds, flour, sugars and spices. Add the butter and mix together until the mixture is crumbly. Set aside.

3. For the cake, combine the butter and sugar in a large bowl with an electric mixer and cream them together on medium speed until the mixture is light and fluffy. Beat in the egg.

4. Sift together the flour, baking powder, and ginger and add them to the butter mixture alternately with the milk, making sure the ingredients are well blended.

5. Spread the batter evenly in the prepared baking pan. Sprinkle the raspberries and peach pieces over the batter in an even layer. Sprinkle the topping over the fruit and bake for about 45 to 55 minutes or until the top is golden brown and bubbling and a toothpick inserted in the center comes out clean. Serve with French vanilla ice cream if desired.

ADVANCE PREPARATION: Can be prepared up to 8 hours ahead and kept at room temperature.

PEAR-RASPBERRY ALMOND TART
S E R V E S 8 T O 10

THIS ELEGANT SHOWSTOPPER of a dessert features pear halves and raspberries baked with an almond filling inside a flaky crust. While this dessert takes some time to prepare, it's not difficult, and the result will make you feel like a professional pastry chef.

PASTRY
1-1/4 cups all-purpose flour or white pastry flour
1 tablespoon powdered sugar
   pinch of salt
1/2 cup unsalted butter, frozen and cut into small pieces
1 large egg yolk
2 tablespoons ice water

ALMOND FILLING
1-1/2 cups sliced blanched almonds
3/4 cup sugar
4 tablespoons unsalted butter
2 tablespoons all-purpose flour
1/4 cup almond liqueur such as Amaretto
2 large eggs at room temperature

PEAR AND RASPBERRY TOPPING
4 medium Bosc pears, peeled, cored, halved, and thinly sliced,
   keeping each half together
1/2 pint raspberries
2 tablespoons unsalted butter
2 tablespoons sugar

APRICOT GLAZE

1   cup apricot preserves

2   tablespoons fresh lemon juice

GARNISH

2   tablespoons sliced almonds

1. For the pastry, combine the flour, sugar, and salt in a food processor fitted with the metal blade. Process for a few seconds to blend. Add the butter and process until the mixture resembles coarse meal, about 5 to 10 seconds. With the motor running, gradually add the egg yolk and then the water until the dough is just beginning to come together and will adhere when pinched.

2. Transfer the dough to a floured pastry board or work surface. Press the dough into a round shape for easy rolling. Roll the dough into a circle large enough to fit a 10-inch tart pan with a removable bottom. Drape the pastry circle over the rolling pin and fit it into the pan. Roll the pin over the pan with moderate pressure to remove excess overlapping dough. Press the pastry with your fingers so it adheres to the sides of the pan. If you're using a tart pan with straight edges, raise the edges of the pastry 1/4 to 1/2 inch above the top of the pan by squeezing the dough from both sides, using your thumb and index finger. Place the pan on a baking sheet.

3. For the almond filling, grind the almonds in a food processor fitted with the metal blade. Add the sugar, butter, flour, and almond liqueur. Turn the machine on and off until a meallike paste is formed. Add the eggs and process for 10 seconds to incorporate. Spread the mixture evenly in the pastry shell.

4. Preheat the oven to 400°F. For the fruit topping, arrange the sliced pear halves on top of the filling with the narrower part of the pear closer to the middle to resemble a pear shape. The top should show 8 pear halves sitting on the filling like a flower. Arrange the raspberries between the pear slices in a consistent pattern. Place a circular pattern of raspberries in the middle. Push the raspberries down so that they are embedded in the almond paste, leaving the tops exposed. Be sure to fit the raspberries tightly together.

5. Dot the pears with the butter and sprinkle them evenly with the sugar. Bake the tart for 50 to 60 minutes or until it is brown on top. If the tart becomes too brown, place foil over it to keep it from burning. Remove the tart from the oven and cool.

6. While the tart is baking, prepare the glaze. In a small saucepan, bring the preserves and lemon juice to a boil over medium-high heat. Strain the glaze

through a fine-mesh nylon strainer into another small saucepan. When you're ready to use it, reheat the glaze just to a boil. Brush the glaze on the cooled pears lavishly to give them a shiny appearance. Garnish with almond slices and serve with French vanilla ice cream if desired.

ADVANCE PREPARATION: Can be prepared up to 8 hours ahead through step 3, covered, and refrigerated. The finished tart can be kept for up to 6 hours in the refrigerator. Remove the tart from the refrigerator 1 hour before serving. This is best served at room temperature.

NOTE: Store any unused glaze in the refrigerator in a jar for up to 2 months.

MANGO AND MACADAMIA NUT BROWN BUTTER TART

SERVES 6

THIS SMOOTH, NUTTY brown butter filling laced with sweet exotic mango and rich macadamia nut pieces is a good example of Hawaiian regional cooking. A classic concept, the brown butter tart, is reinterpreted with local Hawaiian ingredients. Fortunately, mangoes and macadamia nuts are available year-round in most supermarkets. Chop the macadamia nuts into small pieces and finely dice the mango for the best texture.

PASTRY

1-1/4	cups all-purpose or white pastry flour
	pinch of salt
2	tablespoons powdered sugar
1/2	cup unsalted butter, frozen and cut into small pieces
1	large egg yolk
1/4	cup ice water

FILLING

3/4	cup unsalted butter
3	large eggs at room temperature
3/4	cup sugar
3	tablespoons all-purpose flour
1-1/4	cups peeled and finely diced ripe mango, (pieces no larger than 1/4 inch)
1	cup macadamia nuts, rinsed of all salt and chopped into 1/4-inch pieces
1/2	cup apricot glaze (recipe follows)
2	tablespoons finely chopped well-rinsed macadamia nuts

1. For the pastry, preheat the oven to 375°F. Place the flour, salt, and powdered sugar in a food processor fitted with the metal blade and process for 5 seconds. Add the butter, egg yolk, and water and process until you have a crumblike texture, about 5 to 10 seconds.

2. Mold the dough into a round form for easy rolling. On a floured pastry board, roll the dough into a 12-inch circle. Place it in an 11-inch tart pan with a removable bottom or a flan ring, pie pan, or quiche pan. With your fingers, fit the dough into the flan ring or pan. If you're using a tart pan with straight edges raise the fluted edges 1/4 to 1/2 inch above the top of the flan ring or pan by squeezing the dough from opposite sides using your index fingers.

3. To prevent the pastry from puffing up while baking, drape parchment paper or tin foil over it and place pie weights, rice, or dried beans evenly over the paper. Bake for 15 minutes. Remove the weights and paper and prick the pastry with a fork. (The pie weights can be reused.) Return the pastry to the oven and bake until it is light brown, approximately 5 to 7 minutes more. Remove it from the oven.

4. For the filling, place the butter in a small saucepan over high heat and melt it. Watch carefully until the butter is dark brown and then remove it from the heat. Strain the butter through a strainer lined with a double thickness of cheesecloth into a small saucepan. Keep warm. There should be no black specks in the butter.

5. In a medium mixing bowl, beat the eggs together until they are frothy. Beat in the sugar until well incorporated. Sprinkle in the flour and whisk until it is well combined and no lumps appear. Add the warmed brown butter and mix again. Add the mango and macadamia nuts and mix to combine.

6. Reduce the oven temperature to 350°F. Place the baked pie shell on a baking sheet and pour the filling into the crust. Bake for 20 to 25 minutes. The filling should be dark brown and set in the center and should move just slightly when the pan is moved. Remove the tart from the oven and let it cool. When the tart is cool, brush it with a thin layer of apricot glaze. Garnish with chopped macadamia nuts. Refrigerate until serving time.

ADVANCE PREPARATION: Can be prepared up to 8 hours ahead and refrigerated. Remove the tart from the refrigerator 1/2 hour before serving.

Apricot Glaze

MAKES 1/2 CUP

1/2 cup apricot preserves
1   tablespoon fresh lemon juice

1. In a small saucepan, bring the preserves and lemon juice to a boil. Strain through a fine-mesh nylon strainer. When you're ready to use the glaze, heat it just to the boil again. Brush it on the fruit.

BLUEBERRY LEMON TART

SERVES 8

CALIFORNIANS LOVE FRUIT desserts. This two-tiered fruit tart combines a creamy citrus filling with a topping of mild West Coast blueberries. Just a hint of almond flavors the flaky crust. This tart is a delightful finish to Roast Crispy Fish with Warm Lentils (page 172).

PASTRY

1	cup plus 2 tablespoons all-purpose or white pastry flour
2	tablespoons finely ground almonds
2	tablespoons powdered sugar
1/2	cup unsalted butter, frozen and cut into small pieces
1	large egg yolk
1/4	cup ice water

FILLING

4	large eggs at room temperature
1-1/2	cups sugar
2	tablespoons unsalted butter, softened
1	cup fresh lemon juice
2	tablespoons whipping cream
1	tablespoon finely chopped lemon zest

GARNISH

1	pint blueberries
	powdered sugar
	fresh mint leaves
	strip of lemon zest
1	cup cream, whipped

1. For the pastry, combine the flour, almonds, and sugar in a food processor fitted with the metal blade. Add the butter and egg yolk and process until the mixture resembles coarse meal, about 5 to 10 seconds. With the motor running, gradually add water until the dough is just beginning to come together and will adhere when pinched. Wrap the pastry in plastic and chill it for 20 minutes.

2. Transfer the pastry to a floured pastry board or work surface. Press it into a round shape for easy rolling. Roll the pastry out into a circle large enough to fit an 11-inch tart pan with a removable bottom or a flan ring that has been placed on a baking sheet. Drape the pastry circle over a rolling pin and fit it into the pan. Roll the rolling pin over the tart pan or flan ring with moderate pressure to remove excess overlapping dough. Press the pastry with your fingers so that it adheres to the sides of the pan. If you're using a tart pan with straight edges, raise the edges of the pastry 1/4 to 1/2 inch above the top of the pan by squeezing the dough from both sides with your index fingers.

3. Preheat the oven to 375°F. Place the tart pan on a baking sheet. To prevent puffing up while baking, line the pastry with a sheet of parchment paper or foil pressed to fit the sides. Pour pie weights, dried beans, or rice into the center of the paper and distribute evenly.

4. Bake the crust for 15 minutes. Remove the weights and foil; prick the bottom of the pastry shell with a fork. (The beans and rice may be reused.) Return the crust to the oven and bake it for 5 to 7 minutes, until light brown. Do not overbrown because the pastry will be baked further.

5. For the filling, beat the eggs until frothy in a large mixing bowl with an electric mixer on medium speed or in a food processor fitted with the metal blade. Add the sugar and softened butter and beat until thick and lemon colored. Add the lemon juice, cream, and zest and mix well.

6. Pour the filling into the tart crust and bake for 10 minutes. Reduce the oven temperature to 350°F and bake for 12 to 15 minutes, until the filling is light brown and moves just slightly when shaken. Cool the tart in the pan on a wire rack.

7. When the tart has cooled, remove the sides of the pan. Place the tart on a serving platter and carefully arrange the blueberries in concentric circles on top, starting on the outside and going toward the center. Dust with powdered sugar. To serve, garnish each plate with mint, lemon zest, and a large dollop of whipped cream.

ADVANCE PREPARATION: Can be prepared up to 8 hours ahead and kept at room temperature. Can be prepared up to 1 day ahead through step 2, covered with foil, and refrigerated.

TIRAMISU WITH TOASTED HAZELNUTS AND CHOCOLATE

SERVES 6

ITALIAN EVERYTHING HAS swept the restaurant scene in California, and desserts are no exception. Tiramisu, literally "pick-me-up," has become more popular than the hot fudge sundae. This soft, fluffy dessert is easy to prepare. Buy fresh ladyfingers at a bakery and soak them in the espresso quickly, or they will dissolve.

The filling is made with mascarpone, an incredibly rich, soft Italian cheese. Mascarpone has a texture that is a cross between thick crème fraîche and whipped cream cheese, a mildly sweet and slightly acidic flavor. You can find it in Italian markets or in specialty shops.

This version has hazelnut liqueur in the coffee and is garnished with toasted hazelnuts. Tiramisu is very rich, so it's a fitting finale to a relatively light Italian-style dinner. Begin with Roasted Peppers with Mint Vinaigrette and Goat Cheese Croutons (page 15). For a main course, serve either Indian Summer Pasta (page 128) or Wonton Butternut Squash Ravioli with Spinach Pesto (page 134).

2	tablespoons sliced hazelnuts
1	cup whipping cream
1/2	pound (1 cup) mascarpone cheese
1/2	cup powdered sugar
3	tablespoons Frangelico hazelnut liqueur
1-1/2	cups cooled brewed espresso
2	tablespoons brandy or cognac
30	ladyfingers, pulled in half (2 3-ounce packages)
1/4	cup coarsely grated bittersweet chocolate

1. Preheat the oven to 350°F. Toast the hazelnuts on a baking sheet for 5 to 7 minutes or until lightly browned. Watch carefully to avoid burning them.

2. In the bowl of an electric mixer on medium speed, whip the cream until soft peaks form. Set aside. In another bowl of an electric mixer on medium speed, beat the mascarpone for a minute. Slowly add the sugar and 2 tablespoons of the Frangelico to the mascarpone and beat until the mixture is well combined. Carefully fold in the whipped cream.

3. In a medium mixing bowl, combine the espresso, brandy, and remaining tablespoon of Frangelico. Dip half the ladyfingers quickly into the coffee mixture, one by one, and arrange them flat side down in a single layer in an 8-inch square serving dish. You will need to cut a few of the ladyfingers in half to fit the end of the dish.

4. Spread two thirds of the mascarpone mixture on top of the ladyfingers. Sprinkle 2 tablespoons of the grated chocolate evenly on top. Dip the remaining ladyfingers into the coffee mixture and arrange them in a single layer flat side down on top of the mascarpone. Repeat the procedure with the remaining mascarpone mixture, spreading it on the ladyfingers in a thin even layer.

5. Sprinkle the toasted hazelnuts and then the chocolate on top, making sure they are distributed evenly for an attractive presentation. Refrigerate for at least 4 hours. Cut into squares to serve.

ADVANCE PREPARATION: Can be prepared up to 8 hours ahead and refrigerated.

Variation: Strawberries or raspberries may be added in the middle layer and used as a garnish on top if desired.

VANILLA CARAMEL CREAM
SERVES 6

THIS RECIPE MIGHT be the best argument against the false notion that Californians don't like rich desserts. In fact, when Californians dine out, they frequently choose a light first and main course, then dash all pretext of restraint when the dessert menu appears. I don't think it's much different at home.

This soft caramel version of crème brulée is based on the *crema di vanilla* often served in Italian restaurants. Half-and-half, instead of the usual heavy cream, is the basis for the silky custard that is baked, cooled, and then cloaked with a wickedly rich caramel sauce. Dissolving the sugar in half-and-half creates a finer-textured custard. If you like berries, garnish the top with your favorite variety. Obviously, small servings are recommended.

CUSTARD
2   cups half-and-half
1/2 cup sugar
1   vanilla bean, split open or 2 teaspoons vanilla extract
6   large egg yolks at room temperature

CARAMEL
1/2 cup sugar
1/4 cup water
1   teaspoon vanilla extract
1/2 cup whipping cream

1. Preheat the oven to 325°F. In a heavy medium saucepan over medium-high heat, combine the half-and-half, sugar, and the split vanilla bean. Bring the mixture to a boil, stirring constantly to make sure the sugar has dissolved. Remove the mixture from the heat and cool it slightly. If you're using vanilla extract instead of vanilla bean, add it now.

2. In a large electric mixer bowl or with a hand whisk, beat the egg yolks for 1 minute and then add the half-and-half in a slow, steady stream on low speed, trying not to create too much foam.

3. Pour the mixture through a fine-mesh sieve into a pitcher or large measuring cup. Arrange six 1/2-cup soufflé ramekins in a shallow baking pan. Pour the custard evenly into the ramekins. Carefully pour 1 inch of hot water around the ramekins in the pan to help the custard cook evenly.

4. Bake the custard for about 30 to 35 minutes or until a cake tester or skewer inserted in the center comes out almost clean. Remove the ramekins from the water bath and let them cool to room temperature. Place the ramekins in the refrigerator for 2 hours before topping the custard with the caramel.

5. To prepare the caramel topping, combine the sugar and water in a heavy medium saucepan. Do not use a dark-colored pan, or you will not be able to see the color of the caramel. Dissolve the sugar in water over low heat. Turn up the heat and continually swirl the pan over the heat. The mixture will be bubbly. If sugar crystals form on the sides of the pan, cover it for 1 minute to dissolve them. Boil the mixture until it turns a dark golden brown color. Watch carefully, because caramel can burn easily. (If you make the caramel too dark, it will continue to cook and taste burned.) Remove the caramel from the heat and let it cool, making sure it is still liquid. Replace the caramel on low heat, add the vanilla and cream, and continue cooking. The mixture will look as if it has separated, but with patience and constant stirring it will become smooth in a few more minutes. Cool the mixture. It will thicken slightly.

6. Ladle the cooled caramel over each cooled custard ramekin, swirling to distribute the caramel evenly. Refrigerate at least 2 hours or until the caramel is set.

ADVANCE PREPARATION: The custards may be prepared up to 3 days ahead, covered, and refrigerated. Remove them from the refrigerator and serve.

PUMPKIN BREAD PUDDING WITH EGGNOG BRANDY SAUCE

SERVES 8

TIRED OF THE prospect of yet another pumpkin pie ending your holiday dinner? This dessert is familiar comfort when you want the flavor of pumpkin pie but not just the same old dessert. Actually, once you taste this pudding it will become a favorite throughout the fall and winter months.

Bread puddings come in all shapes and flavors. This idea is based on my good friend Kathy Blue's gingerbread pudding, which graces her Thanksgiving dessert table every year. Combining pumpkin bread and a pumpkin custard doubles the flavor and brings an unusual taste to bread pudding.

If you like to bake homemade holiday gifts, you can make this dessert in smaller loaf pans and decorate the pans with colored cellophane. The Eggnog Brandy Sauce is optional.

PUMPKIN CUSTARD

1/2	cup golden raisins
1/2	cup brandy
4	large eggs
3	large egg yolks
1-1/4	cups sugar
1/2	cup canned pumpkin puree
3	cups half-and-half
2	teaspoons vanilla extract
1/4	teaspoon ground cinnamon
1/4	teaspoon ground allspice
1/4	teaspoon ground ginger
1/4	teaspoon freshly grated nutmeg
1	loaf of Spiced Pumpkin-Hazelnut Bread (page 313)
	Eggnog Brandy Sauce (page 424) or whipped cream (optional)

1. In a small saucepan, combine the raisins and brandy and bring to a boil. Remove the raisins from the heat and set them aside for 1 hour to plump them.

2. Preheat the oven to 375°F. Butter a 2-quart oval or round baking dish. Place the dish in a larger pan that will serve as a water bath.

3. In a mixing bowl with electric mixer on medium speed, beat the eggs and yolks until frothy. Slowly add the sugar and beat the mixture until it is thick and lemon colored. Add the pumpkin puree and half-and-half, reducing the speed to low. Add the vanilla, spices, and plumped raisins and brandy and mix.

4. Slice the pumpkin bread into 1/8-inch slices and place the slices overlapping to fill the baking dish. Ladle the custard mixture over the pumpkin bread slices until the baking dish is filled to the top, making sure the raisins are distributed evenly.

5. Pour enough boiling water into the larger baking pan to reach halfway up the sides of the baking dish. Place the pudding in the oven and bake for 40 to 45 minutes.

6. Open the oven using heavy oven mitts and with a large spoon push the bread down. The liquid custard will rise. Spoon the custard evenly over the bread slices. Bake for about 10 minutes or until a skewer inserted in the center comes out clean. Remove the pudding from the oven, sprinkle it with powdered sugar, and cut it into squares. Serve with Eggnog Brandy Sauce or whipped cream if desired.

ADVANCE PREPARATION: Can be prepared up to 1 day ahead through step 3. Refrigerate the custard and bring to room temperature before assembling. You can also prepare the dish up to 1 day ahead through step 4 and refrigerate it before baking. It will be a bit less custardy since the bread will have absorbed the custard.

CHOCOLATE CHIP COFFEE CAKE
SERVES 6 TO 8

THIS UPDATED SOUR cream coffee cake combines a mixture of toasted pecans and almonds with cinnamon and chocolate chips as a filling and a topping. Serve the cake for brunch, tea, or dessert. Don't worry if some of the topping comes off when you invert the cake. A dusting of powdered sugar is all that's needed.

FILLING
1 cup coarsely chopped pecans
1 cup coarsely chopped almonds
2 tablespoons sugar
2 teaspoons ground cinnamon
6 ounces semisweet chocolate chips

BATTER
1 cup unsalted butter
2 cups sugar
2 large eggs at room temperature
1 cup sour cream
2 teaspoons vanilla extract
2 cups all-purpose flour
1 teaspoon baking powder
1/4 teaspoon salt

GARNISH
powdered sugar (optional)

1. Preheat the oven to 350°F. Grease and flour a 9-inch lightweight bundt pan or angel food cake pan.

2. For the filling, toast the nuts on a baking sheet for 5 minutes or until lightly browned. Cool. Combine the nuts, sugar, cinnamon, and chocolate chips in a small bowl and set aside.

3. Cream the butter and sugar with an electric mixer on medium speed until the mixture is light and fluffy. Beat in the eggs one at a time. Stir in the sour cream and vanilla.

4. Combine the flour, baking powder, and salt in a bowl and mix well. Fold this into the butter mixture. Spread half the batter in the prepared pan with a spatula. Sprinkle with half the filling mixture. Spread with the remaining batter and sprinkle the rest of the filling on top in an even layer, pushing the chocolate chips and nuts into the batter.

5. Bake for about 1 hour to 1-1/4 hours or until a tester inserted in the center comes out clean. (You may want to put a piece of aluminum foil on top after 45 minutes of baking so the chocolate does not burn.) Cool the coffee cake in the pan. Invert it onto a cake rack, then invert it back onto a serving platter. Dust with powdered sugar if desired.

ADVANCE PREPARATION: Can be prepared up to 8 hours ahead but is best eaten warm.

BANANA CAKE WITH CHOCOLATE FUDGE FROSTING

SERVES 8 TO 10

FLUFFY BANANA-SCENTED CAKE is sandwiched between layers of creamy fudge frosting in this old-fashioned homage to the classic chocolate-banana combination. While bananas used to come exclusively from the tropics, one farmer in the Montecito area near Santa Barbara has been experimenting with some truly unusual varieties with excellent results.

The frosting is based on a classic ganache, which becomes very thick as it chills, so watch carefully. Be sure to use a good-quality semisweet chocolate. If you like, use 8 ounces of semisweet and 2 ounces of bittersweet for a deeper chocolate flavor. This cake is a perfect ending to a special family dinner or birthday.

CAKE

1-3/4 cups all-purpose flour
1　　teaspoon baking soda
1/4　teaspoon salt
1　　cup unsalted butter, softened
1　　cup sugar
2　　large eggs at room temperature
1　　cup mashed banana (about 2 ripe medium bananas)
2　　teaspoons vanilla extract
1/2　cup buttermilk

FROSTING

1-1/4 cups whipping cream
10   ounces semisweet chocolate, cut into small pieces
4   tablespoons unsalted butter, softened
1   tablespoon vanilla extract

1   medium banana, thinly sliced

1. Preheat the oven to 350°F. Grease the bottom and sides of two 8-inch round cake pans.

2. Combine the flour, baking soda, and salt in a medium bowl.

3. In a large mixing bowl with an electric mixer on medium speed, beat the butter and sugar together until fluffy and light lemon colored. Add the eggs and then the mashed banana and vanilla and beat until well blended. Don't worry if the mixture looks curdled.

4. Alternately add the flour mixture and buttermilk on low speed until they are completely incorporated, ending with the flour. Divide the batter between the prepared cake pans. Bake for 30 to 35 minutes or until the tops spring back to the touch and are golden brown. Cool the cake in the pans on wire racks and then invert them onto the racks and bring them to room temperature.

5. To prepare the frosting, bring the cream to a boil in a heavy medium saucepan over high heat. When boiling, remove the cream from the heat and add the chocolate, butter, and vanilla, stirring until the chocolate and butter are completely melted and the mixture is smooth. Place the pan in the refrigerator and cool, checking every 15 minutes and giving it a stir. The frosting will begin to set after 50 minutes and become quite thick. Check every 5 minutes to get the right consistency.

6. To frost the cake, place one layer flat side up on a 12-inch round platter. Spread with a third of the frosting. Carefully place the banana slices on top of the frosting in an even layer. Place the other cake layer flat side up on the bananas and flatten it with your hand. Frost the top and sides very thickly with the remaining frosting. Make peaks by making quick movements with your hand so the cake looks old-fashioned. Clean the platter with a damp paper towel to remove any excess frosting. Let the frosting set and serve at room temperature.

ADVANCE PREPARATION: Can be prepared up to 1 day ahead and refrigerated. Bring to room temperature before serving.

CHOCOLATE FREAK-OUT

THIS VERY INTENSE CHOCOLATE DESSERT falls somewhere between a cake, a torte, and a cheesecake, and is a chocolate lover's dream. Best of all, you can always store one in your freezer. It tastes almost as good frozen and thawed as it does freshly baked and chilled.

1	pound semisweet or bittersweet chocolate, cut into 1-inch pieces
10	tablespoons unsalted butter
4	large eggs, separated
2	tablespoons all-purpose flour
	pinch of salt
2	tablespoons sugar

GARNISH
powdered sugar or 1 cup whipping cream, whipped

1. Preheat the oven to 425°F. Butter the sides and bottom of an 8-inch springform pan. Place an 8-inch round of wax paper on the bottom.

2. In the top of a large double boiler over medium heat, melt the chocolate, making sure no water touches it. Add the butter, mixing to incorporate it with the chocolate mixture as it melts. Cool the mixture.

3. In the medium bowl of an electric mixer, beat the egg yolks until fluffy and light lemon colored, about 5 minutes. Add the flour and continue mixing just until the flour is incorporated.

4. In another medium bowl of an electric mixer, beat the egg whites and salt until the whites begin to hold their shape. Add the sugar and continue whipping until they are thick and hold their shape but are not dry or overly stiff.

5. Add the cooled chocolate mixture to the egg yolks, mixing well. With a rubber spatula, slowly add one third of the egg whites to the chocolate mixture, mixing from the bottom of the bowl to blend the whites into the chocolate. Add the remaining whites and continue gently blending them in until there are no white streaks left. Pour the mixture into the prepared pan.

6. Bake the cake in the center of the oven for exactly 15 minutes. (It will look almost raw but will continue to cook as it cools.) Remove the cake from the oven and let it cool. To remove the cake from the pan, use a knife to separate the sides from the pan. When the cake is cool, place it on a serving platter and dust it with powdered sugar; or decorate with whipped cream all over the cake and then pipe rosettes all around the top in a circular border. Chill until ready to serve.

ADVANCE PREPARATION: This cake has the best texture when made a day ahead, refrigerated, and removed 1 hour before serving. It also freezes well.

BITTERSWEET CHOCOLATE HAZELNUT TORTE WITH BANANA CUSTARD SAUCE

SERVES 6

REMEMBER HOW DELICIOUS frozen chocolate-covered bananas were when you were a kid? This grown-up dessert features intense bittersweet chocolate as the main flavor, enhanced by a burst of tropical banana essence in the custard sauce. While this torte takes some time to prepare, you can make the cake ahead and freeze it with excellent results.

TORTE
6   ounces bittersweet chocolate, cut into small pieces
3/4 cup unsalted butter
4   large eggs at room temperature
3/4 cup sugar
3   tablespoons all-purpose flour
3   tablespoons ground hazelnuts

GLAZE AND DECORATION
6   ounces bittersweet chocolate, cut into small pieces
1/2 cup unsalted butter
1/2 teaspoon safflower oil
1   tablespoon light corn syrup
20 whole hazelnuts

SAUCE
Banana Custard Sauce (recipe follows)

1. Preheat the oven to 375°F. Cut a round of wax paper to fit an 8-inch round cake pan. Butter the pan and place the paper in the bottom of the pan and butter it generously.

2. Combine the chocolate and butter in the top of a double boiler over medium-low heat and melt slowly, stirring occasionally. Or combine the chocolate and butter in a 2-cup microwave-safe glass measuring cup and heat on 100 percent power for 1-1/2 minutes, until melted, stirring once. Let cool.

3. With an electric mixer on medium speed in a large mixing bowl whisk the eggs until frothy. Slowly add the sugar and beat the mixture until it is pale lemon colored, about 5 minutes. Fold the chocolate mixture into the egg mixture and blend well. Stir in the flour and nuts until well combined.

4. Pour the mixture into the prepared pan. Bake for 25 to 30 minutes, until the outside is firm and the interior is slightly underdone but not runny. A tester inserted in the center should come out slightly wet. Cool the cake in the pan, then unmold it onto a cake rack. Place the cake rack on a cookie sheet lined with wax paper.

5. For the glaze, melt the chocolate and butter in the top of a double boiler over low heat. Stir the chocolate until it is melted and smooth. Or combine the chocolate and butter in a 2-cup microwave-safe glass measuring cup and heat on 100 percent power for 1-1/2 minutes, until melted, stirring once. Stir in the oil and syrup. Allow the glaze to cool to room temperature. (Make sure the glaze stays at room temperature and does not harden. If it hardens, gently soften it in the top of a double boiler until tepid or for 20 seconds on 50 percent power in the microwave.)

6. Pour the glaze over the cooled cake and tilt the cake so that it runs down the sides. Use a long spatula to touch up the sides of the cake. When the glaze is set, carefully place the whole hazelnuts in a circular pattern on the outer edge of the top of the cake. Slide a spatula under the cake and lift it up onto a cake platter lined with a doily. Serve with Banana Custard Sauce.

ADVANCE PREPARATION: Can be prepared up to 1 day ahead, covered, and kept at room temperature. The cake can also be refrigerated. Remove it from the refrigerator 1 hour before serving. The cake can be refrigerated until set, wrapped in foil, and frozen for up to 2 months. Remove it from the freezer 8 hours ahead and keep it at room temperature.

Banana Custard Sauce

MAKES 6 SERVINGS

1-1/3 cups half-and-half
1/2   vanilla bean, split open, or 1 teaspoon vanilla extract
3   large egg yolks
1/3   cup sugar
1   soft banana, cut into small pieces

1. In a small saucepan over medium-high heat, combine the half-and-half and vanilla bean and bring to a simmer. Turn off the heat and cover the pan. Let the vanilla bean steep for 20 minutes. Remove the vanilla bean.

2. Place the egg yolks in the top of a double boiler over medium heat. Add the sugar and whisk until thick and lemon-colored. Slowly pour in the hot half-and-half, whisking constantly. Continue whisking and cook until the mixture has a custardlike consistency. It should coat the bottom of a wooden spoon. *Do not let the custard boil, or it will curdle.*

3. Immediately remove the sauce from the heat and add the banana. If you're using vanilla extract, add it now. With a hand blender, puree the banana into the cream mixture. (If you don't have a hand blender, puree the banana in a food processor and then add it to the sauce.) Pour the sauce through a fine-mesh sieve into a bowl for a silky consistency if desired. Cover the sauce and store in the refrigerator until needed.

ADVANCE PREPARATION: Can be prepared up to 1 day ahead, covered, and refrigerated until serving time.

BANANA SPLIT
ICE CREAM TORTE

SERVES 6 TO 8

ICE CREAM PIES are a big hit in California for several reasons. They're easy to assemble, pretty to look at, and they work well with our warm climate and informal entertaining style.

You can vary the ice cream if you like. Just remember that the crust is chocolate and go from there. Other recommended flavors are Oreo, coffee, English toffee, and layers of vanilla and strawberry, like the flavors of an old-fashioned banana split.

This is a great dessert to keep in your freezer. Remember to remove the torte from the freezer 15 minutes before serving for easy slicing.

CRUST
6   tablespoons sliced blanched almonds
40 chocolate wafers (1 9-ounce box)
5   tablespoons unsalted butter, melted

FILLING
3   bananas, peeled and cut into 1/4-inch slices
1   quart French vanilla ice cream, softened
6   ounces bittersweet chocolate, finely chopped

GARNISH
2   ounces bittersweet chocolate, grated

1. Preheat the oven to 350°F. Toast the almonds on a baking sheet for 7 to 10 minutes or until lightly browned. Reserve 2 tablespoons of the almonds for the garnish.

2. For the crust, process the remaining 1/4 cup of the almonds in a food processor fitted with the metal blade for 10 seconds. Add the cookies and process until they resemble crumbs. Transfer the crumbled cookies and nuts to a medium mixing bowl and add the butter, mixing with your fingers until completely combined. Butter the bottom and sides of a 9-1/2-inch springform pan. Pat the crumb mixture into the bottom and halfway up the sides. (Don't worry if it's not perfectly even.) Refrigerate for at least 4 hours or freeze for 1 hour.

3. For the filling, puree 2 of the bananas in a food processor fitted with the metal blade. Add the ice cream and process until well blended. With a few pulses, blend in the chocolate and then the remaining sliced banana, being sure not to break it up too much.

4. Pour the filling into the crust in the pan in an even layer, smoothing it down. Cover it with wax paper and place it on a baking sheet to keep it level. Freeze for 1 hour. When the ice cream is set but not completely frozen, garnish the top with the reserved almonds and the grated chocolate in an even layer. Freeze the torte for at least 12 hours, then cover it with plastic wrap. Remove the torte from the freezer 15 minutes before serving, place it on a serving platter, and release the sides of the pan.

ADVANCE PREPARATION: Can be prepared up to 1 month ahead, covered tightly, and frozen.

CHOCOLATE TRUFFLE BROWNIES

MAKES 32 BROWNIES

THE BEST PART about preparing these brownies is that you mix everything right in the top of a double boiler. This adaptation of my dear friend Denny Luria's brownie recipe increases the chocolate and reduces the amount of flour, resulting in a crispy-chewy and very moist and chocolaty brownie. If you like nuts, add 1/2 cup toasted pecans or walnuts. Serve these on their own or with a scoop of French vanilla ice cream. Store remaining brownies in an airtight container.

1   cup unsalted butter
6   ounces unsweetened chocolate, cut into small pieces
2   cups sugar
4   large eggs at room temperature
1   teaspoon vanilla extract
1/2 cup all-purpose flour
1/2 teaspoon salt

1. Preheat the oven to 325°F. Grease a 9- by 13-inch baking pan.

2. Combine the butter and chocolate in the top of a double boiler over medium-low heat and melt slowly, stirring occasionally.

3. When the butter and chocolate are melted, remove the pot from the heat, add the sugar, and whisk vigorously. Add the eggs and vanilla and whisk until completely incorporated. Add the flour and salt and blend in, making sure there are no lumps of flour. The mixture should now have a shiny batterlike consistency.

4. Pour the batter into the prepared pan and gently smooth the top. Bake in the center of the oven for 40 minutes or until the top is crisp and dry and a wooden toothpick inserted 1 inch from the center comes out barely moist. Cool to room temperature before cutting into squares or bars.

ADVANCE PREPARATION: Can be prepared up to 1 day ahead and kept in an airtight container until serving time.

WHITE CHOCOLATE AND PISTACHIO COOKIES

MAKES ABOUT 4 DOZEN

THE FIRST TIME I tasted these I couldn't believe how satisfying and sweetly comforting they are. This recipe comes from landscape architect Denise Smith. Based loosely on the Toll House recipe, her adaptation combines creamy white chocolate chunks with roasted unsalted green pistachios. You'll need a good-quality white chocolate like Lindt.

2-1/4 cups all-purpose flour
1   teaspoon baking soda
3/4   teaspoon salt
1   cup unsalted butter
1   cup firmly packed light brown sugar
1/2   cup sugar
2   large eggs at room temperature
1   teaspoon vanilla extract
3/4   pound white chocolate, cut into small chunks, or chips
1   cup coarsely chopped unsalted pistachios

1. Sift together the flour, baking soda, and salt and set aside.

2. In a large bowl with an electric mixer on medium speed, beat the butter and sugar until the mixture becomes creamy. Beat in the eggs and vanilla. Add the flour mixture and continue mixing until well blended. Stir in the chocolate and nuts.

3. Preheat the oven to 350°F. Drop the cookies by rounded teaspoonfuls 2 inches apart onto an ungreased baking sheet. Bake for 10 to 12 minutes or until lightly browned. They should look slightly underdone when removed from the oven. Let the cookies sit in the pan for a minute before removing them to cool. Store in an airtight container.

ADVANCE PREPARATION: Can be prepared up to 1 day ahead and kept in an airtight container.

SPICY CRINKLE COOKIES
MAKES ABOUT 4 DOZEN

THESE MOIST, CHEWY cookies perfumed with sweet spices are perfect with simple fruit desserts or ice cream. I like to serve a plate of these with Mixed Exotic Fruit Gazpacho (page 349) or alongside a platter of Fresh Apricots and Strawberries with Sour Cream and Brown Sugar (page 351).

2-1/4 cups all-purpose flour
2　　teaspoons baking soda
1/4　　teaspoon salt
1/2　　teaspoon ground cloves
1　　teaspoon ground cinnamon
1　　teaspoon ground ginger
1/2　　teaspoon freshly grated nutmeg
1/2　　teaspoon ground allspice
3/4　　cup unsalted butter, softened
1　　cup packed dark brown sugar
1　　large egg at room temperature
1/4　　cup molasses
　　granulated sugar for rolling the cookies

1. In a medium bowl, sift together the flour, baking soda, salt, and spices.

2. In a large bowl with an electric mixer on medium speed, beat the butter and add the brown sugar, beating until creamy. Beat in the egg and molasses. Add the sifted flour mixture and continue mixing until well blended.

3. Chill the dough, covered, in the refrigerator for at least 4 hours.

4. Preheat the oven to 350°F. Grease a cookie sheet. Lay a large sheet wax paper on the counter and sprinkle it with sugar. Roll the dough into balls about the size of a

walnut and then roll them in the sugar, creating an even sugar layer. Place the cookies about 2 inches apart on the prepared cookie sheet. Bake for about 8 to 10 minutes or until just set. (They will puff up when cooking, then fall down, forming the crinkle when cooled.) Cool on a rack. Store in an airtight container.

ADVANCE PREPARATION: Can be prepared up to 1 day ahead and kept in an airtight container.

CALIFORNIA PISTACHIOS

Since the first commercial harvest in 1976, California has become the second-largest producer of pistachio nuts in the world. You can find shelled, unsalted pistachios in most specialty imported food markets or health food stores. If you can't find them shelled, you can do this yourself very easily. Do be certain, however, to use the unsalted variety for cooking.

What makes California pistachios so special? They're usually larger than their imported cousins, with a vivid green color and a wide split shell that makes them easier to open. The Kerman variety has a smooth, buttery flavor.

In the 1930s European importers dyed blemished pistachio shells red because of antiquated harvesting and processing methods that bruised the shells. Most California pistachios are sold in their natural tan shell, but some are still dyed red because many consumers have become accustomed to the red color. To keep shelled and unshelled pistachios fresh and flavorful, store them in an airtight container in the refrigerator for up to a month.

BASICS

EASY BROWN TURKEY OR CHICKEN STOCK   393

EASY BROWN VEAL STOCK   395

TURKEY OR CHICKEN STOCK   397

CORN BREAD FOR STUFFING   399

DOUBLE-TOMATO HERB SAUCE   400

MIXED-HERB PESTO   402

PESTO   403

SUN-DRIED TOMATO PESTO   404

ANCHO CHILE PASTE   406

RED PEPPER AÏOLI   408

ROASTED GARLIC PUREE   409

BASIC VINAIGRETTE   410

HOT PEPPER OIL   412

SPICY TOMATO SALSA   413

TOMATILLO SALSA   414

RUSTIC SALSA   415

SMOKY SALSA   416

ROASTED TOMATO JAM   418

CRANBERRY ALMOND RELISH   419

GINGER-SPICED ASIAN PEAR AND CRANBERRY COMPOTE   421

ASIAN PEAR–QUINCE–APPLE SAUCE   423

EGGNOG BRANDY SAUCE   424

CRÈME FRAÎCHE   425

EASY BROWN TURKEY OR CHICKEN STOCK

MAKES 1-1/2 QUARTS

SOMETIMES I PREFER a dark brown poultry stock instead of the usual white. My friend Kathy Blue makes an incredibly rich brown poultry stock. Her secret lies in reducing the stock for hours on top of the stove. However, this oven technique saves time, requires less cleanup, and doesn't sacrifice any of the delicious results of Kathy's method. I'm not sure I'll ever make brown stock any other way.

4 pounds turkey or chicken necks, backs, and wings, cut up
2 large carrots, cut into 2-inch slices
2 large onions, cut into 2-inch slices
1 bouquet garni*

1. Preheat the oven to 425°F. Place the necks, backs, and wings in a heavy large roasting pan. Roast, turning occasionally, until browned, about 1-1/2 hours.

2. Using oven mitts, open the oven door carefully, pull the oven rack with the pan on it halfway out, and pour about 2 cups of water or enough to cover the bones into the pan. Deglaze the pan by stirring and scraping the bits from the bottom of the pan. The water will become a rich brown color. Add the vegetables, an additional 10 cups of water, and the bouquet garni. Return the pan to the oven and continue cooking for another 1-1/2 to 2 hours. Add more water as it reduces.

3. Remove the pan from the oven, being sure to use heavy oven mitts, and let the stock cool. Remove the bones and pour the stock through a fine-mesh strainer (a conical strainer is excellent for this purpose) into a large bowl. Let it cool to room temperature. Cover the bowl and refrigerate for at least 6 hours or overnight.

---

* To make a bouquet garni, wrap a parsley stem, a bay leaf, and a sprig of fresh thyme in cheesecloth and tie with string. Tie the string to the handle of your pan so you can retrieve it easily.

4. With a large spoon, remove the hardened fat from the surface and discard it. The stock should be clear. If you're not using it immediately, pour it into small containers and refrigerate.

ADVANCE PREPARATION: If not used within 3 days, the stock should be frozen and then reboiled before being used. Freeze in small containers for convenient use.

EASY BROWN VEAL STOCK

MAKES ABOUT 3 QUARTS

CALIFORNIA SAUCES AND reductions often rely on veal stock for their light, meaty richness rather than beef stock, which tends to be heavy and overpowering. Veal stock has another virtue: it assimilates the flavors it's blended with in a most appealing way. Prepare this stock in large quantity and divide it into small containers to keep in your freezer. Making veal stock from scratch may seem like a big fuss, but this oven method makes it a snap, and the stock is so delicious that you'll want to have it on hand.

1 tablespoon olive oil
4 pounds veal knuckles with some meat on them
1 large carrot, cut into 2-inch slices
1 large onion, cut into 2-inch slices
2 celery ribs, cut into 2-inch slices
2 medium leeks, white part only, cleaned and finely chopped
1 cup full-bodied dry red wine like Merlot or Cabernet Sauvignon
2 tablespoons tomato paste
18 cups water
1 bouquet garni*

1. Preheat the oven to 425°F. Lightly oil the veal bones in your hands and place them in a heavy large roasting pan. Roast for 1 hour. Add the vegetables and continue roasting for 1/2 hour, turning occasionally, until well browned, making sure the vegetables are browned but not burned.

---

* To make a bouquet garni, wrap a parsley stem, a bay leaf, and a sprig of fresh thyme in cheesecloth and tie with string. Tie the string to the handle of your pan to retrieve it easily.

2. Using oven mitts, open the oven door carefully, pull out the rack with the pan on it halfway, pour the wine into the pan, and deglaze the pan by stirring and scraping the bits from the bottom of the pan. Add the tomato paste; the mixture will become a rich brown color. Add 3 quarts of the water and the bouquet garni, making sure the bones are just covered with the water. Return the pan to the oven, reduce the heat to 325°F, and continue cooking for 1 hour. Add the remaining 6 cups of water. Reduce the oven temperature to 300°F and roast for 1 hour.

3. Remove the pan from the oven, being sure to use heavy oven mitts, and let the stock cool. Remove the bones and pour the stock through a fine-mesh strainer (a conical strainer is excellent for this purpose) into a large bowl. Let the stock cool to room temperature. Cover it and refrigerate for at least 6 hours or overnight.

4. With a large spoon, remove the hardened fat from the surface and discard it. The stock should be clear. If you're not using it immediately, pour it into small containers and refrigerate again.

ADVANCE PREPARATION: If not used within 3 days, the stock should be frozen and then reboiled before being used. Freeze it in small containers for convenient use.

TURKEY OR CHICKEN STOCK

MAKES 3 QUARTS

SOUPS AND SAUCES always benefit from a rich homemade stock. Make this up and keep it in your freezer in 1- and 2-cup containers.

4 pounds turkey or chicken necks and backs
3 celery ribs
3 medium carrots, peeled
2 medium onions, root ends cut off, cut into halves
2 medium leeks, both white and green parts, cleaned and sliced
1 bouquet garni*
   salt to taste

1. Combine all the ingredients except the salt in a 6-quart stockpot. Add enough cold water to fill the pot three-quarters full. Bring slowly to a boil over medium heat, uncovered.

2. Turn down the heat as low as possible and simmer for 3 hours. Add salt to taste. Taste for seasoning.

3. Strain the stock through a colander or strainer lined with cheesecloth. Let it cool and refrigerate for at least 6 hours or overnight. With a large spoon, remove the hardened fat from surface and discard it.

4. If you're not using it immediately, pour the stock into containers and refrigerate.

ADVANCE PREPARATION: If not used within 3 days, the stock should be frozen and then reboiled before being used. Freeze in small containers for convenient use.

---

* To make a bouquet garni, wrap a parsley stem, a bay leaf, and a sprig of fresh thyme in cheesecloth and tie with string. Tie the string to the handle of your pan to retrieve it easily.

COOKING WITH LESS FAT

There's no question that reducing fat has become a way of life for many of us. But that doesn't mean that you can't have intense, flavorful food. Here are some ways to reduce fat without sacrificing flavor:

• Use olive oil spray instead of coating the ingredient with oil. You still get the same flavor with a far less oily texture. This works particularly well on breads, potatoes, and vegetables.

• Substitute nonfat yogurt when possible for cream or sour cream. The key is to remember that you can't simmer yogurt, but you can add it as a zippy garnish to cold and warm soups, salad dressings, and even mashed potatoes.

• Whipping cream is still preferable for finishing certain sauces, but you can reduce the amount and add roasted garlic puree, pureed cooked vegetables, or vegetable or chicken stock to the sauce for extra body with a fine result (make crème fraîche, page 425, out of your leftover whipping cream, and it will keep for at least a week in the refrigerator.)

• Add a tablespoon or two of boiling water instead of some of the oil to an emulsified vinaigrette to lighten the consistency and fat level or add a few tablespoons of nonfat yogurt or chicken stock.

• Choose dry-aged cheeses like Parmesan, Pecorino Romano, or dry Jack to flavor a dish by garnishing it with thin shreds.

• Consider chopped fresh herbs, Dijon mustard, and citrus as low-fat flavor enhancers that really work.

• Make a crust of mustard, coat with fresh herbs or hoisin sauce, and then coat with scallions, ginger, and sesame seeds for fish or poultry.

• Use your favorite vegetable salsa as a sauce.

• Try smoking meat, poultry, seafood, or vegetables to add flavor without fat.

CORN BREAD FOR STUFFING

MAKES 8 CUPS

DON'T TRY TO save time by using a packaged corn bread mix, usually cloyingly sweet and too moist. Making corn bread from scratch is a snap. This basic recipe is studded with corn kernels and is slightly dry, which works well for most stuffing recipes. Because the holidays tend to be such a hectic time, I always make this corn bread right after Halloween and stick it in my freezer in a tightly sealed plastic bag. Before using, defrost to room temperature and proceed with your recipe.

1   cup all-purpose flour
1   cup yellow cornmeal
1   tablespoon baking powder
1   teaspoon sugar
1   teaspoon salt
1/4 teaspoon pepper
1/3 cup vegetable oil or melted unsalted butter
1   large egg
1   cup buttermilk
1/2 cup fresh corn kernels (about 1 medium ear) or thawed frozen

1. Preheat the oven to 425°F. Grease an 8- or 9-inch square baking pan.

2. Combine the flour, cornmeal, baking powder, sugar, salt, and pepper in a large mixing bowl. Add the oil, egg, and buttermilk and whisk until all the ingredients are just blended. Add the corn kernels and mix just to combine.

3. Spoon the mixture into the prepared pan and bake for 20 to 25 minutes or until a skewer inserted in the center comes out clean. Cool the mixture in the pan, turn it out, and cut it into small chunks. Proceed with the recipe or freeze until ready to use.

ADVANCE PREPARATION: Can be prepared up to 2 months ahead, wrapped tightly in a plastic bag, and frozen. Thaw before using.

DOUBLE-TOMATO HERB SAUCE

MAKES ABOUT 2 QUARTS

THIS CALIFORNIA REWORKING of the classic marinara sauce includes both canned and sun-dried tomatoes for extra-rich flavor. This thick home-style sauce is equally good on pasta, pizza, meatballs, or eggs.

1   3-ounce package dry-packed sun-dried tomatoes
2   tablespoons olive oil
1   medium onion, finely chopped
1   medium carrot, peeled and finely chopped
1   celery rib, finely chopped
1   28-ounce can crushed tomatoes
1   14-ounce can tomatoes, diced
2   garlic cloves, minced
1   cup full-bodied red wine like Chianti or Merlot
2   cups water
1/4 cup finely chopped parsley
1   teaspoon finely chopped fresh thyme or 1/2 teaspoon dried
1/4 cup finely chopped fresh basil or 2 tablespoons dried
     salt and pepper to taste

1. Place the sun-dried tomatoes in a small mixing bowl and pour boiling water over them. Let them steep for 5 minutes. Drain the softened tomatoes and reserve.

2. Heat the oil in a large nonaluminum pot over medium heat. Add the onion, carrot, and celery and cook until soft, stirring frequently to prevent burning, about 10 minutes. Add both the canned tomatoes and the softened sun-dried tomatoes, the garlic, wine, water, and herbs. Partially cover and reduce the heat to medium-low. Simmer for 1-1/2 hours, stirring occasionally. Add salt and pepper.

3. Puree the mixture in the pot with a hand blender or in a food processor fitted with the metal blade until the sauce is a fine puree with no large pieces of tomato. You may need to add more water for a saucelike consistency since the sun-dried tomatoes provide extra thickness. Taste for seasoning, adding more salt and pepper and herbs if desired. Serve hot.

ADVANCE PREPARATION: Can be prepared up to 5 days in advance, covered, and refrigerated. It also can be frozen in small containers for up to 2 months.

MIXED-HERB PESTO

MAKES 1-1/4 CUPS

BASIL, PARSLEY, CHIVES, and thyme are combined in this recipe for a spirited pesto. Most herbs are now available year-round, so you can serve this anytime. I prefer to add the cheese right before serving so that I can use the sauce with or without it. Pesto is excellent added to soups, dressings, and sauces and as a glaze for tomatoes.

2   garlic cloves, peeled
2   cups firmly packed fresh basil leaves (about 1 medium bunch)
1/4 cup firmly packed parsley leaves
1   medium bunch of chives, chopped (about 1/3 cup)
1   tablespoon fresh thyme leaves
3   tablespoons pine nuts
1/2 cup olive oil
1/4 teaspoon black pepper
1/2 cup freshly grated Parmesan

1. While the motor is running, add the garlic to a food processor fitted with the metal blade. Process until pureed. Add the basil, parsley, chives, and thyme and process until finely chopped. Add the pine nuts and finely chop.

2. With the motor running, slowly pour in the olive oil in a fine stream. Scrape down the sides of the bowl to blend the ingredients. Add the pepper.

3. Just before serving, add the cheese and process until well blended. Taste for seasoning. Refrigerate the pesto in a tightly covered container until ready to use.

ADVANCE PREPARATION: Can be prepared up to 1 week ahead through step 2 and refrigerated. Add the cheese just before serving.

PESTO

MAKES 1 TO 1-1/2 CUPS

I COOK WITH this uncomplicated pesto when I'm in the mood for the straight-forward classic flavors of basil and Parmesan.

2   garlic cloves, peeled
2   cups firmly packed fresh basil leaves (about 2 medium bunches)
1/2 cup firmly packed parsley leaves
2   tablespoons pine nuts
1/2 cup olive oil
1/4 teaspoon black pepper
3/4 cup freshly grated Parmesan

1. With the motor running, add the garlic cloves to a food processor fitted with the metal blade. Process until pureed. Add the basil and parsley and process until finely chopped. Add the pine nuts and finely chop.

2. With the motor running, slowly pour in the olive oil in a fine stream. Add the pepper.

3. Just before serving, add the cheese and process until well blended. Taste for seasoning. Refrigerate the pesto in a tightly covered container until ready to use.

ADVANCE PREPARATION: Can be prepared up to 1 week ahead through step 2 and refrigerated. Add the cheese just before serving.

WHAT TO DO WITH SUN-DRIED TOMATO PESTO OR ANCHO CHILE PASTE

- Add to crème fraîche, sour cream, or mayonnaise for a quick and easy dip for raw vegetables.
- Add to baby potatoes and roast them in foil or parchment.
- Add to mayonnaise and spread on a sandwich with grilled red peppers, grilled eggplant, and fresh goat cheese.
- Use to season steamed vegetables.
- Use as part of a sauce for sautéed chicken breasts or turkey scaloppini.
- Use as a paste for chicken breasts that will be grilled.
- Use as an addition to basic vinaigrette.

SUN-DRIED TOMATO PESTO

MAKES ABOUT 1/2 CUP

WHETHER THIS RECIPE originated in Italy or here in California, this luscious pesto is incredibly versatile. It flavors cheese, main courses, dressings, sauces, and pasta. It's also good on lightly toasted bread.

1 garlic clove, peeled
1/2 cup oil-packed sun-dried tomatoes, drained
2 tablespoons finely chopped fresh basil leaves
2 tablespoon pine nuts
1/4 teaspoon salt
1/8 teaspoon pepper

1. With the motor running, add the garlic to a food processor fitted with the metal blade. Add the tomatoes, basil, pine nuts, salt, and pepper and process until a thick paste is formed. If it is very thick, you may need to add a bit of olive oil. Place the pesto in a covered container and refrigerate.

ADVANCE PREPARATION: Can be prepared up to 1 week ahead and stored in the refrigerator.

Variation: For a simpler paste, puree the garlic, tomato, salt, and pepper together and add enough oil to form a thick paste.

ANCHO CHILE PASTE

MAKES 1/2 CUP

ANCHO CHILES ARE a dried version of the poblano chile with a moderately hot flavor. If you can't find ancho chiles, substitute any dried red chile such as New Mexico or California dried chiles.

Garlic and ancho chiles are toasted in a dry skillet, which is a Mexican technique for releasing their flavor. Additions of mild balsamic vinegar and sweet honey bring out the toasted chile flavor. The chiles are then softened, pureed, and strained into a thick paste. This is a wonderful flavoring to have on hand. Try adding it to sour cream, mayonnaise, or butter. It's also a spicy coating for meat that will be grilled or roasted.

2   large garlic cloves, unpeeled
6   large ancho chiles (about 3 ounces)
3   tablespoons olive oil
1   tablespoon balsamic vinegar
1   teaspoon honey
1/2 teaspoon salt

1. Place the garlic in a small skillet over medium-high heat. Toast the garlic cloves by heating and turning them as they begin to brown. When light brown in color, remove them from the skillet and peel them. Set aside.

2. In the same skillet, heat the chiles over medium heat until they begin to expand and the flesh is soft, about 1 to 2 minutes. (If you have an overhead fan, turn it on, because the chiles may make you cough.) The chiles should smell rich but should not be charred. Remove the chiles from the heat and cool.

3. Wear rubber gloves when handling chiles. Slit the chiles open and remove the seeds, stems, and any veins. Place the chiles in a small bowl. Pour boiling water over them to cover and let them soften for 15 minutes. Remove them from the water, drain well, and pat dry.

4. With the motor running, add the garlic cloves to a food processor fitted with the metal blade. Process the garlic until pureed. Add the chiles, oil, vinegar, honey, and salt and process until the mixture is pureed, scraping down the sides as needed. Strain through a fine-mesh strainer to remove all coarse pieces and taste for seasoning. Store the chile paste in an airtight container in the refrigerator.

ADVANCE PREPARATION: Can be prepared up to 1 month ahead and refrigerated.

RED PEPPER AÏOLI

M A K E S   1 - 1 / 4   C U P S

THIS SIMPLE SAUCE relies on store-bought mayonnaise to avoid any health risks that might occur from using raw eggs in homemade mayonnaise. Sometimes I add the pulp from a head of roasted garlic for a milder version.

4 garlic cloves
1 roasted, peeled (page 287), seeded, and finely chopped medium red bell
    pepper
1 cup mayonnaise
    salt and white pepper to taste
    pinch of cayenne pepper

1. With the motor running, add the garlic cloves to a food processor fitted with the metal blade and process until pureed. Add the red pepper and process until well blended. Add the mayonnaise and process. Add the salt, pepper, and cayenne and taste for seasoning. Refrigerate the sauce in a tightly covered container until serving time.

ADVANCE PREPARATION: Can be prepared up to 5 days ahead and refrigerated.

ROASTED GARLIC PUREE
MAKES ABOUT 2 TO 3 TABLESPOONS

2 heads of garlic
2 teaspoons olive oil

1. Preheat the oven to 425°F. With a sharp knife, cut off the top quarter of the whole head of garlic, then score gently, just cutting through a few layers of the papery skin, all around the diameter. Pull off the loose skin from the top half, trying not to remove every shred. (This will make it easier to squeeze out the cooked cloves later.)

2. Place each garlic head on a piece of aluminum foil. Sprinkle with olive oil and wrap tightly. Place on a baking sheet and bake for 45 to 60 minutes or until the garlic is soft when pierced with a knife. Remove from the oven and cool. Using your fingers, squeeze the soft garlic pulp into a small bowl.

ADVANCE PREPARATION: Can be prepared up to 3 days ahead, covered well, and refrigerated.

BASIC VINAIGRETTE

MAKES 3/4 CUP

THIS VINAIGRETTE IS my standby salad dressing that will brighten up any variety of salad greens. If you like the full-bodied flavor of balsamic vinegar, you can replace part of the red wine vinegar with balsamic, but the dressing will be stronger.

1   medium shallot, finely chopped
1   garlic clove, minced
1   tablespoon finely chopped parsley
1   tablespoon finely chopped fresh chives
1   teaspoon Dijon mustard
1   tablespoon fresh lemon juice
3   tablespoons red wine vinegar
3/4 cup olive oil
1/2 teaspoon salt
1/4 teaspoon black pepper

1. Combine the shallots, garlic, parsley, chives, mustard, lemon juice, and vinegar in a medium bowl and whisk until well blended. Or place in a food processor fitted with the metal blade and process until well blended.

2. Slowly pour the olive oil into the bowl, whisking continuously (or processing) until blended. Add the salt and pepper and taste for seasoning.

ADVANCE PREPARATION: Can be prepared up to 1 week ahead and refrigerated. Bring to room temperature and whisk before using.

VINAIGRETTE

These splendid sauces are not just for salads. You can also use them to accompany grilled or steamed vegetables or grilled chicken, fish, or meat, a particularly appealing idea when you want a sauce but don't want to spend hours reducing stock.

A successful vinaigrette depends on excellent ingredients, the ratio of oil to vinegar, and making sure the two have emulsified. I prefer a ratio of three oils to one vinegar. If you're watching your fat content, add a little hot water or chicken stock in lieu of some of the oil to lighten the dressing. You can use a food processor or a hand blender to make vinaigrette because it automatically creates an emulsion that will last at least a few hours. If you don't have a food processor, just put the ingredients in a small lidded jar and shake vigorously to emulsify or whisk them together in a bowl. Always add the oil last. Vinaigrette will keep in the refrigerator for weeks. Bring it to room temperature before using and emulsify again.

There is an enormous variety of excellent oils and vinegars available that allow you to be really creative. Keep on hand extra virgin olive oil, safflower oil, aged sherry vinegar, a quality red wine vinegar, and balsamic vinegar. Imported hazelnut oil and walnut oil should be used sparingly because their flavors are very intense. I usually use half nut oil and half olive oil.

Almost all vinaigrettes should include a minced shallot and a garlic clove. Dijon mustard is also an excellent flavor enhancer. I like to use just a touch of cream to smooth out the acid in the vinegar for a milder vinaigrette.

Here are some other combinations:

- grilled corn and red onion vinaigrette
- tomato basil vinaigrette
- mixed-herb vinaigrette with chervil, dill, chives, burnet
- chunky tomato–fresh mint vinaigrette
- black bean, tomato, and cilantro vinaigrette
- fennel, garlic, and balsamic vinaigrette
- ginger, orange, and toasted sesame seed vinaigrette
- chopped Niçoise and green olive, caper, and anchovy vinaigrette
- roasted mixed red and yellow pepper vinaigrette
- mixed yellow and red pear tomato vinaigrette
- roasted garlic and blue cheese vinaigrette

HOT PEPPER OIL

M A K E S   1   C U P

USE THIS SPICY oil sparingly. It enlivens many dishes from soup to salad dressings and will keep in the refrigerator almost indefinitely.

1/4 cup hot red pepper flakes
1   cup vegetable or canola oil

1. Combine the pepper flakes and oil in a small saucepan over medium heat; bring to a boil and then immediately turn off the heat. Cool the mixture.

2. Strain the oil into a small glass jar that can be sealed. Keep refrigerated.

Variation: Leave the pepper flakes in the oil. They will fall to the bottom and can be used in seasoning. The oil will become hotter as it stands.

SPICY TOMATO SALSA
MAKES ABOUT 1 QUART

ALL OVER MEXICO you find this traditional salsa in restaurants and in home kitchens. This all-purpose Mexican condiment, sometimes called *pico de gallo* in Texas and *salsa cruda* or *salsa fresca* in Mexico, can be used as a flavoring agent in many dishes from soups to vegetables.

You can regulate the hotness by the number of chiles included. If you like a more rustic salsa, don't bother to peel and seed the tomatoes. Typical of California cooking style, you can change the underlying flavor of this salsa to an Italian accent. Simply replace the jalapeños, cilantro, and lime juice with crushed red pepper flakes, chopped fresh basil, and lemon juice.

4 large fresh tomatoes, peeled, seeded, and finely chopped
2 jalapeño chiles, seeded and finely chopped*
2 tablespoons finely chopped cilantro
1 small red onion, finely chopped
1 garlic clove, minced
1 teaspoon fresh lemon or lime juice
1 teaspoon salt
  pinch of black pepper

1. Combine all the ingredients in a medium bowl and mix well. Taste for seasoning. Cover the salsa and refrigerate.

ADVANCE PREPARATION: Can be prepared up to 3 days ahead and refrigerated. Remove from the refrigerator 1/2 hour before serving.

Variation: Canned jalapeños may be used if fresh are unavailable. Do not add lemon juice if you're using canned chiles.

---

* When you're working with chiles, always wear rubber gloves. Wash the cutting surface and knife immediately.

TOMATILLO SALSA
MAKES 2-1/2 CUPS

LIGHT AND SPICY, tomatillo sauce is an important basic in California cooking. Here the onion is cooked briefly in stock, which is added to the sauce to lighten it. If fresh tomatillos are unavailable, you can substitute drained canned tomatillos with a pinch of sugar; you won't need to cook them. Use this salsa on grilled meat or fish, or to flavor sauces. It's also great with eggs and fresh corn tortillas.

3/4 cup chicken stock (page 397)
1   small onion, coarsely chopped
1   pound tomatillos, husked and quartered
2   jalapeño chiles, seeded and finely chopped*
2   garlic cloves, minced
3   tablespoons finely chopped cilantro
1/4 teaspoon ground cumin seed
1/2 teaspoon salt
1   tablespoon fresh lemon juice

1. In large skillet over medium heat, heat the chicken stock, add the onion, and simmer for about 5 minutes, covered. Add the tomatillos and cook, covered, for another 5 minutes.

2. Pour the contents of the skillet into a food processor fitted with the metal blade and process until coarsely chopped. Add the remaining ingredients and taste for seasoning. Pour the salsa into a storage container and let it cool. Refrigerate until using.

ADVANCE PREPARATION: Can be made up to 5 days ahead and refrigerated in an airtight container.

---

* When you're working with chiles, always wear rubber gloves. Wash the cutting surface and knife immediately.

RUSTIC SALSA

MAKES ABOUT 2 CUPS

THIS CHUNKY, RUSTIC salsa is a combination of red tomatoes and green tomatillos. Unlike other salsas, this one is refined through cooking and coarsely chopping.

1   tablespoon olive oil
6   large Roma tomatoes, halved
2   tomatillos, husked, cored, and quartered
1   small red onion
2   tablespoons finely chopped cilantro
2   garlic cloves, minced
1/2 teaspoon salt
1/4 teaspoon pepper
1/2 teaspoon mild ground red chile powder
1/2 cup chicken stock (page 397)

1. In a large skillet over medium heat, heat the oil, add the tomatoes and tomatillos, and sauté for about 6 to 8 minutes. Stir in the onion, cilantro, and garlic and continue cooking for 8 minutes or until the tomatoes and onion are soft. Stir in the salt, pepper, and chile powder. Remove from the heat and let cool.

2. In a food processor fitted with the metal blade, puree the cooled vegetable mixture, being sure to leave some texture. Add the stock and taste for seasoning. Pour the mixture into a storage container and cool. Refrigerate until using. Spoon over goat cheese or use as a dip for chips.

ADVANCE PREPARATION: Can be made up to 5 days ahead and refrigerated in an airtight container.

SMOKY SALSA

MAKES 2 CUPS

HUGO MOLINA, THE executive chef of The Parkway Grill in Pasadena, created this recipe for The Crocodile Cantina, a fun party of a restaurant serving Central American and Mexican food.

Chipotle chiles canned in adobo sauce, which can be found in Mexican markets, are used here. Chipotles are smoked jalapeño chiles that take on a charred flavor when dried.

Grilling the ingredients first provides a smoky undertone. Try this on Ricotta Corn Cakes (page 33) or as sauce for grilled flank steak (page 235). This salsa is great with a big basket of warm crisp tortilla chips (page 324).

5   large Roma tomatoes, halved
1   small red onion, cut into thick slices
3   scallions, white and light green parts only
1/3 medium bunch of cilantro, bottom stems removed
1   garlic clove
1   teaspoon canned chipotle peppers
1   teaspoon apple cider vinegar
1   teaspoon salt
1/4 cup chicken stock (page 397)

1. Prepare a barbecue for medium-high-heat grilling. Grill the tomatoes, onion slices, and scallions until partially charred, turning occasionally. The red onions will take the longest. Transfer to a plate. Grill the cilantro for about 30 seconds, just to wilt it and give off a slight smoky flavor.

2. With the motor running, add the garlic clove to a food processor fitted with metal blade. Process until pureed. Add the grilled vegetables and remaining ingredients and process until all the vegetables are pureed. Taste for seasoning. (For a thinner consistency, add more chicken stock.) Serve with chips and guacamole or as a condiment for grilled chicken or meat.

ADVANCE PREPARATION: Can be prepared up to 1 week ahead, covered tightly, and refrigerated.

Variation: Add a few tablespoons of beer.

ROASTED TOMATO JAM

MAKES 1-1/2 CUPS

IF YOU'VE NEVER roasted a tomato, you should try it. The juices of the tomato slowly evaporate, leaving them sweet and slightly caramelized. I usually make this in the summer and early fall months, when tomatoes are as they should be—juicy, vine-ripened, and full of flavor.

Farmer's markets have sprouted up all over California in small and big cities alike. You can find just about any variety of tomato in these markets—from the simple beefsteak to zebra tomatoes—in every imaginable size.

While this rustic condiment requires a long cooking time, it needs little hands-on attention. Serve Roasted Tomato Jam warm alongside Grilled Veal Chops with Zucchini-Corn Relish (page 254) or any simple flavored chicken breast. Roasted Onions and Baby Potatoes (page 299) make a nice side dish. This is also good added to warm pasta.

6   pounds tomatoes (about 6 large), peeled, seeded, and coarsely chopped
4   garlic cloves, finely chopped
2   tablespoons olive oil
1   teaspoon finely chopped fresh thyme leaves
1   teaspoon salt
1/4 teaspoon black pepper

1. Preheat the oven to 425°F. In a large nonaluminum baking pan, combine the tomatoes, garlic, oil, and thyme and mix until well blended. Roast for about 2 to 2-1/2 hours, stirring every 30 minutes. The liquid will slowly evaporate, and the mixture will begin to thicken and lightly caramelize. Remove it from the oven and let it cool. Add the salt and pepper and taste for seasoning. Store in an airtight container.

ADVANCE PREPARATION: Can be prepared up to 1 week ahead and refrigerated.

CRANBERRY ALMOND RELISH
SERVES 6 TO 8

THIS IS A standard dish on my Thanksgiving table. A hot sugar syrup briefly cooks the cranberries so that the fruit is slightly undercooked and crunchy. Raspberries and toasted almonds add a unique touch. This is also good with roast chicken or duck.

1/2 cup slivered blanched almonds
1   12-ounce bag fresh cranberries, washed and picked over
1   cup sugar
1   cup water
1   medium Pippin apple, peeled, cored, and quartered
1   medium pear, peeled, cored, and quartered
2   teaspoons minced orange zest
3/4 cup fresh or thawed frozen raspberries
1/4 cup light rum
    pinch of freshly grated nutmeg

GARNISH
fresh mint sprigs

1. Preheat the oven to 350°F. Toast the almonds on a baking sheet for 7 to 10 minutes or until lightly browned. Reserve.

2. Spoon the cranberries into a food processor fitted with the metal blade and chop them coarsely by pulsing the machine a few times. Transfer the cranberries to a large mixing bowl.

3. Combine the sugar and water in a medium saucepan over medium heat and bring to a simmer. Cook the syrup until the sugar is dissolved and the liquid is clear. Immediately pour the syrup over the cranberries and mix well.

4. Place the apple and pear in the food processor fitted with the metal blade and coarsely chop. Transfer to the cranberry mixture. Add the orange zest, raspberries, rum, and nutmeg and mix gently to combine. Taste for seasoning.

5. Spoon into a serving bowl and garnish with fresh mint. Add the almonds just before serving.

ADVANCE PREPARATION: Can be prepared up to 2 days ahead through step 4, covered, and refrigerated. Add the almonds just before serving.

GINGER-SPICED ASIAN PEAR AND CRANBERRY COMPOTE

MAKES ABOUT 6 CUPS

SOMETIMES I WANT a simple sauce with clear flavors. This recipe, inspired by Deborah Madison's cranberry quince sauce, is a lively blending of exotic produce (the Asian pear) with the native American cranberry.

According to Elizabeth Schneider in *Uncommon Fruits and Vegetables*, more than 25 varieties of Asian pear were planted by Chinese prospectors as they crossed through the Sierra Nevada mountains during the gold rush days. Asian pears have a mild aroma and a granular texture, making them difficult to overcook. Oddly enough, their flavor intensifies through long cooking, yet they always retain a slight crunch.

Balsamic vinegar provides a sweet-tart finish to the sauce. Fresh ginger is infused during cooking and is also stirred in at the end to create a layering of flavors. Serve this compote with turkey, poultry, or lamb. I like to serve it at room temperature.

10 cloves
1   2-inch piece of fresh ginger, peeled
1   2-inch piece of cinnamon stick
15 allspice berries
1   cup sugar
2   cups water
2   large Asian pears, peeled, cored, and chopped into 1-inch chunks
1   12-ounce bag fresh cranberries, washed and picked over
2   tablespoons balsamic vinegar
2   teaspoons finely chopped fresh ginger

1. Make a bouquet garni by enclosing the cloves, ginger, cinnamon stick, and allspice berries in a piece of cheesecloth tied together with a piece of string. Tie the string to the handle of a large saucepan.

2. Combine the bouquet garni, sugar, and water in the saucepan and bring the syrup to a boil. When the sugar is dissolved, lower the heat and add the Asian pear pieces. Cover the pan and simmer the pears for about 40 to 45 minutes. They will still offer slight resistance when pierced with a knife.

3. Stir in the cranberries and turn up the heat so that the cranberries will cook and begin to pop, stirring frequently; this should take about 8 to 10 minutes. When the cranberries have cooked, remove the pan from the heat and cool. Remove the bouquet garni from the compote. Add the vinegar and ginger and taste for seasoning. The sauce will firm up as it cools. Refrigerate until serving time. Taste for seasoning just before serving.

ADVANCE PREPARATION: Can be prepared up to 5 days ahead, covered, and refrigerated. Taste before serving. You may need to add a bit more vinegar.

ASIAN PEAR-QUINCE-APPLE SAUCE

MAKES ABOUT 5 CUPS

SOMETIMES SIMPLE ADDITIONS to a basic recipe can make a grand difference. Quince gives off a tropical fruit perfume, and Asian pears maintain a crisp quality, adding unexpected taste and texture to traditional applesauce. I like to serve this as an accompaniment to Crispy Potato Pancakes with Vegetables (page 296) and Braised Beef with Sun-Dried Tomatoes, Zinfandel, and Thyme (page 237). It's also nice heated gently and spooned over French vanilla ice cream.

1 cup sugar
2 cups water
1 cinnamon stick
2 quinces, peeled, cored, and cut into 2-inch chunks
2 Asian pears, peeled, cored, and cut into 2-inch chunks
2 Pippin apples, peeled, cored, and cut into 2-inch chunks

1. In a large casserole over medium heat, combine the sugar, water, and cinnamon stick and cook until the sugar is dissolved. Add the quince and bring it to a low simmer. Cover and cook for about 40 minutes, stirring occasionally.

2. Add the pears and apples and continue cooking for about 1/2 hour, stirring occasionally, until the apples have softened. Remove the cinnamon stick. If you prefer a pureed saucelike consistency, puree the sauce in the pot with a hand blender to reach the desired consistency. Spoon the sauce into containers until ready to use. It is delicious served warm, at room temperature, or chilled.

ADVANCE PREPARATION: Can be prepared up to 1 week ahead and refrigerated.

EGGNOG BRANDY SAUCE

MAKES ABOUT 2-1/2 CUPS

A VERSION OF this versatile sauce using raw eggs first appeared in *The Cuisine of California.* This updated recipe cooks the eggs with superfine sugar to achieve a silky texture and also to avoid any health problems. Brandy and a sprinkling of freshly grated nutmeg enliven this fluffy dessert sauce. This is an exceptional finish to Nectarine Cobbler with Dried Cherries (page 357), Pumpkin Bread Pudding (page 373), or any fruit holiday dessert. You can make your own superfine sugar by briefly whirling regular white sugar in the food processor.

3	egg yolks
3/4	cups superfine sugar
2	tablespoons unsalted butter, softened
3	large egg whites
1	cup whipping cream
1/2	teaspoon vanilla extract
2 to 3	tablespoons brandy, cognac, or applejack
1/8	tablespoon freshly grated nutmeg

1. In the top of a double boiler over medium heat, combine the egg yolks, sugar, and butter and whisk until thick and lemon colored. (The mixture will be very thick until it begins to cook.) Be careful not to overcook and curdle the eggs. The mixture is done when you can coat a spoon with it. Let it cool.

2. In a medium mixing bowl, whip the egg whites until they are stiff.

3. In a medium mixing bowl, whip the cream until it is stiff.

4. Fold the egg whites and cream alternately into the egg yolk mixture until no streaks remain. Fold in the vanilla, brandy, and nutmeg. Serve immediately.

ADVANCE PREPARATION: Can be prepared up to 2 hours ahead and refrigerated. Serve cold. Be careful of the mixture starting to separate. Whisk well if separation begins.

CRÈME FRAÎCHE

MAKES 1 CUP

CRÈME FRAÎCHE IS a versatile substitute for whipping cream in sauces and desserts. Unlike sour cream, it won't break down when added to warm sauces. You might want to sweeten it when serving it with fresh fruit. This is a great way to use up extra whipping cream and to extend its shelf life.

1 cup whipping cream, preferably not ultrapasteurized
2 tablespoons cultured buttermilk

1. Combine the cream and buttermilk in a glass jar or crockery bowl (not metal) and whisk until well blended. Loosely cover the jar or bowl with foil, letting some air in. Leave it in a warm place for at least 24 hours and up to 36 hours. The cream will become thick enough for a spoon to stand up in it and will have a sour, nutty taste.

2. Stir the cream after it has thickened. Cover the cream and refrigerate it until ready to use.

ADVANCE PREPARATION: Can be prepared up to 1 week ahead and refrigerated.

MENUS

THANKSGIVING OR CHRISTMAS

Pear, Pistachio, and Chicken Liver Mousse (page 3)
Marinated Roast Turkey (page 216)
Rich Turkey Gravy (page 218)
Ginger-Spiced Asian Pear and Cranberry Compote (page 421)
OR
Cranberry Almond Relish (page 419)
Onion, Prune, and Chestnut Compote (page 288)
Corn Bread, Leek, and Red Pepper Stuffing Terrine (page 285)
Sautéed Green and Yellow Beans with Garlic and Basil (page 271)
Spiced Sweet Potato Pudding (page 300)
Pumpkin Bread Pudding with Eggnog Brandy Sauce (page 373)

SUMMER CELEBRATION FOR WEDDINGS OR GRADUATIONS

THIS MENU WORKS BEAUTIFULLY ON A BUFFET TABLE.

Asian Gravlax with Ginger-Mustard Sauce (page 8)
Asian Guacamole (page 24)
Focaccia (page 337)
Indonesian Leg of Lamb (page 250)
Rice Pilaf with Corn and Peanuts (page 306)
Tricolor Vegetable Sauté (page 272)
Mango and Macadamia Nut Brown Butter Tart (page 364)
Bittersweet Chocolate Hazelnut Torte with Banana Custard Sauce
(page 381)

WEEKEND BRUNCH

Herbed Scrambled Eggs with Goat Cheese (page 122)
Chicken and Apple Sausage (page 223)
OR
Turkey Sausages with Sun-Dried Tomatoes (page 225)
Roasted Onions and Baby Potatoes (page 299)
Fresh Pear Bread (page 318) and Orange–Poppy Seed Bread
(page 317) with Assorted Preserves
Fresh Melon and Berries

SUNDAY SUPPER

Blood Orange, Mushroom, and Avocado Salad (page 89)
Turkey Vegetable Cobbler (page 220)
Baked Pears in Burgundy and Port Glaze (page 345)

A SUMMER PICNIC

Shrimp Salsa (page 11)
Green Pea Guacamole (page 22)
Crisp Tortilla Chips (page 324)
Grilled Chicken, Black Bean, and Corn Salad with Salsa Dressing
(page 103)
Fresh Apricots and Strawberries with Sour Cream and Brown
Sugar (page 351)
White Chocolate and Pistachio Cookies (page 387)

INFORMAL HOLIDAY BUFFET

Green Olive Tapenade (page 19)
Sun-Dried Tomato Tapenade (page 21)
Parmesan Toasts (page 311)
Peppery Greens with Gorgonzola and Pine Nuts (page 80)
Grilled Orange Mustard Chicken (page 195)
Baked Vegetable Rigatoni with Tomatoes and Provolone (page 130)
Sliced Oranges and Fresh Berries
Orange, Almond, and Olive Oil Cake (page 353)

NO-HASSLE ELEGANT DINNER PARTY

Baked Brie with Sun-Dried Tomato Pesto (page 27)
Broccoli Leek Soup with Parmesan Cream (page 47)
OR
Farmer's Market Chopped Salad (page 78)
Grilled Lamb Chops with Cranberry-Rosemary Marinade (page 242)
Confetti Rice Pilaf (page 305)
Home Ranch Butternut Squash (page 279)
Chocolate Truffle Brownies (page 386)

A COLD BUFFET

Assorted Grilled Vegetables (page 13)
Chilled Artichoke Halves with Red Pepper Aïoli (page 17)
Crispy Roast Chicken (page 208)
Long-Grain and Wild Rice Salad with Corn and Salmon (page 96)
Caesar Salad with Mixed Baby Lettuces and Parmesan Toasts
(page 76)
Walnut Bread (page 332) with Assorted Cheeses
Peach Melba Buckle (page 359)

WINTER DINNER

Sweet Potato–Jalapeño Soup with Tomatillo Cream (page 45)
Grilled Steaks with Olivada and Port Wine Sauce (page 240)
White Bean Stew with Spinach and Tomatoes (page 283)
Roasted Winter Vegetables (page 274)
Banana Cake with Chocolate Fudge Frosting (page 377)

FARMER'S MARKET DINNER

Roasted Peppers with Mint Vinaigrette and Goat Cheese Croutons
(page 15)
Warm Grilled Vegetable and Shrimp Salad (page 111)
Indian Summer Pasta (page 128)
Fresh Fruit Basket with Assorted Cookies

SPRING LUNCH

Mixed Green Salad with Chilled Asparagus
West Coast Crab Cakes with Grapefruit Sauce (page 183)
Country Sourdough Bread (page 327)
Essencia Zabaglione with Fresh Fruit Compote (page 347)
Spicy Crinkle Cookies (page 388)

LAST-MINUTE DINNER PARTY

Smoked Fish Mousse (page 7) with Toasts
Glazed Orange-Hoisin Chicken (page 210)
Spicy Almond Couscous (page 303)
Tricolor Vegetable Sauté (page 272)
Chocolate Freak-Out (page 379)

INDEX

A

Aïoli, red pepper, 408
  chilled artichoke halves with, 17–18
  grilled seafood bisque with, 65–66
Almond(s):
  caper relish, grilled scallop brochettes
    with, 190–91
  chocolate chip coffee cake, 375–76
  couscous, spicy, 303–4
  cranberry relish, 419–20
  orange, and olive oil cake, 353–54
  pear-raspberry tart, 361–63
Appetizers and first courses, 1–37
  Asian gravlax with ginger mustard
    sauce, 8–9
  Asian guacamole, 24
  assorted grilled vegetables, 13–14
  baked Brie with sun-dried tomato
    pesto, 27–28
  California caponata, 31–32
  chilled artichoke halves with red
    pepper aïoli, 17–18
  goat cheese with rustic salsa, 25
  green olive tapenade, 19–20
  green pea guacamole, 22–23
  griddled quesadillas with caramelized
    onions, chicken, and Jack cheese,
    29–30
  pear, pistachio, and chicken liver
    mousse, 3–4
  ricotta corn cakes with smoky salsa
    topping, 33–34
  roasted peppers with mint vinaigrette
    and goat cheese croutons, 15–16
  shrimp salsa, 11–12
  smoked fish mousse, 7
  smoked salmon and caviar torta, 5–6
  sun-dried tomato tapenade, 21
  tuna tartare, 35–36
Apple:
  -Asian pear-quince sauce, 423
  and chicken sausage, 223–24
  orange oven pancake, puffed,
    119
Apricot(s):
  fresh strawberries and, with sour
    cream and brown sugar, 351
  glaze, 366
Artichoke halves, chilled, with red
    pepper aïoli, 17–18
Asian pear:
  and cranberry compote, ginger-spiced,
    421–22
  -quince-apple sauce, 423
Asparagus:
  scrambled eggs with smoked salmon
    and, 120–21
  springtime salmon salad, 113–14
Avocado(s), 91
  Asian guacamole, 24
  blood orange, and mushroom salad,
    89–90
  cucumber, and dill salsa, grilled
    salmon fillet with, 167–68
  cucumber gazpacho, 69–70

Avocado(s) (*cont.*)
  green pea guacamole, 22–23
  tomato salsa, grilled skirt steak with, 229–30

B

Bacon:
  barbecued pizza with leeks, mozzarella, tomatoes, and pancetta, 156–57
  fava beans with red onions and, 281–82
  tomato vinaigrette, warm, spinach and mushroom salad with, 87–88
Balsamic vinegar, 53–54
  lentil soup with thyme and, 55–56
  vinaigrette, pasta with tomatoes, basil and, 132–33
Banana:
  cake with chocolate fudge frosting, 377–78
  custard sauce, bittersweet chocolate hazelnut torte with, 381–82
  split ice cream torte, 384–85
Barley risotto, two-mushroom, 145–46
Basil:
  mixed-herb pesto, 402
  pasta with tomatoes, balsamic vinaigrette and, 132–33
  pesto, 403
  sautéed green and yellow beans with garlic and, 271
Bass, sea:
  grilled, with caponata, 165–66
  roast crispy, with warm lentils, 172–73
  roasted, with mustard salsa, 163–64
Bean(s):
  black, grilled chicken, and corn salad with salsa dressing, 103–4
  black, soup with lime cream, 61–62
  chicken minestrone with mixed-herb pesto, 63–64

fava, with red onions and bacon, 281–82
La Scala chopped salad, 92–93
lentils, 171
lentil soup with thyme and balsamic vinegar, 55–56
pesto sauce, grilled chicken with, 199–200
pinto, soup with gremolata, 59–60
roast crispy fish with warm lentils, 172–73
sautéed green and yellow, with garlic and basil, 271
spinach, pasta, and fagioli soup, 49–50
white, and vegetable salsa, grilled tuna with, 186–87
white, soup with leeks, carrots, and eggplant, 51–52
white, stew with spinach and tomatoes, 283–84
Beef:
  braised, with sun-dried tomatoes, Zinfandel, and thyme, 237–39
  grilled flank steak with smoky salsa, 235–36
  grilled roast, with shallot-chive sauce, 233–34
  grilled skirt steak with avocado-tomato salsa, 229–30
  grilled steak and potato salad, 100–102
  grilled steaks with olivada and port wine sauce, 240–41
  grilling of, 189
  panfried noodles with vegetables, 252–53
Beets:
  mixed greens with peppers and, 85–86
  orange-glazed, 276
Blenders, hand, 42
Blueberry lemon tart, 367–68
Bourbon mustard sauce, grilled turkey breast in, 214–15

Brandy eggnog sauce, 424
  pumpkin bread pudding with, 373–74
Bread(s), 309–41
  Ciji's scones with currants, 315–16
  corn, for stuffing, 399
  corn, leek, and red pepper stuffing terrine, 285–86
  corn tortillas, 322–23
  country sourdough, 327–29
  crisp tortilla chips, 324
  dough, preparation of, 325–26
  focaccia, 337–39
  fresh pear, 318–19
  jalapeño cheese, and rustic bread sticks, 334–36
  maple corn muffins, 320–21
  orange–poppy seed, 317
  Parmesan toasts, 311
  pizza dough, 340–41
  pudding, pumpkin, with eggnog brandy sauce, 373–74
  sourdough rye rolls, 330–31
  spiced pumpkin-hazelnut, 313–14
  sun-dried tomato toasts, 312
  walnut, 332–33
Broccoli leek soup with Parmesan cream, 47–48
Brownies, chocolate truffle, 386
Buckle, peach melba, 359–60
Bulgur, tomato-mint, 302

C

Cakes:
  banana, with chocolate fudge frosting, 377–78
  chocolate chip coffee cake, 375–76
  glazed lemon sour cream, 355–56
  orange, almond, and olive oil, 353–54
  peach melba buckle, 359–60
Caper almond relish, grilled scallop brochettes with, 190–91

Caponata:
  California, 31–32
  grilled sea bass with, 165–66
Caramel vanilla cream, 371–72
Carrots, white bean soup with leeks, eggplant and, 51–52
Cauliflower puree with two cheeses, 273
Caviar and smoked salmon torta, 5–6
Cheese(s):
  baked Brie with sun-dried tomato pesto, 27–28
  baked vegetable rigatoni with tomatoes and provolone, 130–31
  barbecued pizza with leeks, mozzarella, tomatoes, and pancetta, 156–57
  broccoli leek soup with Parmesan cream, 47–48
  butternut squash gratin with tomato fondue, 277–78
  Caesar salad with mixed baby lettuces and Parmesan toasts, 76–77
  California caponata, 31–32
  goat, croutons, roasted peppers with mint vinaigrette and, 15–16
  goat, herbed scrambled eggs with, 122–23
  goat, with rustic salsa, 25
  holiday lasagne with roasted vegetables and pesto, 137–39
  Jack, griddled quesadillas with caramelized onions, chicken and, 29–30
  jalapeño bread and rustic bread sticks, 334–36
  La Scala chopped salad, 92–93
  oven-roasted potatoes with Parmesan, 298
  Parmesan, 140
  Parmesan toasts, 311
  pasta salad with Parmesan dressing, 98–99
  peppery greens with Gorgonzola and pine nuts, 80–81

Cheese(s) (*cont.*)
  pesto, 403
  potatoes Vaugirard, 294–95
  ricotta corn cakes with smoky salsa
    topping, 33–34
  ricotta pancakes with sautéed spiced
    pears, 124–25
  smoked salmon and caviar torta, 5–6
  two, cauliflower puree with, 273
Cherries, dried, nectarine cobbler with,
  357–58
Chestnut, onion, and prune compote,
  288–89
Chicken:
  and apple sausage, 223–24
  arroz con pollo, 206–7
  crispy roast, 208–9
  farmer's market chopped salad, 78–
    79
  with garlic and lime, 204–5
  glazed orange-hoisin, 210
  griddled quesadillas with caramelized
    onions, Jack cheese and, 29–30
  grilled, black bean, and corn salad
    with salsa dressing, 103–4
  grilled, Niçoise, 197–98
  grilled, with pesto bean sauce, 199–
    200
  grilled orange mustard, 195–96
  grilling of, 189
  lemon, with roasted garlic sauce,
    201–2
  liver, pear, and pistachio mousse, 3–4
  marinating of, 249
  minestrone with mixed-herb pesto,
    63–64
  panfried noodles with vegetables,
    252–53
  salad, wine country, 109–10
  salad with Chinese noodles, 107–8
  sausage, making of, 226
  stock, 397
  stock, easy brown, 393–94
  warm grilled, salad with pesto, 105–6

Chile pepper(s), 231–32
  ancho, and tomato cream, pasta with,
    126–27
  ancho, cream, roasted garlic and
    butternut squash soup with, 41–42
  ancho, paste, 406–7
  ancho, paste, uses for, 405
  jalapeño, sweet potato soup with
    tomatillo cream, 45–46
  jalapeño cheese bread and rustic bread
    sticks, 334–36
  peeling of, 232
  smoky salsa, 416–17
  spicy tomato salsa, 413
  tomatillo salsa, 414
  types of, 231–32
Chive(s):
  mixed-herb pesto, 402
  orange sauce, glazed halibut with,
    176–77
  shallot sauce, grilled roast beef with,
    233–34
Chocolate:
  banana split ice cream torte, 384–85
  bittersweet, hazelnut torte with
    banana custard sauce, 381–82
  chip coffee cake, 375–76
  freak-out, 379
  fudge frosting, banana cake with,
    377–78
  tiramisu with toasted hazelnuts and,
    369–70
  truffle brownies, 386
  white, and pistachio cookies, 387
Cobblers:
  nectarine, with dried cherries, 357–
    58
  turkey vegetable, 220–22
Compotes:
  fresh fruit, Essencia zabaglione with,
    347–48
  ginger-spiced Asian pear and
    cranberry, 421–22
  onion, prune, and chestnut, 288–89

Condiments. *See also* Sauces.
 cranberry almond relish, 419–20
 hot pepper oil, 412
 roasted garlic puree, 409
 roasted tomato jam, 418
Confit of red onions and prosciutto, 153
Cookies:
 chocolate truffle brownies, 386
 spicy crinkle, 388–89
 white chocolate and pistachio, 387
Corn:
 corn bread for stuffing, 399
 grilled chicken, and black bean salad
  with salsa dressing, 103–4
 long-grain and wild rice salad with
  salmon and, 96–97
 maple muffins, 320–21
 rice pilaf with peanuts and, 306
 ricotta cakes with smoky salsa
  topping, 33–34
 and tomato soup, 67–68
 zucchini relish, grilled veal chops
  with, 254–55
Cornish hens, roasted, with honey
 tangerine marinade, 212–13
Cornmeal:
 corn bread, leek, and red pepper
  stuffing terrine, 285–86
 corn bread for stuffing, 399
 crisp tortilla chips, 324
 grilled instant polenta, 149–50
 grilled polenta with confit of red
  onions and prosciutto, 149–50
 instant vs. traditional polenta, 152
 maple corn muffins, 320–21
 ricotta corn cakes with smoky salsa
  topping, 33–34
 soft polenta with sun-dried tomato
  pesto, 147–48
 tortillas, 322–23
 yellow, grilled polenta using, 151–52
Couscous, spicy almond, 303–4
Crab cakes with grapefruit sauce, West
 Coast, 183–85

Cranberry:
 almond relish, 419–20
 and Asian pear compote, ginger-
  spiced, 421–22
 rosemary marinade, grilled lamb
  chops with, 242–43
Crème fraîche, 425
Cucumber:
 avocado, and dill salsa, grilled salmon
  fillet with, 167–68
 avocado gazpacho, 69–70
 pasta, grilled swordfish on a bed of,
  with Asian salsa, 178–79
Currants, Ciji's scones with, 315–16
Custard:
 banana sauce, bittersweet chocolate
  hazelnut torte with, 381–82
 Essencia zabaglione with fresh fruit
  compote, 347–48
 vanilla caramel cream, 371–72

D

Desserts, 343–89
 baked pears in burgundy and port
  glaze, 345–46
 banana cake with chocolate fudge
  frosting, 377–78
 banana split ice cream torte, 384–85
 bittersweet chocolate hazelnut torte
  with banana custard sauce, 381–82
 blueberry lemon tart, 367–68
 chocolate chip coffee cake, 375–76
 chocolate freak-out, 379–80
 chocolate truffle brownies, 386
 Essencia zabaglione with fresh fruit
  compote, 347–48
 fresh apricots and strawberries with
  sour cream and brown sugar, 351
 glazed lemon sour cream cake, 355–
  56
 mango and macadamia nut brown
  butter tart, 364–66
 mixed exotic fruit gazpacho, 349–50

Desserts (*cont.*)
nectarine cobbler with dried cherries, 357–58
orange, almond, and olive oil cake, 353–54
peach melba buckle, 359–60
pear-raspberry almond tart, 361–63
pumpkin bread pudding with eggnog brandy sauce, 373–74
quick fruit, 352
spiced sweet potato pudding, 300–301
spicy crinkle cookies, 388–89
tiramisu with toasted hazelnuts and chocolate, 369–70
vanilla caramel cream, 371–72
white chocolate and pistachio cookies, 387
Dessert sauces:
Asian pear-quince-apple, 423
banana custard, 383
crème fraîche, 425
eggnog brandy, 424
Dill, avocado, and cucumber salsa, grilled salmon fillet with, 167–68

E

Eggnog brandy sauce, 424
pumpkin bread pudding with, 373–74
Eggplant:
California caponata, 31–32
white bean soup with leeks, carrots and, 51–52
Eggs:
golden frittata with tomatillo salsa, 117–18
herbed scrambled, with goat cheese, 122–23
scrambled, with asparagus and smoked salmon, 120–21

F

Fat, reducing of, 398
Fat separators, 219

First courses. *See* Appetizers and first courses.
Fish. *See* Seafood.
Focaccia, 337–39
Frittata, golden, with tomatillo salsa, 117–18
Fruit(s). *See also specific fruits.*
desserts, quick, 352
dried, loin of pork with Gewürztraminer and, 264–65
fresh, compote, Essencia zabaglione with, 347–48
mixed exotic, gazpacho, 349–50

G

Garlic, 203
chicken with lime and, 204–5
roasted, and butternut squash soup with ancho chile cream, 41–42
roasted, mashed potatoes with leeks, 290–91
roasted, puree, 409
roasted, sauce, lemon chicken with, 201–2
sautéed green and yellow beans with basil and, 271
Gazpacho:
cucumber avocado, 69–70
mixed exotic fruit, 349–50
Ginger:
mustard sauce, Asian gravlax with, 8–9
-spiced Asian pear and cranberry compote, 421–22
Grapefuit sauce, West Coast crab cakes with, 183–85
Gratin, butternut squash, with tomato fondue, 277–78
Gravlax, Asian, with ginger mustard sauce, 8–9
Gravy, rich turkey, 218–19
Gremolata, pinto bean soup with, 59–60

Grilling, tips for, 188–89
Guacamole:
  Asian, 24
  green pea, 22–23

H

Halibut:
  glazed, with orange-chive sauce, 176–77
  grilled, with red pepper-mint sauce, 174–75
  roast crispy, with warm lentils, 172–73
Hand blenders, 42
Hazelnut(s):
  bittersweet chocolate torte with banana custard sauce, 381–82
  pumpkin bread, spiced, 313–14
  toasted, tiramisu with chocolate and, 369–70
Honey tangerine marinade, roasted Cornish hens with, 212–13

I

Ice cream torte, banana split, 384–85

L

Lamb:
  brochettes with crunchy raita, 247–48
  chops, grilled, with cranberry-rosemary marinade, 242–43
  grilling of, 189
  Indonesian leg of, 250–51
  panfried noodles with vegetables, 252–53
  rack of, with mint crust, 244–46
Lasagne, holiday, with roasted vegetables and pesto, 137–39
Leek(s):
  barbecued pizza with mozzarella, tomatoes, pancetta and, 156–57

broccoli soup with Parmesan cream, 47–48
corn bread, and red pepper stuffing terrine, 285–86
risotto with tomatoes, Niçoise olives and, 141–42
roasted garlic mashed potatoes with, 290–91
white bean soup with carrots, eggplant and, 51–52
Lemon:
  blueberry tart, 367–68
  chicken with roasted garlic sauce, 201–2
  sour cream cake, glazed, 355–56
Lentil(s), 171
  soup with thyme and balsamic vinegar, 55–56
  warm, roast crispy fish with, 172–73
Lime:
  chicken with garlic and, 204–5
  cream, black bean soup with, 61–62
Liver, chicken, pear, and pistachio mousse, 3–4

M

Mango and macadamia nut brown butter tart, 364–66
Maple corn muffins, 320–21
Marinades, 249
Meat, 227–67. *See also* Bacon; Beef; Lamb.
  Asian glazed pork tenderloin, 266–67
  braised stuffed shoulder of veal, 260–63
  easy brown veal stock, 395–96
  grilled veal chops with zucchini-corn relish, 254–55
  grilling of, 189
  Indian summer pasta, 128–29
  light meatballs with double-tomato herb sauce, 256–57

Meat (*cont.*)
  loin of pork with dried fruits and
    Gewürztraminer, 264–65
  marinating of, 249
  panfried noodles with vegetables,
    252–53
  veal stew with orange sauce, 258–59
Menus, 427–30
Minestrone, chicken, with mixed-herb
    pesto, 63–64
Mint:
  crust, rack of lamb with, 244–46
  lamb brochettes with crunchy raita,
    247–48
  red pepper sauce, grilled halibut with,
    174–75
  tomato bulgur, 302
  vinaigrette, roasted peppers with goat
    cheese croutons and, 15–16
Muffins, maple corn, 320–21
Mushroom(s):
  blood orange, and avocado salad, 89–
    90
  and spinach salad with warm tomato-
    bacon vinaigrette, 87–88
  two-, barley risotto, 145–46
  yellow split pea soup with smoked
    turkey and, 57–58
Mustard:
  bourbon sauce, grilled turkey breast
    in, 214–15
  ginger sauce, Asian gravlax with, 8–
    9
  orange chicken, grilled, 195–96
  salsa, roasted sea bass with, 163–
    64

N

Nectarine cobbler with dried cherries,
    357–58
Noodles. *See also* Pasta.
  Chinese, chicken salad with, 107–8
  panfried, with vegetables, 252–53

O

Oil. *See also* Olive oil.
  hot pepper, 412
Oil misters, 336
Olivada:
  grilled steaks with port wine sauce
    and, 240–41
  uses for, 241
Olive(s), 37
  green, tapenade, 19–20
  Niçoise, risotto with leeks, tomatoes
    and, 141–42
Olive oil, 82
  orange, and almond cake, 353–54
Onion(s):
  California caponata, 31–32
  caramelized, griddled quesadillas with
    chicken, Jack cheese and, 29–30
  prune, and chestnut compote, 288–89
  red, confit of prosciutto and, 153
  red, fava beans with bacon and, 281–
    82
  red, grilled polenta with confit of
    prosciutto and, 149–50
  red, sauce, baked salmon with, 169–
    70
  roasted baby potatoes and, 299
Orange(s):
  almond, and olive oil cake, 353–54
  apple oven pancake, puffed, 119
  blood, mushroom, and avocado salad,
    89–90
  chive sauce, glazed halibut with, 176–
    77
  Essencia zabaglione with fresh fruit
    compote, 347–48
  -glazed beets, 276
  -hoisin chicken, glazed, 210
  mustard chicken, grilled, 195–96
  poppy seed bread, 317
  sauce, veal stew with, 258–59
Orange roughy, broiled, with salsa glaze,
    181–82

P

Pancake(s):
  crispy potato, with vegetables, 296–97
  puffed apple-orange oven, 119
  ricotta, with sautéed spiced pears, 124–25
Pancetta, barbecued pizza with leeks, mozzarella, tomatoes and, 156–57
Pasta:
  with ancho chile and tomato cream, 126–27
  baked vegetable rigatoni with tomatoes and provolone, 130–31
  chicken salad with Chinese noodles, 107–8
  holiday lasagne with roasted vegetables and pesto, 137–39
  Indian summer, 128–29
  panfried noodles with vegetables, 252–53
  salad with Parmesan dressing, 98–99
  spinach, and fagioli soup, 49–50
  with tomatoes, basil, and balsamic vinaigrette, 132–33
  wonton butternut squash ravioli with spinach pesto, 134–36
Pea:
  green, guacamole, 22–23
  yellow split, soup with mushrooms and smoked turkey, 57–58
Peach melba buckle, 359–60
Peanuts, rice pilaf with corn and, 306
Pear(s):
  baked, in burgundy and port glaze, 345–46
  fresh, bread, 318–19
  pistachio, and chicken liver mousse, 3–4
  raspberry almond tart, 361–63
  sautéed spiced, ricotta pancakes with, 124–25

Pepper(s), bell:
  mixed greens with beets and, 85–86
  peeling of, 287
  red, aïoli, 408
  red, aïoli, chilled artichoke halves with, 17–18
  red, aïoli, grilled seafood bisque with, 65–66
  red, corn bread, and leek stuffing terrine, 285–86
  red, mint sauce, grilled halibut with, 174–75
  roasted, with mint vinaigrette and goat cheese croutons, 15–16
Pepper, chile. *See* Chile pepper.
Pepper, hot, oil, 412
Pesto, 403
  bean sauce, grilled chicken with, 199–200
  holiday lasagne with roasted vegetables and, 137–39
  mixed-herb, 402
  mixed-herb, chicken minestrone with, 63–64
  spinach, wonton butternut squash ravioli with, 134–36
  sun-dried tomato, 404
  sun-dried tomato, baked Brie with, 27–28
  sun-dried tomato, soft polenta with, 147–48
  warm grilled chicken salad with, 105–6
Pilaf:
  confetti rice, 305
  rice, with corn and peanuts, 306
Pine nuts, peppery greens with Gorgonzola and, 80–81
Pistachio(s), 389
  pear, and chicken liver mousse, 3–4
  and white chocolate cookies, 387
Pizza:
  barbecued, with leeks, mozzarella, tomatoes, and pancetta, 156–57

Pizza (*cont.*)
  dough, 340–41
  Jewish breakfast, 154–55
  toppings for, 158
Polenta:
  grilled, using yellow cornmeal, 151–52
  grilled, with confit of red onions and prosciutto, 149–50
  grilled instant, 149–50
  instant vs. traditional, 152
  soft, with sun-dried tomato pesto, 147–48
Poppy seed-orange bread, 317
Pork:
  grilling of, 189
  loin of, with dried fruits and Gewürztraminer, 264–65
  tenderloin, Asian glazed, 266–67
Potato(es):
  baby, roasted onions and, 299
  and grilled steak salad, 100–102
  light and fluffy mashed, 292–93
  oven-roasted, with Parmesan, 298
  pancakes with vegetables, crispy, 296–97
  roasted garlic mashed, with leeks, 290–91
  Vaugirard, 294–95
Poultry, 193–226. *See also* Chicken; Turkey.
  grilling of, 189
  marinating of, 249
  roasted Cornish hens with honey tangerine marinade, 212–13
  sausage, making of, 226
  trussing of, with skewers, 215
Prosciutto:
  confit of red onions and, 153
  grilled polenta with confit of red onions and, 149–50
Prune, onion, and chestnut compote, 288–89

Puddings:
  pumpkin bread, with eggnog brandy sauce, 373–74
  spiced sweet potato, 300–301
Pumpkin:
  bread pudding with eggnog brandy sauce, 373–74
  hazelnut bread, spiced, 313–14

Q

Quesadillas, griddled, with caramelized onions, chicken, and Jack cheese, 29–30
Quince-Asian pear-apple sauce, 423

R

Raita, crunchy, lamb brochettes with, 247–48
Raspberry-pear almond tart, 361–63
Ravioli, wonton butternut squash, with spinach pesto, 134–36
Relish, cranberry almond, 419–20
Rice:
  arroz con pollo, 206–7
  garden risotto, 143–44
  long-grain and wild, salad with corn and salmon, 96–97
  pilaf, confetti, 305
  pilaf with corn and peanuts, 306
  risotto with leeks, tomatoes, and Niçoise olives, 141–42
  spinach timbales, 307–8
Rigatoni, baked vegetable, with tomatoes and provolone, 130–31
Risotto, 142
  garden, 143–44
  with leeks, tomatoes, and Niçoise olives, 141–42
  two-mushroom barley, 145–46
Roasting, high-heat, 275
Rolls, sourdough rye, 330–31

Rosemary-cranberry marinade, grilled lamb chops with, 242–43

S

Salad dressings. *See also* Salads.
  basic vinaigrette, 410
Salads, 73–114
  blood orange, mushroom, and avocado, 89–90
  Caesar, history of, 75
  Caesar, with mixed baby lettuces and Parmesan toasts, 76–77
  California, 83–84
  chicken, with Chinese noodles, 107–8
  farmer's market chopped, 78–79
  grilled chicken, black bean, and corn, with salsa dressing, 103–4
  grilled steak and potato, 100–102
  La Scala chopped, 92–93
  long-grain and wild rice, with corn and salmon, 96–97
  mixed greens with beets and peppers, 85–86
  pasta, with Parmesan dressing, 98–99
  peppery greens with Gorgonzola and pine nuts, 80–81
  spinach and mushroom, with warm tomato-bacon vinaigrette, 87–88
  springtime salmon, 113–14
  warm grilled chicken, with pesto, 105–6
  warm grilled vegetable and shrimp, 111–12
  wheatberry vegetable, 94–95
  wine country chicken, 109–10
Salmon:
  Asian gravlax with ginger mustard sauce, 8–9
  baked, with red onion sauce, 169–70
  grilled, fillet with avocado, cucumber, and dill salsa, 167–68
  Jewish breakfast pizza, 154–55
  long-grain and wild rice salad with corn and, 96–97
  salad, springtime, 113–14
  smoked, and caviar torta, 5–6
  smoked, scrambled eggs with asparagus and, 120–21
Salsa, 180
  Asian, grilled swordfish on a bed of cucumber pasta with, 178–79
  avocado, cucumber, and dill, grilled salmon fillet with, 167–68
  avocado-tomato, grilled skirt steak with, 229–30
  dressing, grilled chicken, black bean, and corn salad with, 103–4
  glaze, broiled orange roughy with, 181–82
  mustard, roasted sea bass with, 163–64
  rustic, 415
  rustic, goat cheese with, 25
  shrimp, 11–12
  smoky, 416–17
  smoky, grilled flank steak with, 235–36
  smoky, topping, ricotta corn cakes with, 33–34
  spicy tomato, 413
  tomatillo, 414
  tomatillo, golden frittata with, 117–18
  tomatillo grilled shrimp, 161–62
  vegetable and white bean, grilled tuna with, 186–87
Sauces, dessert:
  Asian pear-quince-apple, 423
  banana custard, 383
  crème fraîche, 425
  eggnog brandy, 424
Sauces, savory. *See also* Condiments.
  basic vinaigrette, 410
  confit of red onions and prosciutto, 153
  double-tomato herb, 400–401

Sauces, savory (cont.)
  ginger mustard, 9–10
  ginger-spiced Asian pear and
    cranberry compote, 421–22
  green olive tapenade, 19–20
  mixed-herb pesto, 402
  pesto, 403
  red pepper aïoli, 408
  rustic salsa, 415
  smoky salsa, 416–17
  spicy tomato salsa, 413
  sun-dried tomato pesto, 404
  tomatillo salsa, 414
  vinaigrette, 411
Sausage(s):
  chicken and apple, 223–24
  Indian summer pasta, 128–29
  poultry, making of, 226
  turkey, with sun-dried tomatoes,
    225–26
Scallop(s):
  brochettes, grilled, with almond caper
    relish, 190–91
  grilled seafood bisque with red pepper
    aïoli, 65–66
Scones with currants, Ciji's, 315–16
Seafood, 159–91
  Asian gravlax with ginger mustard
    sauce, 8–9
  baked salmon with red onion sauce,
    169–70
  broiled orange roughy with salsa
    glaze, 181–82
  glazed halibut with orange-chive
    sauce, 176–77
  grilled, bisque with red pepper aïoli,
    65–66
  grilled halibut with red pepper-mint
    sauce, 174–75
  grilled salmon fillet with avocado,
    cucumber, and dill salsa, 167–68
  grilled scallop brochettes with
    almond caper relish, 190–91
  grilled sea bass with caponata, 165–66

  grilled swordfish on a bed of
    cucumber pasta with Asian salsa,
    178–79
  grilled tuna with vegetable and white
    bean salsa, 186–87
  grilling of, 188–89
  Jewish breakfast pizza, 154–55
  long-grain and wild rice salad with
    corn and salmon, 96–97
  marinating of, 249
  roast crispy fish with warm lentils,
    172–73
  roasted sea bass with mustard salsa,
    163–64
  scrambled eggs with asparagus and
    smoked salmon, 120–21
  shrimp salsa, 11–12
  smoked fish mousse, 7
  smoked salmon and caviar torta,
    5–6
  springtime salmon salad, 113–14
  tomatillo grilled shrimp, 161–62
  tuna tartare, 35–36
  warm grilled vegetable and shrimp
    salad, 111–12
  West Coast crab cakes with grapefruit
    sauce, 183–85
Shallot-chive sauce, grilled roast beef
  with, 233–34
Shrimp:
  grilled seafood bisque with red pepper
    aïoli, 65–66
  salsa, 11–12
  tomatillo grilled, 161–62
  and vegetable salad, warm grilled,
    111–12
Side dishes, 269–308
  butternut squash gratin with tomato
    fondue, 277–78
  cauliflower puree with two cheeses,
    273
  confetti rice pilaf, 305
  corn bread, leek, and red pepper
    stuffing terrine, 285–86

crispy potato pancakes with vegetables, 296–97

fava beans with red onions and bacon, 281–82

home ranch butternut squash, 279–80

light and fluffy mashed potatoes, 292–93

onion, prune, and chestnut compote, 288–89

orange-glazed beets, 276

oven-roasted potatoes with Parmesan, 298

potatoes Vaugirard, 294–95

rice pilaf with corn and peanuts, 306

roasted garlic mashed potatoes with leeks, 290–91

roasted onions and baby potatoes, 299

roasted winter vegetables, 274–75

sautéed green and yellow beans with garlic and basil, 271

spiced sweet potato pudding, 300–301

spicy almond couscous, 303–4

spinach rice timbales, 307–8

tomato-mint bulgur, 302

tricolor vegetable sauté, 272

white bean stew with spinach and tomatoes, 283–84

Soups, 39–72

black bean, with lime cream, 61–62

broccoli leek, with Parmesan cream, 47–48

chicken minestrone with mixed-herb pesto, 63–64

corn and tomato, 67–68

cucumber avocado gazpacho, 69–70

grilled seafood bisque with red pepper aïoli, 65–66

lentil, with thyme and balsamic vinegar, 55–56

mixed exotic fruit gazpacho, 349–50

pinto bean, with gremolata, 59–60

roasted garlic and butternut squash, with ancho chile cream, 41–42

roasted vegetable, 43–44

spinach, pasta, and fagioli, 49–50

squash vichyssoise, 71–72

sweet potato-jalapeño, with tomatillo cream, 45–46

white bean, with leeks, carrots, and eggplant, 51–52

yellow split pea, with mushrooms and smoked turkey, 57–58

Sourdough:

bread, country, 327–29

rye rolls, 330–31

Spinach:

and mushroom salad with warm bacon-tomato vinaigrette, 87–88

pasta, and fagioli soup, 49–50

pesto, wonton butternut squash ravioli with, 134–36

rice timbales, 307–8

white bean stew with tomatoes and, 283–84

Squash:

butternut, and roasted garlic soup with ancho chile cream, 41–42

butternut, gratin with tomato fondue, 277–78

butternut, wonton ravioli with spinach pesto, 134–36

grilled veal chops with zucchini-corn relish, 254–55

home ranch butternut, 279–80

vichyssoise, 71–72

Stews:

veal, with orange sauce, 258–59

white bean, with spinach and tomatoes, 283–84

Stock:

easy brown turkey or chicken, 393–94

easy brown veal, 395–96

turkey or chicken, 397

Strawberries:
  Essencia zabaglione with fresh fruit
    compote, 347–48
  fresh apricots and, with sour cream
    and brown sugar, 351
Stuffed shoulder of veal, braised, 260–
  63
Stuffing:
  corn bread, leek, and red pepper,
    terrine, 285–86
  corn bread for, 399
Sweet potato:
  jalapeño soup with tomatillo cream,
    45–46
  pudding, spiced, 300–301
Swordfish, grilled, on a bed of cucumber
    pasta with Asian salsa, 178–79

T

Tangerine honey marinade, roasted
    Cornish hens with, 212–13
Tapenade:
  green olive, 19–20
  sun-dried tomato, 21
Tarts:
  blueberry lemon, 367–68
  mango and macadamia nut brown
    butter, 364–66
  pear-raspberry almond, 361–63
Thyme:
  braised beef with sun-dried tomatoes,
    Zinfandel and, 237–39
  lentil soup with balsamic vinegar and,
    55–56
  mixed-herb pesto, 402
Timbales, spinach rice, 307–8
Tiramisu with toasted hazelnuts and
    chocolate, 369–70
Toasts:
  Parmesan, 311
  Parmesan, Caesar salad with mixed
    baby lettuces and, 76–77
  sun-dried tomato, 312

Tomatillo(s):
  cream, sweet potato-jalapeño soup
    with, 45–46
  grilled shrimp, 161–62
  rustic salsa, 415
  salsa, 414
  salsa, golden frittata with, 117–18
Tomato(es):
  avocado salsa, grilled skirt steak with,
    229–30
  bacon vinaigrette, warm, spinach and
    mushroom salad with, 87–88
  baked vegetable rigatoni with
    provolone and, 130–31
  barbecued pizza with leeks,
    mozzarella, pancetta and, 156–57
  and corn soup, 67–68
  double-, herb sauce, 400–401
  double-, herb sauce, light meatballs
    with, 256–57
  fondue, butternut squash gratin with,
    277–78
  fresh vs. canned, 236
  mint bulgur, 302
  pasta with basil, balsamic vinaigrette
    and, 132–33
  risotto with leeks, Niçoise olives and,
    141–42
  roasted, jam, 418
  rustic salsa, 415
  salsa, spicy, 413
  smoky salsa, 416–17
  white bean stew with spinach and,
    283–84
Tomato(es), sun-dried, 26
  and ancho chili cream, pasta with,
    126–27
  braised beef with Zinfandel, thyme
    and, 237–39
  double-tomato herb sauce, 400–401
  grilled chicken Niçoise, 197–98
  light meatballs with double-tomato
    herb sauce, 256–57
  pesto, 404

pesto, baked Brie with, 27–28
pesto, soft polenta with, 147–48
pesto, uses for, 405
tapenade, 21
toasts, 312
turkey sausages with, 225–26
Torta, smoked salmon and caviar, 5–6
Tortes:
   banana split ice cream, 384–85
   bittersweet chocolate hazelnut, with
     banana custard sauce, 381–82
Tortilla(s):
   chips, crisp, 324
   corn, 322–23
   griddled quesadillas with caramelized
     onions, chicken, and Jack cheese,
     29–30
Tuna:
   grilled, with vegetable and white
     bean salsa, 186–87
   tartare, 35–36
Turkey:
   breast, grilled, in mustard bourbon
     sauce, 214–15
   gravy, rich, 218–19
   grilling of, 189
   La Scala chopped salad, 92–93
   light meatballs with double-tomato
     herb sauce, 256–57
   marinated roast, 216–17
   sausage, making of, 226
   sausages with sun-dried tomatoes,
     225–26
   smoked, yellow split pea soup with
     mushrooms and, 57–58
   stock, 397
   stock, easy brown, 393–94
   vegetable cobbler, 220–22

V

Vanilla caramel cream, 371–72
Veal:
   braised stuffed shoulder of, 260–63

chops, grilled, with zucchini-corn
   relish, 254–55
light meatballs with double-tomato
   herb sauce, 256–57
stew with orange sauce, 258–59
stock, easy brown, 395–96
Vegetable(s). *See also specific vegetables.*
   assorted grilled, 13–14
   chicken minestrone with mixed-herb
     pesto, 63–64
   crispy potato pancakes with, 296–97
   garden risotto, 143–44
   grilling of, 189
   high-heat roasting of, 275
   Indian summer pasta, 128–29
   marinating of, 249
   panfried noodles with, 252–53
   pasta salad with Parmesan dressing,
     98–99
   rigatoni, baked, with tomatoes and
     provolone, 130–31
   roasted, holiday lasagne with pesto
     and, 137–39
   roasted, soup, 43–44
   roasted winter, 274–75
   sauté, tricolor, 272
   and shrimp salad, warm grilled, 111–12
   turkey cobbler, 220–22
   wheatberry salad, 94–95
   and white bean salsa, grilled tuna
     with, 186–87
Vichyssoise, squash, 71–72
Vinaigrette, 411
   balsamic, pasta with tomatoes, basil
     and, 132–33
   basic, 410

W

Walnut bread, 332–33
Wheatberry vegetable salad, 94–95
Wine:
   baked pears in burgundy and port
     glaze, 345–46

Wine (*cont.*)
  braised beef with sun-dried tomatoes,
    Zinfandel, and thyme, 237–39
  Essencia zabaglione with fresh fruit
    compote, 347–48
  loin of pork with dried fruits and
    Gewürztraminer, 264–65
  port, sauce, grilled steaks with olivada
    and, 240–41

Wonton butternut squash ravioli with
    spinach pesto, 134–36

Z

Zabaglione, Essencia, with fresh fruit
    compote, 347–48
Zucchini-corn relish, grilled veal chops
    with, 254–55